PENGUIN BOOKS

THE BENEFITS OF PASSION

Catherine Fox was born in 1961. After reading English at Durham University she went on to do a doctorate in theology at London. Her first novel, *Of Angels and Men*, is also published in Penguin. She now lives in Tyneside with her husband, who is a vicar, and their two sons.

THE BENEFITS OF PASSION

Catherine Fox

PENGUIN BOOKS

PENGUIN BOOKS

Published by the Penguin Group
Penguin Books Ltd, 27 Wrights Lane, London W8 5TZ, England
Penguin Putnam Inc., 375 Hudson Street, New York, New York 10014, USA
Penguin Books Australia Ltd, Ringwood, Victoria, Australia
Penguin Books Canada Ltd, 10 Alcorn Avenue, Toronto, Ontario, Canada M4V 3B2
Penguin Books (NZ) Ltd, 182–190 Wairau Road, Auckland 10, New Zealand

Penguin Books Ltd, Registered Offices: Harmondsworth, Middlesex, England

First published by Hamish Hamilton 1997
Published in Penguin Books 1998
1 3 5 7 9 10 8 6 4 2

Printed in England by Clays Ltd, St Ives plc

For
Bridget, Mary, Katy, Kate
and the other Cathy

CHAPTER I

Isabella Deane was downwardly mobile. Her elder sister Hermione, who was not, deplored this tendency. So did their mother. Their father was a solicitor and made no comment either way. Poor Isabella had always been like it, even as a little girl. She had gone quite happily to the local village primary school and made friends with girls like Debbie Ambridge – the sort of girl who used to do handstands against the school wall to show her knickers when the RAF apprentices were going past. Hermione had thrown a tantrum after her first day at Nettledon County Primary and had to be sent instead as a day girl to a little private school in the next town, where they wore a uniform and learnt to play tennis. Isabella and Debbie played in the quarry and on building sites or up on the railway line where Isabella was once almost cut in two by an express train.

However, she lived long enough to pass her eleven plus and join Hermione at the grammar school (the only kind of state school Hermione would countenance). Mrs Deane was optimistic about the school's polite influence; but it soon became apparent that Isabella had waved goodbye to the likes of Debbie Ambridge only to meet up with the Tracy Wattses of this world, who were like Debbie Ambridge only they had brains. The sort of girl who rolled her school skirt over and over at the waist to make it short enough. She and Isabella and their kind went out illegally during the lunch hour to ogle the men, tacking back and forth across the busy high street (where Isabella was once almost crushed by a lorry) in pursuit of the local talent. They ate large slices of Black Forest gateau from the baker's as they went.

Walking the streets and eating! The headmistress was speechless when the matter was brought to her attention. Letters were sent to the relevant parents. Mrs Deane despaired. Mr Deane made no comment.

Then there was a turn for the better. Isabella, having lived long enough to reach the sixth form, surprised everyone by getting a place at Cambridge to read English. Mrs Deane was an old Girtonian herself and her spirits rose again. Hermione, now in her first year at the Other Place, was thoughtful when she heard the news. It was as though in some obscure way her younger sister's success undermined the value of her own Oxford scholarship. On reflection she was pleased. She shared her mother's belief that Cambridge would reverse the unfortunate downward trend.

Isabella's wedding dress three years later – like an outward and visible sign of an inward and spiritual truth – showed them just how wrong they were. Tight oyster satin split to the thigh.

'You look unspeakably vulgar,' said Hermione as Isabella postured in front of the spare bedroom mirror a week before the wedding.

'Barney will like it,' said Isabella.

'I imagine he will,' replied Hermione coolly.

He did. Oh my, oh my – didn't he just.

'Barney, we can't possibly!'

'Why not? We're married.'

'But . . .'

She was on her back on the spare bed with the unspeakable dress ruched up round her waist. Voices and chinking glasses from the marquee on the lawn, and Barney on top of her, consummating their marriage in long, unhurried thrusts.

'Barney, I can't believe you're doing this!'

He grinned.

A sudden cramp stabbed into her right hip joint and she squealed and squirmed, and in the end had to wrap her legs round his waist to dislodge the pain. This was mistaken for passion and the dress was in sudden crisis. She heard a couple of stitches crack, but those seams held. Polite voices on the lawn. She clung on like a shipwrecked sailor to a mast. A tap at the door. Her mother's voice.

'Everything all right, darlings?'

'Just coming,' said Barney. A pause. He came.

Isabella's thighs shook as she scrambled into her going away outfit. She looked up and saw Barney rub a towel over his fair curly head and smile his slow smile at her. It struck her that marriage might be one long process of interesting discovery. But that was on her wedding day.

Annie sat cross-legged on a chair with her notebook. She was hovering about twenty feet above the lawn looking down on the guests and trying to decide what kind of weather to have. It should have been one of those blazing August days which melted the tarmac on the roads and turned the marquee into an oven, but as she watched she could see that a stiffish breeze was blowing and making Mrs Deane clutch her hat as she talked to one of Barney's older sisters. Hermione seemed to shiver slightly in her bridesmaid's dress, but it might simply have been a fastidious shudder. Barney's family were decidedly *not* her sort of people. Her frown transformed into a frigid smile as one of Barney's brothers-in-law bore down on her with a video camera. 'Give us a nice smile, love.' A wedding video. Good God. How incredibly tacky. The other bridesmaid, a tall blonde, received the camera's attentions with amused contempt. The lawn was very green. Barney's sisters' stilettos (shudder) kept sinking into it.

Annie rose up higher for a moment and scanned the suburban gardens spread out beneath her. Lush as far as the eye could see. A rainy August, then. The tiny guests circulated. Annie watched the progress of Mrs Deane's custard-coloured hat among the groups. She would be smiling and checking that glasses were full, glancing every now and then at her watch. What on earth was keeping Barney and Isabella? A stuck zip? A sudden flood of tears? Perhaps she should –? Annie watched her go into the house.

Some of Barney's nieces and nephews had got underneath Mr Deane's raspberry nets and were busy scrumping. There was Barney's father's bald head. He'd spotted what his grandchildren were up to. Little buggers. Still, no wonder they were hungry. Pinwheel smoked-salmon sandwiches. Fresh bloody dates stuffed with cream cheese. And only wine to drink. I ask you. Plenty of everything, he had to admit, but he knew that he and Maureen would be stopping for steak and chips that evening before they got half-way up the M1.

At last Annie saw the guests being herded round to the front of the house by the best man. He was tall and thin. Dark-haired. He flapped his long arms at them, encouraging them on with a kind of despairing good humour, like a shepherd who loves sheep tenderly but is under no illusions about their intellectual powers. Who was he? An old school-friend of Barney's probably. Perhaps they had played cricket together in the First XI.

The guests gathered on the drive. The couple emerged. Cheers. Confetti. Photos. Isabella was wearing a minute black dress and a straw hat as wide as a cartwheel. Barney's father winked and mimed some paternal encouragement to his son. His wife cuffed him, a practised back-handed blow to the chest. Her face did not change at all. Nobody was quite sure whether she liked Isabella. The couple climbed into a red car crammed with balloons, and bearing the shaving-foam motto 'Vicars do it on their knees'. They drove off amid more cheers.

Annie watched the car climb the hill and head out of town, balloons bobbing and scraps of shaving foam blowing away in the wind. The guests stood about on the pink gravel drive. They looked like passengers diverted to a strange station on a Sunday afternoon. Barney's father rubbed his hands together briskly and said, 'Well, now.' But everyone continued to stand.

The car was a red dot heading north, a mite crawling across an endless green carpet. Annie could hear the larks as her chair rode along in the sky.

'Can I tempt you?' Edward appeared beside her on a cloud holding out a treacle tart. Annie jumped in surprise.

'Yes. Just a small slice, thanks.'

Edward peered over her shoulder. She shut the book, although it was written in her own secret shorthand. 'What's this?' he asked. 'Doctrine essay?'

'Well . . .' she shrugged to avoid telling an outright lie. The cloud had given way to grey theological-college carpet.

'What about a cup of tea?' His brown hair was wet from a recent shower. He'd probably been out rowing.

'Thank you.' He left the room. She listened to his brogues clumping along the corridor to the kitchen. The green August day had vanished and Annie could see the miserable north-eastern rain speckling her window. She hated February.

'Earl Grey all right?' He had a hearty voice. Coverdale Hall chapel sounded more like a packed stand at Twickenham than divine worship when Edward and his kind were in full cry.

'Lovely, thanks.'

Edward began singing, '"Thine be the glory, risen conquering Son!"' Annie waited, tense, wondering whether she could snatch another moment for her novel. 'Milk?'

'Yes, please.' Silence. She opened her book again. The car crawling northwards like a –

'How strong do you like it?'

Annie pounded her fists noiselessly on the desk. Just give me the tea and go!

'As it comes.' It was there the whole time, this murderous irritability, crackling away like background radiation. '"Endless is the victory thou o'er death hast won!"' boomed Edward's fine baritone from the kitchen. Clump, clump, came his brogues along the corridor. She reminded herself that Edward was a good friend and that she liked him. He brought in the tea and cake. The problem was hers, not his. She was guiltily aware she would have found him even more irritating if he hadn't stood a good-looking six foot two in his rugby socks.

'You're busy,' he said. 'Shall I leave you in peace?'

'Would you mind? Sorry, Edward.'

He was gone with a polite wave of the hand. She ate his cake and hated herself. Why do I feel like this? She had always assumed that the dark night of the soul was a noble thing. A solitary wrestling with your Maker. 'Comforter, where, where is your comforting?' But this felt like a case of permanent pre-menstrual tension. Waking one morning to find yourself doubting the divinity of Christ was one thing, but to be locked in perpetual crabbiness with your fellow ordinands was another. She looked down at her notebook again, aware that this was the one thing in her life that she enjoyed at the moment, but that there was always something else she ought to be doing instead. Preparing the prayers for tomorrow's service, for instance. Later. Later.

Now, where were Barney and Isabella going on their honeymoon? Northumberland. A long journey, but that was nothing to the happy couple. Barney and Isabella would not have to broil for hours in contraflows like us lesser beings. Their red car could travel three hundred miles in seven words: 'They arrived at last at the cottage . . .' But how had they met in the first place?

Isabella first saw Barney in the catalogue room of Cambridge University Library and she hunted him down and married him. It was the summer term of her second year and she was fiddling around one morning looking something up and not revising for her part ones because it was almost time for the tea room to open. Ten minutes to cheese-scone time. She glanced around and there was Barney: big and blond and beautiful, walking through the catalogue room minding his own business. All thought of cheese scones fled from her mind and she pursued him through the library and up several flights of stairs to South Wing 4.

It was a room she had never previously visited and it looked out across some playing fields. He settled down to work not knowing he was a marked man. April sunshine was coming through the window and turning his fair hair into a halo round his head. He had a sort of bruised and bewildered beauty, like an overgrown cherub after a night on the tiles. You, she thought, are gorgeous. She pulled a volume at random from a nearby shelf. *The New Testament and the People of God.* Her jaw dropped. Don't tell me this is the *theology* section. She looked across at the broad shoulders and fair head. You can't be one of those Bible bashers. I won't let you be. She brightened at the idea that he might only be there because it was a pleasant sunny place to study with a good view of the prep-school rounders matches if you got bored with your work. Isabella slid the volume back onto the shelf and stood watching him. She was sucking a lock of her dark hair, a vulgar habit she had never outgrown and which undermined the impact of her expensive bob. As she loitered past she noticed that he had a pile of books beside him with reservation slips in them. She bent down and whispered in her husky voice, 'Are these yours?'

He looked up in surprise. 'Yes.'

She whisked the slip of paper out of the top volume. *B. Hardstaff*. She tucked it into her pocket and smiled her nicest smile. 'Thank you.'

She glanced back at him when she reached the doorway. He was watching her. Then she saw him shake his head briskly as though clearing the inexplicable incident from his mind before settling down to work again.

'I've just seen *the* most *gorgeous* man,' said Isabella to her friend Camilla as they went out through the library's revolving doors a couple of hours later.

'Yeah?' said Camilla. They paused on the steps while she lit a cigarette. She shook out the match and threw it away. 'What's he like, then?' Camilla herself was a tall blonde, aloof and cool as the stratosphere, the sort of woman who in a previous era would never have had to resort to lighting her own cigarette. Her expression implied that she found life faintly amusing.

'Oh, he's –' Isabella broke off. 'Don't look! It's him!' Camilla looked. He walked past them down the steps. 'Don't you think he's beautiful?' But Camilla had her eyebrow up.

Her incredulity acted as a dare on Isabella. 'Excuse me,' she called. He turned. 'I just want you to know you're the sexiest man I've ever met and I think I'm in love with you.'

He stared at her in blank astonishment. There was a ripple of amusement among those close enough to overhear. Camilla laughed mockingly. Oh, Gawd, thought Isabella. Why did I do that? But then he smiled at her, a slow, broad smile. Her heart raced. He turned and walked off towards the bikes without a word.

'I take it back,' said Camilla.

'Oh, you like him? Do you really?'

Camilla curled a wisp of smoke back up her nostril then blew a cloud away. 'He has a certain *je sais exactement quoi*. What's his name?' Isabella pulled out the slip of paper and handed it over.

'Hardstaff. Hmm. That has a promising phallic ring to it. What does the B stand for? Barry? Bert? Brian?'

'Oh, God! Please not!'

'He'll be bald and fat before he's forty,' said Camilla as he cycled past. 'That sort always are.'

Isabella put two fingers in her mouth and whistled. 'Hey, big boy – what's your name?'

But there was no answer, just another grin. They watched him disappear along the road.

'Self-satisfied bastard,' said Camilla, almost to herself.

That evening they were in Camilla's room finishing off a second bottle of wine because it was Friday, and anyway, there was a limit to how much revision a sane person could do. Smoke rose in a straight line from Camilla's cigarette. She was lying on the bed with her feet up on the wall examining her legs. Her long blonde hair fanned out over the duvet cover and she looked like a 1940s advert for nylons.

'I just wish I had nicer boobs, that's all,' said Isabella, from in front of the mirror. She scrunched them up in her hands and wondered if an underwired bra might be the answer. 'I mean, they look so *arbitrary*. What are they doing there, exactly? If I didn't have tits I'd look like a boy, wouldn't I?' There was some truth in this. She had a straight, slim-hipped figure and broadish shoulders. 'They don't *work*, do they? Be honest.' Camilla blew a perfect smoke ring.

'You've got good legs, though.' There was a tiny pause in which Isabella did not say, as she should have done, So have you. Despite their length and slenderness there was just the slightest suggestion of teddy-bear ankle about Camilla's legs.

'But I've got piggy eyes.'

'Brian won't be looking at your eyes,' said Camilla.

'He's not called Brian, for God's sake.' Isabella polished a smear off the mirror. 'He's Ben, or something. He *has* to be.'

'Bruce,' murmured Camilla. 'Bernard. Boris. Bertram.'

'Shut up.' Isabella poured the last of the wine and Camilla writhed to a sitting position. *Sinuous*, thought Isabella, with tipsy aggression. She always felt hoydenish in Camilla's company.

'So how will you catch him?' asked Camilla.

'I'll think of something.'

'Well, when you've finished with him, hose him down and send him round to me.'

But I might never finish with him, thought Isabella, surprised at this new idea. A man you might never tire of. Hmm. She downed the last of her Chardonnay thoughtfully.

Her tactics were simple: she went up to South Wing 4 on Monday morning in a very short skirt and sat beside him. After a moment he turned and looked at her. She smiled and fluttered her eyelashes. His eyes held a look of tired resignation. Beautiful grey eyes with deep laughter lines and long, long lashes. Older than your run-of-the-mill student. He must be a postgrad, she decided. He went back to work.

'What's your name?' she whispered. But he only laid a finger on his lips and shook his head without looking up from his book. He sat reading – she timed him – for three solid hours without a break. When he finally gathered his books and left at twelve thirty, he cycled off so fast that she had no hope of following.

The next day he wasn't there. Nor the next. By the third she began to think she must have scared him off, but on the Friday she saw him going out of the revolving doors at twelve thirty-one, and realized he must have been hiding in a different bit of the library. The following Monday she tracked him down in the Rare Books room and sat next to him with her thigh almost touching his. He glanced up and gave her another long, weary look. She fluttered her eyelashes and smiled again, and he returned to his work. And so it went on. He hid in increasingly devious places. Sometimes she found him, sometimes she didn't.

After a fortnight of him steadfastly refusing to talk to her or be distracted from his work, she thought up a different strategy. She lay in wait in the bike park at nine o'clock, watched him arrive, then chained her bike to his after he had gone into the library. She came back at twelve thirty-two and found him waiting with his bike-clips on and his arms folded. He was not surprised to see her.

Hee hee! This is going to be *fun*! She went up to him, smiling.

'Would you mind unlocking your bike?' he said.

'If you tell me your name.'

Eventually he sighed. 'Look, there's something about me I think you ought to know.'

Her heart gave a nasty lurch. 'You're gay!' She saw a fleeting grin.

'Worse than that, I'm afraid.' Another lurch.

'You're married!'

'Worse than that, even. I'm an ordinand.'

'A what?'

'An ordinand. A trainee priest.'

She grasped at the word in bewilderment. 'A *priest*? You mean, like . . . Are you a virgin?' Several heads swivelled their way at this.

He was struggling not to smile. 'Actually I'm not, as it happens, Isabella.'

He knew her name! 'You know my name! How?'

'Can I have my bike now, please?'

'No. I haven't finished with you yet.' He looked at his watch, sighed again and waited. She savoured that look of sweet resignation, thinking how she would share it with Camilla later. 'You're Catholic, then?'

'Well yes.' A dismal bell rang. Something about celibacy.

'Not Anglican?' she pleaded.

'Actually, yes.'

'Oh, *Anglo*-Catholic, you mean?'

He rubbed his hand over his face wearily. 'I'm an evangelical. We're all catholic, but I wouldn't worry about it.' He shrugged apologetically at the complexity of the issue. There was a pause.

'Does that mean you *can* have it off or you *can't*?' asked Isabella, cutting briskly through all this nonsense.

I don't believe this, said his look. 'It means I can't.'

'Why not? Vicars can get married, can't they?'

'They can't just *have it off* when they feel like it.'

She felt a slight rush of shock at hearing him repeat this expression. 'I bet some of them do.'

'Not this one. Look, I'm late. Can I have my bike?'

'In a minute. Why can't you?' She lit triumphantly on a good argument. 'I mean, sex must be OK. After all, God created it, didn't he?' She slid closer and smiled up at him encouragingly.

'You might like to take a look at the Maker's instructions some time, Isabella.'

She stared, then drew back a little and began to suck her hair. A blush crept up her neck towards her face. 'I've read the Bible. Well, bits of it. Adam and Eve and the Sermon on the Mount.' Suddenly she wasn't sure she had. She knew what it was about, though. Roughly. 'I mean, I know the Ten Commandments.'

He raised his eyebrow enquiringly, and she turned away in case he asked her to recite them. The only one she could remember off-hand was the one about not committing adultery. The whole thing was going horribly wrong. She bent down to unlock her bike and to hide her embarrassment.

'There you are.' Her tone was almost as flippant as ever. 'Have I made you late for your prayers, Father?'

He mounted his bike. 'Lunch, actually.'

'Wait. Do you belong to some kind of college, or something?' He grinned at her and cycled off. 'Hey! Which college? Come back!' But he was gone.

Isabella stood a long time chewing her hair. Her insides felt raw, as though some meanness in her had been exposed and brought to light. I was only teasing him, she thought. He didn't have to put up with it. He could have told me to get lost. But the feeling wouldn't go away. She had always imagined that despite her outrageousness she was essentially an OK sort of person. Now she felt as though there was some vast overshadowing standard she was failing to measure up to.

She climbed on her bike and headed back to college, busy tailoring the incident into an amusing anecdote for Camilla. She was back in her room before she realized she still didn't know the bastard's name.

CHAPTER 2

'I want you to imagine, if you would, a town or city you know well,' said Muriel. 'At night,' she added.

The group obediently shut its eyes. It was four o'clock on Thursday afternoon; Annie's least favourite time of the week. After a moment's skirmish with irritation she closed her eyes too, and pictured the town where she had grown up. She was standing on the high street outside the Nonconformist chapel where her father was a deacon. Rain was spotting the puddles on the pavement.

'The street lights are on,' continued Muriel's voice. Well, of course they are, thought Annie crossly. It's night. She loathed these contemplative exercises. 'Imagine, now, that you are hovering over this town or city.' Pleased by this unexpected development, Annie rose up. 'In a helicopter.' She bumped down again angrily. Why a helicopter? Annie was capable of crossing the Rockies on a *chaise-longue*, but loyalty to Muriel made her call up a helicopter. She hovered over the town in the noisy cockpit as the blades chopped round overhead.

'Approaching high street, over,' said the pilot beside her.

'Proceed to Western Road, over,' crackled Control. Chop chop chop.

'It is totally silent,' said Muriel. Annie tried to stifle the racket. 'And now I want you to imagine that a figure steps forward from the shadows. You haven't noticed him or her before.'

Oh, honestly! Annie's eyes popped open in exasperation. How could anyone conceal themselves in the cockpit of a helicopter?

She scanned the group, but no one else seemed to be having difficulty with the idea.

'The figure says something.' Annie shut her eyes again.

'Listen, could you drop me off at that wine bar on Frogmore Street?' said the figure.

'And you respond,' went on Muriel.

Helicopter banks round out of control. 'Where the bloody hell did you spring from, mate? You nearly gave me a heart attack!' Annie spiralled down clutching her seat. We're going to crash! The hacking of blades filled her head.

'And now,' said Muriel, 'let's spend about ten or fifteen minutes in silence thinking about this exercise.'

Annie fought the temptation to open her eyes. Most of the time Muriel was a normal middle-aged woman, but under the pressure of preaching or leading a small group she broke out into peculiar stilted gestures a little out of sync with her words as though she were a badly dubbed foreign film. 'Let's try to explore, in the silence, what God might be trying to say to us about our calling.'

Annie crossed her legs restlessly. Ideas like *God* and *Calling* had long been the staples, the bread and rice of her spiritual diet. But now they seemed more like French black truffles: so hard to get hold of they may as well not exist at all. The time had long passed when she should have gone to talk to a member of staff, or even her bishop, about this. Her self-imposed deadlines came and went: summer, Advent, Christmas. And now Lent was bearing down on her. It was cowardice that held her back, or pride; for although it was not uncommon for people to drop out of their training at Coverdale, Annie could not bear to be one of them. She had put herself forward for the ministry in opposition to her parents. Bad enough to become an Anglican, let alone seek out a role which was in flat contradiction to the Scriptures. A woman could preach (under certain circumstances), but she certainly couldn't have charge of a congregation. The Bible was quite clear on the subject. And as for wanting to be a priest – *well*. Where do you read anything about *priests* in the New Testament? To say nothing of academic theology. What had a bunch of atheist intellectuals got to do with the Word of God? People who studied theology lost their faith. It had been proven time and time again. You see, Anne? We warned you it would happen. The slippery slope.

I really must go and talk to someone, thought Annie. Dr Pollock, the Principal of Coverdale Hall and Jesus College, was a terrifying woman. Annie couldn't imagine approaching her. David Tuckerman, who was the Warden of Coverdale Hall, was a nice man, but she couldn't confide in him either. It was his very niceness that made the idea impossible. Her doubts weren't strong, clean and brave. They were furtive and unpleasant. They were to do with hating church and wanting to get off with an entire rugby team. If this was her biological clock ticking, then it was built like Big Ben.

Annie made an effort to drag herself back to the group. What were they supposed to be pondering? God and Calling. The wrecked helicopter smoked on the street below. A camera crew circled its remains. Annie could make out the shape of a smart young correspondent with a microphone. 'The cause of this tragic accident hasn't been established yet.' An unknown figure stepping out from the shadows and saying something. Who was it? The dark stranger of the tea leaves, for ever in the future waiting to be met. Dark and thin. Intelligent. Intense . . .

'GOD AND CALLING,' said Annie firmly to herself. Outside, the cathedral clock struck quarter past four. She wondered if the other members of the group were sitting thinking about sex as well. Perhaps everyone found the session illuminating except her. Her imagination was too finely tuned. It resented being jerked around by other people's inexpert handling. She had escaped to private worlds of her own for as long as she could remember; places where things didn't require engines and propellers to make them fly. All you needed was a stiff breeze and you could circumnavigate the globe in Grandma's bloomers. The problem for Annie was remembering that it was the real world that was real. Half the time the characters in her novel seemed more convincing than the people around her. If she were to run into Barney or Isabella on the riverbank it would be a while before she thought, Just a minute – you're not supposed to be here.

She opened her eyes and looked round the rest of the group again. There were five of them sitting with her in Dave's room in Coverdale Hall. On the wall were several batiks – women with waterjars, elephants – which dated back to Dave's various stints overseas as a voluntary worker. Annie's eyes twitched away from the colourful squares. They made her think of her ex-fiancé Graham, who was now a missionary in Africa. Eleven years after the event, she could no more remember why she had ditched him than why she had ever got engaged to him in the first place. Well, you'll end up never getting married if you carry on like this, Anne, said her mother. Right so far. Annie was thirty-one and still single. Her mother hadn't particularly liked Graham, but women shouldn't expect too much.

Dave had his eyes shut. He was about thirty as well, but looked younger. Annie sympathized. People were constantly mistaking her for an undergraduate, or worse still, a teenager. It was a serious disadvantage in her chosen profession. The Ten Commandments seemed more like ten diffident hints when she pronounced them. She had been a fairly hopeless teacher, as well; but fortunately she had only ever taught in a polite girls' private school so she had just about got away with it. The girls had expressed their rebellion in furtive novel-reading and yawns rather than in flying desktops. Dave had grown a beard to disguise his absurdly youthful appearance, but it only made him look like a small boy peeping through a hedge.

Next to him sat Ted Watts, a big gentle man in his fifties. Annie was fond of him, and they shared a lot of silly jokes which nobody else really understood. Their current craze was odd notices seen in shops. 'This door is alarmed', was Ted's latest discovery. Annie was waiting to tell him about the one she had spotted the previous day: 'Free-range thighs'. Their favourite was on the wall of the local greengrocer's: 'The assistants will cut up large cabbages on request.' Edward could not be brought to see why this was funny.

Annie suspected that she was a surrogate daughter for Ted. His own family had remained down south while he was training, and he seldom saw his wife and two teenage girls except during the vacation. Annie had once been on holiday with them in

Northumberland in a cottage owned by a doctor friend of Edward's. She had spent half the time not having a clue what they were talking about. Years of accumulated jokes, Spoonerisms and varieties of pig Latin made their conversation unintelligible to outsiders. Annie felt doubly left out. Her own family had never enjoyed things that much.

Ted's large form partially obscured Muriel. Muriel had been a midwife before coming to Coverdale, and she still wore one of those little upside-down nurse's watches pinned to her front, although her bosom was a mantelpiece worthy of a carriage clock at least. Annie couldn't see her face, but her hands were visible, palm-upwards on her knees, cupped as though waiting to receive something. Julian of Norwich's hazelnut, perhaps.

On the opposite side of the room from Annie sat Isobel. Without Isobel around Annie would have qualified as a *jolly attractive woman* by Coverdale standards. Isobel was tall and willowy and blonde. Annie was only of medium height and build, with round brown eyes, dark rusty brown hair and freckles. Isobel could sit on her long silky tresses, but Annie had had to reconcile herself to the fact that the only way she was ever going to be able to sit on her own hair was if she cut it all off and stuffed a cushion with it. She had been growing it for two years and it was still only shoulder length. It was coarse and bushy and why didn't she get herself a decent haircut? she looked a mess, said Mother.

Annie could not like Isobel. She wrestled dutifully with her failure, calling to mind all those helpful sermons she had heard on the subject. Christian love – *agape* – was not a matter of human emotion. It was an act of will. You could love someone by God's grace without actually liking them. Annie applied herself to the task as though Isobel were the spiritual equivalent of having to eat school cabbage. They ought to have been friends, since they were the only two young single women in their year at Coverdale, but Isobel was so cool and distant. People were a little scared of her. She would put a headmistress-like menace into the Ten Commandments: 'Any individuals caught breaking them and spoiling it for everyone else will be severely punished.' Isobel lacked something. An earthy streak, perhaps; a raunchy sense of humour. This was precisely what Annie had bestowed on her when she took hold of Isobel and put her into her novel as Isabella's friend Camilla.

Annie glanced at her watch. Surely fifteen minutes were up? She suppressed her rising annoyance. If she'd had any sense she would have boycotted the sessions as Edward had. He couldn't bear open-agenda groups, either because of his temperament or as a result of all those years in the Army. He had walked out way back in their first term, muttering that it was a complete bloody waste of time and he had an essay to do. The rest of them had sat asking, 'How do we feel about Edward's actions? We feel hurt, rejected.' No, we don't. We feel jealous, thought Annie. We wish we had his nerve.

It would have been nice, once in a while, to feel that the fault lay out there in other people, in the system, and not in her sinful heart. A woman's place is in the wrong, as Annie's mother was fond of saying whenever she considered herself unfairly accused (which was any time anyone accused her). Annie felt that although there were three women in her immediate family – herself, her elder sister and their mother – the task of being in the wrong always seemed to fall to her. Both her mother and sister were constitutionally unable to be wrong about anything, so whenever someone put empty milk bottles back in the fridge or squeezed the toothpaste in the middle, it always had to be Anne. If anything got lost or broken: Anne. Windows open, doors unlocked, lights left on: Anne. Yes, everyone knew that when something was amiss in the Brown household, stupid, inconsiderate, spendthrift, clumsy old Anne had to be behind it.

Annie had grown up never knowing what her next offence would be. She was always trying to apologize and placate in advance. And over everything lay the long shadow of the Cross. The death of a loving saviour for which she was personally responsible. 'And I want you to know, boys and girls,' the preacher might say, 'that even if you were the only sinner in the whole world, Jesus would have come to die for you. That's how much God loves you. He sent his only son to die in your place. And if there's any boy or girl here today who hasn't asked the Lord Jesus into their heart, I want you to do it now.' By the time she was seven, Annie must have asked the Lord Jesus into her heart about fifty times; as though Jesus spent his time dithering on the threshold, doing a kind of spiritual hokey-cokey – right foot in, right foot out, in, out, in, out . . .

Beside her the last member of the group stirred. Ingram. A smooth thirty-five-year-old possessed by the evil spirit of a Californian therapist. One of his numerous concerns was the inability of the British to get in touch with their feelings, although he was as English as the rest of them. It was largely his influence that kept the group locked in a cycle of what Edward dismissed as navel-gazing. Ingram was pompous, pedantic, pretentious and Annie (NAME THAT EMOTION!) hated him. It was the only time in her life she had given way to hatred. She felt guilty, of course, but what surprised her was that giddy sense of release. Not having to excuse him the whole time, or see the other point of view, or blame herself for his faults. The other members of the group found him trying, but nobody else, as far as she knew, Had A Problem With Ingram the way she did.

His real name was Charles Ingram Wallis, and Annie liked to think of him as Chuck (with connotations of *out* or *up*). 'Ingram' was alleged to be the name of his ancestral Northumbrian village, and this had prompted another of Ted and Annie's games: finding the most appropriate English place-name for Chuck. It had become almost obsessive for Annie. Everywhere she went her eyes darted to signposts. She pored over Ordnance Survey maps. Goonbell, Fry Up, Pratts Bottom, Pity Me, Great Tarpots. And her favourite: Blubberhouses. More recently they had begun inventing their own villages, and Ted would often lean close to Annie in Morning Prayer and murmur something like, 'Foppingham', to which she would reply, 'Gitford'. It took them till half-way through the psalm to recover. Annie made herself look at Ingram. He had shoulder-length fairish hair and little round glasses of the fiercely intellectual kind. Today he was wearing a red blazer and a navy blue silk shirt, red and navy striped tie, navy blue trousers and socks and red patent leather shoes. He was probably wearing navy blue silk boxer shorts monogrammed in red, too. Great Poncington.

'Well,' said Muriel. 'If we could just gather our thoughts together . . .' There was a corporate rustle of clothing as people straightened up from their prayerful positions.

'Whose turn is it to lead us next week?' asked Dave, as he got up to put the kettle on.

'Annie's,' said Ingram, looking up from his Filofax. He was the only one who kept a record of these things, so there was no arguing with him. Annie imagined a petty triumph in his voice. She had her plan ready, however. The next session was going to be called 'Learning from the Quaker tradition', and they would all sit in silence for forty-five minutes.

'Actually,' said Isobel, 'I've got a suggestion. I've got tickets for *King Lear* at the Theatre Royal next Thursday. Why don't we make that our session for the week?'

The group, apart from Ingram, fell on the idea with enthusiasm. Isobel began gazing out of the window, her foot tapping silently as though she were bored by their gratitude.

'Is it a matinée performance?' asked Ingram.

'Evening,' replied Isobel.

Oh, help, thought Annie, seeing what was coming.

'Well, I see no reason why we should forgo Annie's contribution,' said Ingram. 'We could meet as usual, and then go –'

'Certainly not.' If it hadn't been Isobel speaking, the interruption would have seemed rude. 'One or the other.'

'*King Lear, King Lear!*' chorused the group.

'Unless Annie's already prepared something,' said Muriel, always quick to spot a potential cause of hurt.

'No, no,' smiled Annie. Dave began to pass round cups of ideologically sound coffee.

But Ingram was not beaten yet. 'Well, perhaps Annie – as a former English teacher – could prepare a response to the performance for the week after?' His gold-plated fountain pen stooped like a bird of prey over his Filofax. Why does he have to act as though he were our tutor all the time? 'Themes of atonement in *Lear*?' Annie resented his thespy abbreviation of the play's title. He probably referred to *Macbeth* as 'the Scottish play', too.

'Oh, lighten up, Ingram,' said Dave. 'Let's just enjoy ourselves for once.'

Ingram clapped his Filofax shut with a shrug of goodwill. Annie pictured him lightening up as if buoyed by helium, rising to the ceiling and bobbing there against the plaster – 'Help, help! Pull me down, someone!' – while the rest of them drank their coffee and ignored him.

Outside the cathedral bell began to chime for Evensong. It nagged away like her conscience. How long will you go on living a lie? How long? How long? But it was all too huge. Her faith was not a worn-out dress she could simply discard. It would be like trying to set aside the earth she stood on. All at once she could not bear to remain in the same room as the rest of them.

'I'll see you in chapel.' She backed, smiling, out of the door and hurried to her room to write till it was time for the service.

Isabella's view that all clergymen were wankers had not been challenged by her encounters with the college chaplain. He was not bad-looking – tall, dark and thin with round glasses – but Isabella knew she could never think well of a man who sat with one leg wound right round the other and both hands clamped between his thighs. She was, however, prepared to issue a small quantity of charm now that she wanted something from him. Not the full a-thousand-ships quota, but certainly enough to send a couple of smallish fishing smacks slithering down the slipway. With this in mind she went to the trouble of finding out his name before going and knocking on his office door.

He rose politely to his feet as she entered.

'I hope I'm not disturbing you, Tim.' She cast him a three-dinghy-launching smile.

'No, no. Not at all. I was just . . .' He waved at a chair. 'Won't you . . .?' They both sat. 'So how can I . . .?'

By finishing a sentence, for a start, thought Isabella, but before she could speak he sprang to his feet again.

'Tea? Coffee?'

'Coffee, please.' Was he always this twitchy, or was it just the shortness of her skirt? She wriggled it an inch or so back down her thighs with a little squirming movement. He fiddled violently with the coffee machine, then sat down again.

'So, um . . . what can I do for you, um, Isabella?'

Well, um, full marks for knowing her name. She crossed her legs. His glance ricocheted away.

'I'd like to borrow a Bible.'

'Certainly.' He was on his feet again. 'Which version?'

Isabella paused, thrown off course for a minute. Tim hovered in front of his shelves. Surely there was only one Bible? She took a wild stab. 'The traditional one.'

'Ah, the King James, you mean.' He handed her a black volume and she flipped through, peering at the tiny print. 'A bundle of myrrh is my beloved to me,' read Isabella. 'He shall lie all night betwixt my breasts.' She snapped the book shut in shock.

Tim sat down again. He had a concerned look on his face. 'Can I ask . . . Is this a . . . well, a spiritual quest?'

She saw he had slipped into professional mode. 'Oh, no. A carnal one. I'm trying to seduce a priest.'

'Ah, and you're doing some background reading. Good.' Isabella stared. He was supposed to blanch in horror. He had even stopped umming. 'Do you have a particular priest in mind?'

Well, she thought, looking him over with surprised interest. He was young and male. And he had that Everest-like quality of being there. She decided to give him the full battleships-away! treatment.

'I *did* have someone in mind, but now I've met you I'm not so sure . . .' She recrossed her legs at him and fluttered her eyelashes.

He sighed gallantly. 'Is he here in Cambridge?' She nodded, sensing that the conversation had a firm hand at the helm and was heading rather boringly back to port. 'A chaplain or something?' The coffee maker was starting to pop and bubble. 'Tell me all about him.'

Encouraged by having such a nice responsive audience, she poured out the whole story as they sat drinking his surprisingly good coffee.

'Well, if he's an ordinand he should be easy enough to track down,' said Tim. 'There are only two Anglican training colleges in Cambridge.'

'I'm shocked!' said Isabella in glee. 'You're a priest and you're assisting me in a premeditated act of fornication.'

He shrugged as though implying God moved in mysterious ways. 'So what's his name?'

'He won't say. It begins with B. – B. Hardstaff.'

Tim's collusive smile vanished. 'Not Barney!'

Isabella was on him in a flash, clutching at his arm. 'Barney? Barney? That's his name? You know him?' He escaped across the room. 'Tell me!' She pursued him to his noticeboard where several photographs were pinned. He pointed to what seemed to be a picture of a school First XI cricket team.

'Is that him?'

'Yes!' Younger, but clearly the same man, sitting in the captain's place with a clutter of trophies at his feet. On his right-hand side sat Tim. 'Oh, you were at school together, then? So which college is he at?' But Tim was standing on one leg looking thoughtful and starting to um at her again. 'Look, you may as well tell me. I can find out easily enough now you've told me his name.'

'Um . . . yes. True. Well, Latimer Hall, then.'

Isabella hugged herself and giggled. She cycled past it most days. Brace yourself, Barney Hardstaff.

Tim was looking even more worried. He stared at the floor as though scanning around for a safe place to put his hovering foot. She felt a sudden qualm. 'What's wrong?'

'It's just . . . Um, what do you know about him, exactly?'

'Nothing. Only that he's gorgeous and sexy and I want him.' She thought for a moment, then added, 'And he's very stubborn.'

'Ah!' said Tim, seizing on this as though she were a dim pupil who had unexpectedly come up with the right answer. 'Extremely stubborn. It's just that you're so *wonderfully* enthusiastic, Isabella. I wouldn't want –'

'Oh, don't worry about me, Father. I won't be disappointed.'

'Well . . .' He looked doubtful.

'Look, I know he's into all that celibacy crap, but I mean, honestly! Come *on*, Tim. All that went out with the Reformation, didn't it?' He didn't reply. 'Oh, don't tell me *you're* celibate?' she said impatiently, seeing his expression.

'Well, yes. For the foreseeable future, anyway.' He was standing on one leg again as though his whole life were one long balancing trick. 'Until the Church changes its mind about the likes of me.'

'The likes of . . .' Oh, God. He's gay. She had some vague recollection of being told this before, but she hadn't been paying attention. She blushed at the memory of all her superfluous leg-crossings. Bloody waste of time all that was, she thought. 'You mean you manage without sex? *Totally?*'

'Now why should I tell you that?'

'You must do *something*. I mean, you must . . .' Isabella caught herself and converted the gesture into a vague wave of the hand. 'Ahem. Tell me about Barney.'

Tim scratched his head. 'Well, I've known him half my life, and when Barney says no he means it.'

'Hah! Fifty quid says I get him into bed by the end of term.'

'Done,' said Tim, holding out his hand with such alacrity that she hesitated.

'Done. And don't you bloody well warn him!'

'I wouldn't dream of it.'

She eyed him doubtfully. Supposing he was right? Well, you may know Barney, she thought with a smile, but you don't know *me*. She turned to leave. 'Thanks, Tim.'

'Let me know how you get on.'

'Or off.'

He laughed, and she went back along the corridor with the Bible in her hand, wondering how it would all turn out.

Not that Annie was sure she knew that, either. Her own life was slipping out of control, and now her imaginary world was displaying similar tendencies. Nice young chaplains coming out unexpectedly, Isabella getting tiresome. This is supposed to be escapism, thought Annie. I'm supposed to be in charge here. The bells chimed seven, and she leapt up. Damn. I've completely forgotten to go to chapel.

CHAPTER 3

Annie's alarm went off at six a.m. She washed and dressed before settling down to read her Bible and pray as she did every morning. It was what was known in evangelical circles as a Quiet Time. Well, it was quiet. It was a time. But Annie knew that it did not count as a Quiet Time in the proper sense, for instead of studying and praying, her thoughts roamed around freely.

That morning she found herself reflecting on prayer itself. When she was a child, God had always been someone who must be placated. Every night she did her best to please him, searching the crannies of her mind for sin, worrying about like her mother with a duster. First there were the big blatant sins to deal with – lies, disobedience – which lay like clods of mud on the carpet. Then there was pride, a fine film of dust over all her good deeds. But, oddly enough, what troubled her most were the old sins. They had all been confessed long ago and washed in the Blood of the Lamb, but the stains still remained, faint yet stubborn, as though the Blood were an inferior washing powder incapable of shifting deep-down dirt. Impossible. The fault must lie in the application. Perhaps if she had the faith to believe she was truly forgiven, then she would feel spotless. 'Though your sins be as scarlet, they shall be as white as snow,' promised the Good Book, sounding rather like an advert for biological. More faith. That was what was required. Like more elbow-grease. Only that made faith perilously close to Works, and nobody would be saved by their Works. Annie's heart had been washed a thousand times, tumbled wearily round in the drum of confession every night, but it was still grey. On the Last Day, when all laundry would be held up to the light, Annie knew hers would fail the whiteness test. But what was she meant to do? You weren't supposed to wash your own things – that was the error of Rome. God of his free grace did it for you. But why did free grace seem to leave grubby collars?

This must have been in part what drew her to Anglicanism. It relieved her of the terrible burden of keeping on the right side of God. The Anglican Church year rolled on regardless of her spiritual state. Advent, Christmas, Lent, Easter, the long green weeks of Trinity, all revolving calmly round like the eternal spheres. After years of bobbing about alone and terrified in her little dinghy, it was a relief when the great Ark of Salvation hove into her view. You hardly felt the pitch and swell on a deck that broad.

Her concentration was broken by the sound of Edward's brogues clumping down the corridor to the bathroom. She could also hear voices, the sound of running water and a chain being flushed. This had to be the grimmest aspect of college life, the communal bathing and bowel moving. There were plywood partitions, of course, but in Annie's unfortunate imagination they all washed and shat as though the huge old bathroom had never been divided up. This was the real reason why she got up so early – not piety so much as an attempt to avoid coinciding with her colleagues on the early-morning bathroom run. A very lower-middle-class hang-up. She didn't even have the proper vocabulary for it, still accidentally saying *toilet* when flustered, and feeling her common origins showing like a petticoat beneath a skirt hem. Edward could boom words like *crap* in his posh voice, but she was always at a loss. Shit was far too rude, defecate too medical, and as for *number twos* . . . The process had not been referred to at all in the Brown household, even when someone had galloping diarrhoea and could be heard lunging into the smallest room and voiding themselves in wild spluttering explosions.

This coyness made it all whoopingly funny for Annie and her older brother and sister as they were growing up. They were even more prone than most children to snort with suppressed mirth if anyone broke wind. Laughing at such things was strictly forbidden, which spelt hours of prolonged agony for the Brown children. The toilet was situated above the dining room and every last splash and droplet was clearly audible to the family gathered round the table below. 'I'll just go and make myself comfortable,' the visiting preacher might say right before Sunday lunch. The Brown children would hum the tune of the Sunday School offertory hymn, 'Hear the Pennies Dropping', trying in vain to disguise their hoots as coughs and being sent from the room in disgrace before the final crescendo when the refilling cistern howled like a werewolf and all the pipes shook.

When adolescence arrived their hilarity gave way to excruciating embarrassment. Annie's sister Dawn found it all unendurable. She had got on and out and up as fast as possible, ditching her vulgar chapel background with its brown suits and forest-glade air fresheners, reincarnating herself as a journalist under the name Hermione. Silly, said Mrs Brown. Dawn's a perfectly good name. You'll always be Dawn to us. They were not on speaking terms. Annie called her Hermione to her face, but always thought of her as 'Damn', after an unfortunate spelling mistake by their brother Colin who was slightly dyslexic and apt to muddle up his Ms and Ws. Damn now lived in London in a terrifyingly smart flat done out in shades of string white relieved by the occasional splash of cardboard beige. She worked for a snooty magazine, damning other people's taste in interior design, having resolved to have nothing in her house except what she believed to be fashionable and knew to be expensive. Annie had sent her a crocheted crinoline-lady loo-roll cover as a house-warming present and received no reply.

Annie would never be as grown up as Damn. She still found herself betrayed into unseemly mirth on bathroom matters. There had been one dreadful occasion in Coverdale: she was seated ready to pee when someone shifted slightly in the cubicle next to her. All wee-power abruptly deserted her. Then there was the sound of a page turning. Oh, no! It was probably Edward. He was known behind his back as the Bishop of Lewes (pronounced wrongly) for his long daily occupancy of this particular stall. Annie could almost feel the radiant heat of his body glowing through the plywood. Her own face burned as she pictured corduroy trousers round ankles, Bible commentary on hairy thighs. Oh, come on! Pee. Pee. She tried to conjure up images of plunging waterfalls, cascading mountain streams, dripping taps even, but to no avail. There was a sniff from two feet away. In desperation Annie put her fingers in her ears, fearing she was about to hear grunts followed by a sigh of satisfaction. 'Hear the pennies dropping,' she hummed mentally. I can't possibly go out without weeing at all. He'll know I haven't. Suddenly she was seized with the urge to make a loud farting noise. A real six-lagers-and-a-Vindaloo style fanfare. She sat with her hand clamped over her mouth, trying desperately not to laugh.

'Is that you, Annie?' came Edward's voice from beside her. Horror! 'Yes.'

'What are you giggling about?'

'I can't *go* with you sitting there!' Annie wailed. She pulled the chain and fled. Later, when she met him in the street, he laughed and called her a funny girl. He was clearly puzzled by the whole incident. But, then, he had been to boarding school.

Isabella wouldn't be at all fazed by bodily functions, decided Annie. It was one of the reasons she liked her. Isabella had all the directness Annie lacked. Barney wouldn't be disconcerted, either. Annie wondered briefly if she had borrowed a bit of Edward here. Her characters were a magpie's hoard of stolen bits and bobs. An eyebrow here, an accent there. But what never ceased to amaze her was the way these cobbled-together creatures would stand up and live lives of their own with very little reference to her.

Barney was a good example. She had first seen him, as Isabella had, walking through the catalogue room of Cambridge University Library. Big, blond and beautiful, minding his own business. Not being Isabella, however, she didn't pursue him, but went on looking things up in the catalogue instead. She had seen him only once more, crossing John's playing fields in cricket whites one June lunchtime. She didn't even know his name, but now there was Barney, kitted out with a whole existence – home town, upbringing, family, education, vocation. He was more real than the blond stranger striding past her one June twelve years earlier.

★

Isabella set off for Latimer Hall at lunchtime the following day, intending to track down Barney and compel him to come to a May ball with her. It was a bright and breezy day, which fitted her mood perfectly. She had spent the morning revising, and her mind buzzed with fragments of Shakespeare's sonnets as she cycled along. Isabella was neither a very diligent nor a very brilliant scholar, but she had tremendous self-belief which kept her skating with great speed and flair over the thinnest of academic ice.

'"Unthrifty loveliness!"' she recited as she hurtled over Clare bridge, '"Why dost thou spend upon thyself thy beauty's legacy?"' She felt at one with the Bard in her pursuit of golden obstinacy, although more confident in achieving her goal than he appeared to have been.

She reached Latimer and chained up her bike. In the big arched entrance she stopped someone and asked where Barney's room was. G-staircase. Isabella set off across a wide grassy quad with Victorian red-brick buildings standing graciously round it. Some students were playing croquet on the lawn and there were a lot of mothers and toddlers roaming around.

Her heels clipped demurely down the long path. She was wearing a pretty dress with a blue pansy print. Exactly the thing for visiting a clergyman-to-be in, except that on windy days – *whoops!* – the skirt would fly up round her ears like Marilyn Monroe's on the subway grille. Under this she was wearing a slight hint of knicker and the kind of stockings which were supposed not to need a suspender belt but which usually did. 'Hold-ups' they were not. That, however, in Isabella's book, was the whole point of them.

She reached G-staircase. There was a list of names and room numbers at the foot of the stairs. *Barnaby Hardstaff.* She felt a flutter and began to climb. It was quiet. She glanced at the closed oak doors as she passed, wondering what effete clerical types were cringing behind them. When she found Barney's room she paused and listened. He was there! Brushing his teeth by the sound of it. She knocked and went straight in. He was at the sink, back to her, stark naked. Isabella let out a shriek. He turned, toothbrush in mouth.

'Barney! You're *huge!*' Her voice echoed round the stairwell. She was outside before she knew it, staring at the firmly closed door. Bugger. She tried the doorknob and heard the sound of the catch being dropped.

'Let me in, Barney. Please. I want to talk to you.' She knocked. No answer. There was a quality to the silence which convinced her that other people were listening behind all those closed doors. She dismissed the idea of wailing, *I think I'm pregnant!* 'Barney, I want to ask you something.'

The door opened. He'd got his cricket trousers on. She ducked under his arm and darted into the room before he could stop her.

'The answer's no,' he said.

'You don't know what the question is.' She perched on the edge of his desk and admired his torso and chest hair.

Surprise me, said his expression.

'I've been reading the Bible,' she improvised, as he pulled on his shirt. 'I'd no idea it was so complicated. I keep getting all confused. Will you explain it to me?'

His lips twitched as he struggled to remain serious. 'Why not ask your college chaplain? That's what he's there for.' He reached for his pullover.

'Please, Barney. I'm sure you're really good at it.'

'I'm sure Tim is, too.'

'But he's gay.'

His head emerged through the pullover neck, smiling. 'I thought we were talking about Bible study, Isabella.'

'Of *course* we are. So you will, then?'

'No.' There was silence as Isabella rethought her tactics. He was putting on his socks. She looked round the room. Books, sports stuff, beer cans. A bachelor's room. It smelt of Imperial Leather soap. The window looked out over Newnham. Some girls were sunbathing on a flat roof. Good God. One of them was –

'There's a nude woman out there!' she said.

Barney glanced. 'So there is.' He picked up his boots calmly.

'What kind of man *are* you?' He was smiling again. 'Oh! You knew. I bet you've spent the last hour leching!'

'No, I haven't.' He had a foot up on the desk chair in front of her and was tying his laces. 'She's only been out there ten minutes.'

Hah! 'So you admit you're interested in women?'

'I wasn't aware I'd denied it.' I'm just not interested in you, his tone implied. He was lacing the other boot now. We'll see about that. She hitched up her skirt and began adjusting her stockings. His bent head was just inches from her thighs.

'The buggers work their way down when I walk,' she explained innocently when he looked up at her.

A second later she was studying the outside of the locked door again.

'Let me in, Barney.' She rattled the knob. 'I promise I'll be good.' There was no answer. She decided to play to her unseen audience. 'Oh, come on, Barney. You can't possibly waste an erection like that. It's sacrilege! I'm sure God wouldn't want you to.'

The door opened abruptly. She leapt back in case she had pushed him too far. He came out with his cricket bat, looking completely unconcerned, and headed down the stairs. She scampered to keep up with him, heels clacking on the wooden steps.

'Barney, will you come to a May ball with me?'

'No.' They were at the bottom.

'Why not?' No reply. He began striding across the quad. 'Please.'

'I said no.' When Barney says no, he means it.

'Why not? Have you got someone else? Is that it?' Still no answer. She tugged at his arm. He stopped.

'What?' He was exasperated at last.

'I love you, Barney.'

'Well, you've got a funny way of showing it, Isabella.' Her mouth dropped open.

'*Funny?* What do you mean *funny*? I want to go to *bed* with you, for God's sake! What better way of showing it is there?' A small child was gazing up at her in wonderment from the lawn. Piss off, she thought. Barney simply shook his head and began walking again. Her cheeks burned.

'What am I supposed to do? Buy a bloody vibrator?' she muttered at his retreating back.

But he heard her and turned round. 'Why not buy a six-pack while you're at it? I'll give you a donation.'

With that he walked off, leaving her spluttering in the middle of the path. He really *did* mean no. Here was a healthy red-blooded male who was genuinely not interested in a quick no-strings-attached legover. She tried to shrug it off. Perhaps she wasn't his type. But what if he thought she was a slut? And suddenly she could think of no good reason why he shouldn't think that. It's only a game, for God's sake. Why was he taking it all so seriously? She stood, amazed at how much it hurt. I'm getting out of here, she thought. But, unfortunately, the only way out seemed to be along the path after Barney. She was going to have to walk past him and the other cricketers gathering in the archway. The small child was still staring at her. She stuck out her tongue at him, summoned her dignity and walked off.

She was a few yards from the group of chatting men when her skirt, which had been docile all day, chose to leap up like a playful hound. She squeaked and clutched at it. There was a tactful silence and she scurried past the men and their averted smirks. Bloody vicars. It wouldn't be half so embarrassing if they bayed and whistled like normal men.

She heard them setting off and walking past her while she was bending to unlock her bike. She clamped her skirt firmly between her thighs and wrestled with the lock until she re-membered something else about that dress. She straightened up hurriedly, but not before she had given the Latimer Hall First XI a generous glimpse of cleavage. If she had been able to meet Barney's eye as he passed her, she would have seen that he had a distinctly unsaintly expression on his face.

They had just –

There was a knock at Annie's door. She shut her notebook and hid it swiftly under her Bible.

' "Reject battered fishcakes", ' said Ted coming up behind her. She laughed. ' "We offer a full range of sundries." '

'I'm just off to chapel. Do you want to walk down with me?'

31

She sensed an undercurrent of concern. Damn damn damn it all. What if her friends had got together and said, 'We're a bit worried about Annie,' and chosen Ted as the best person to tackle her?

'Yes. Yes, of course.' She rubbed her forehead.

'Headache?' asked Ted.

'No. I'm fine.' There was a pause.

'Good.'

She hated fobbing him off like this. 'I expect it's just my hormones running amok.'

Ted gave her shoulder a friendly pat. 'Poor old Annie.'

She got to her feet. He was probably used to fielding this kind of thing – teenage daughters, menopausal wife. She pictured him in rubber waders venturing out into a dangerous tide of oestrogen. They set off along the corridor.

'It's my age,' she apologized. 'Big Ben. Ticking away. I expect it'll fade.'

'Into a small folding travel clock, maybe,' he suggested, taking up her image as she'd expected him to.

'Good. I can stifle it under my pillow.'

'Or throw it against the wall.' They went down the stairs.

Edward came crashing down three at a time and caught them up. 'Morning!' He might have been addressing a parade ground.

'I sometimes forget to wind my clock up, these days,' said Ted.

Don't, pleaded Annie's look. She could feel herself starting to giggle.

'Why don't you get one with batteries, then?' asked Edward.

Annie yelped.

'It's got a snooze button,' went on Ted. 'In case I want to nod off again.'

'What's the matter with her?' Edward demanded.

'I've given up asking,' replied Ted.

They went out onto the street and crossed over to the college chapel. It was a cold grey morning. The cathedral bells chimed. Ding dong ding *dong*! Ted glanced at Annie and made her laugh again, but she was aware how easily her laughter could slide over the edge into tears. If she were to plunge off down the street sobbing they would understand. The time of the month. Her age. Poor old Annie. They stood aside and let her enter chapel first. It was just politeness, of course, but it felt as though they were police officers escorting her into the dock.

CHAPTER 4

They were just –

They were just what? wondered Annie as she stared at the page. She couldn't remember how that sentence had been going to finish before Ted had interrupted her the previous day. There was no time at present to reconstruct the scene in her mind. She was supposed to be at a doctrine lecture.

Dr Mowbray was already passing round handouts when Annie entered Coverdale lecture room. She slid into an empty seat beside Edward. He gave her his wide flashing smile, and her sex-drive came bounding up like a friendly dog with its tail wagging. *In your basket, Libby!* ordered Annie. Libby was short for Libby-doo, which was how one of Annie's former pupils had thought libido was pronounced. Libby sat panting quietly as Dr Mowbray cleared his throat and put on his glasses.

'Right. Models of atonement today.' He flapped a piece of orange paper. 'Does everyone have one of these salmon-coloured handouts?' There were some smothered grins. Dr Mowbray was very alert to subtle colour gradations. Ted and Annie had wasted many moments devising fanciful names for white paper (polar-bear-coloured, shaving-foam-tinted). Annie looked at the sheet. Quotations from the Early Fathers and great Reformers. It was complemented shortly by a mature Cheddar-coloured sheet with extracts from more recent theologians. Dr Mowbray began.

At first Annie concentrated, on the grounds that if he could be bothered to say it she should be bothered to listen. Dr Mowbray was a kind man with a thorough but rather monotonous lecturing style. He had been a tutor in Coverdale since about the mid-sixteenth century. Before long, however, her thoughts were deflected along a path of their own.

The Crucifixion was supposed to be the pivot of human history. It was the point at which the eternal intersected with the temporal. Somehow Christ was reconciling the world to God by his death on the Cross. Somehow. But how? Annie's eyes scanned the yellow and orange sheets. So many answers to this one question. They all seemed to glance off the surface of the problem. Annie no longer had any answers of her own. As a child she had always pictured the Crucifixion taking place in the back garden at home under the shadow of the horse-chestnut tree. The scribes and Pharisees walked up and down the dusty lane beside it, wagging their heads. They were dressed in long stripy robes from the Sunday School dressing-up box and they had tea-towels on their heads. The wind stirred in the sticky buds while Christ hung motionless on his Cross.

> There is a green hill far away
> Without a city wall,
> Where the dear Lord was crucified,
> Who died to save us all.

It was a strangely dispassionate Passion. Where was the violence, the man nailed up on a plank of wood and left to die in the Middle-Eastern sun?

Edward's biro was racing busily. Annie knew he was just going through the motions, though. He'd already got the Cross sorted out. He made no secret of the fact that his aim was to get through Coverdale with his faith unscathed. Annie suspected he viewed theological college as a sort of boot camp – lots of pretty tedious square-bashing and assault courses, but you knuckled down and got on with it for the sake of what lay beyond. He attended lectures and went on placements stoically, knowing it would soon be over. He'd be ordained, and then he could get on with the real business of proclaiming the Gospel and making disciples. Edward had no room for words like *contextualization* and *dialogue* in his vocabulary. 'Load of bull,' he could be heard booming above the throng in a voice that was clearly going to render some church PA system obsolete when he arrived there as curate.

Annie sighed. Edward was a dear friend, but his theology suffocated her. It marshalled and harried everything into order and began sentences with the words *the Bible says*, as though this automatically silenced any counter-arguments. It dealt with Facts and Proofs. There was little room for the 'what ifs' and 'yes buts' of this world, and Annie was a terrible yes-butter. There were no buts. The Cross was God's solution to Man's sin, as amply demonstrated by the Bridge Illustration.

Oh, that old Bridge Illustration. Annie doodled an arch on the salmon sheet. She had first encountered it at the age of five in a children's address. The visiting preacher (Mr Winter from Watford) got out his flannelgraph. He stuck a felt square saying GOD on the left-hand side of the board and a felt square saying MAN on the right. Between the two was a gap. They were separated by SIN. Man tried in vain to straddle the gulf of green baize with such jerry-built bridges as Good Works and Church Attendance, but in the end (lo and behold) it was a sturdy cross which fitted the hole perfectly. *Ergo*, you could only be saved by Christ's atoning death. Annie was tempted to point out to Edward that a Koran of the right size would also fit. Or a doughnut, even, if you tamped it down properly. But Edward would think that it was just another of her mad, semi-sacrilegious notions.

It wasn't as if Edward had no sense of humour, thought Annie. He was quite capable of laughing at himself, once he'd worked out what the joke was. Annie smiled as she remembered a skit he had done in the Coverdale Christmas revue. Bishop inspects the troops. He had marched onto the stage in a purple shirt with a short crozier tucked under his arm and barked at a line of cassocked recruits: 'All right. Straighten up, you lot. You're in the Church now, you know.' He had paused in front of Annie, who was hopeless at acting and had spent the entire sketch weeping with laughter, and bellowed, 'What's that you've got under your uniform, soldier?'

'Bosoms, sir.'

'Bosoms? Never heard of them! Not regulation!'

'She's a woman, sir,' Ted had interjected. 'We have women in the Church these days, Bishop, sir.'

'Eh? What? Oh. Very good. Carry on, soldier.'

She felt herself starting to giggle again at the memory.

Edward looked up. 'Hopeless!' he hissed, not even bothering to find out what was amusing her this time.

Annie tried to read the quotations in front of her, but found her mind returning to that flannelgraph. She had stared at it, rapt, as the preacher was saying, 'And so, boys and girls, it's no good thinking you can earn your way to God by going to Sunday School.' His voice went kindly on, urging them to invite the Lord Jesus into their heart if they hadn't already done so, while behind him the felt cross was slowly unpeeling itself from the board. It flipped to the floor without a sound, leaving God and Man as estranged as ever.

'Right. Well. Any questions?' asked Dr Mowbray, rubbing his hands together briskly.

Ingram, of course, had a question. He'd been sitting at the back reading a book to demonstrate that doing two things simultaneously hardly engaged one fifth of his vast intellect. He shouldn't even have been there. The lecture was designed for Coverdale students doing the Certificate in Theology, but Ingram was bright and therefore doing the university theology degree. He was attending this lecture simply to show off. Everyone knew he would get a first in his finals in June. Unless Annie was right and he wasn't actually that bright, after all. It would all depend on whether the examiners had the patience to sift through his polysyllabic phraseology to see if an idea was lurking there or not. If they took him at his own estimation he would certainly get a first. Annie scribbled 'Little Pinhead, Rambledon' on a piece of paper and threw it to Ted.

Meanwhile, Ingram's question had drawn to a close. Dr Mowbray looked thoughtful.

'I'm not really sure what you're asking, Ingram,' he said at length. Annie smirked as Ingram flipped back his floppy hair.

'I *think* what I'm saying is this,' he said patiently, and off he went again.

'Get your bloody hair cut,' muttered Edward into his notes.

This was overheard by half the room, but Ingram forged on, impervious to their tittering. Dr Mowbray answered him. He's probably as intelligent as Ingram would like to be, thought Annie. Why doesn't he just swat him aside like a bumptious bluebottle? But Dr Mowbray was endlessly long-suffering and unassuming. Perhaps he'd seen it all before. He must have watched hundreds of ordinands come and go over the years. He was stroking his silvery beard and saying, 'Yes! Ah, yes, indeed! That's a very good point,' to a question from Dave. He tidied it generously into the proper theological categories as though this was what Dave had meant all along. Annie decided that Dr Mowbray should marry Barney and Isabella. She'd have to find a new name for him. Manning? Mayhew? Moore?

'You may now kiss the bride.' Barney did. Not a perfunctory peck, but a long, deep, passionate kiss. Isabella was on her toes almost squeaking with surprise. The moment went on and on. A bee droned up the aisle towards the mass of flowers and Dr Moore cleared his throat. The congregation, who had started to shift a little in their pews, laughed. Barney released her and gave her his wonderful slow smile. My God, thought Isabella. My *God*. What's tonight going to be like?

Libby thumped her tail eagerly in her basket, and Annie snatched her thoughts back. What am I doing here? she wondered, in a kind of amused despair. She thought again about the hundreds of ordinands, picturing them like an early black-and-white film, shuffling with frantic jerky gestures into the lecture room, tackling tricky doctrinal or ethical issues, then juddering out again. Wave after wave of nice, white, middle-class people. We'll go on to live out our faithful, not-very-glamorous lives in parishes up and down the country. What difference will we make? We stake everything on the belief that it makes all the difference in the world, but when we look around, what do we see? Empty churches. Locked churches. Redundant churches. What's the point? We might as well not bother. Don't think that way, she chided herself. Faith was like the apostle Peter walking on water. If you looked round at the wind and the waves and asked yourself how you were doing it, you were bound to sink.

How many others had slid despairingly under the waves in their time at Coverdale? Perhaps they had managed to thrash their way to the shore and were successful barristers and bankers now, attending church on Sundays, looking at the slightly pathetic figure in the pulpit and thinking, Phew. What would she do under those circumstances? She heard her mother tut angrily. You're hopeless, Anne Brown. You're always giving up. There's that pegbag you never finished. You can't go through life never finishing things, you know. But Annie did. Her whole history was a mess of loose ends. She seldom had the courage to cut things off properly and make a clean break. They just petered out. She was always trying to convince herself that she'd come back to them one day and maybe finish them. She still had that pegbag somewhere.

If she left Coverdale she'd have to skulk back to teaching. God, you're so boring, Anne, Damn used to say; and Annie had to admit Damn was right. It would be nice to go out with a little style, for once. To scorch across Coverdale like a bad comet. But that wasn't *done*, of course. Or at any rate, not often. The college had produced one *enfant terrible* in its time, famed for his boozing, bonking and bad language. It was ten years ago, but people still spoke of Johnny Whitaker with a kind of awe. He'd somehow managed to scramble aboard ship again and get ordained, so maybe there was hope. Annie had only contemplated these things, not done them. Maybe he'd sat listening to this very lecture ten years ago with a hangover, plotting the fate of the next sexy undergraduate. She smiled in fellow-feeling. There were several extremely attractive young men in Jesus College next door. *Woof woof. Get down, Libby!*

A bit of folded paper landed on the table in front of her. She opened it. 'Much Blether'. She glanced across at Ted and grinned. He was looking as deadpan as ever.

That evening Annie looked again at the words *They were just*, and crossed them out.

'Stop writing now, please, ladies and gentlemen.'

Isabella's pen made a final desperate lunge towards the end of the sentence. Her arm was dropping off. It was her last exam, thank God, and she knew she had done disastrously. All around the students stretched and exchanged grimaces while the exam scripts were collected up. Isabella wiped her sweaty hands on the skirt of her cream slub-silk dress. It was new and outrageously expensive, and she had bought it in the firm belief that if you looked good, you felt good; and if you felt good, you worked well. The system seemed to have broken down somewhere, though. She was heavily overdrawn and felt lousy. Still, she thought, as she got to her feet, being overdrawn made the sums easier. You just added to your total. And in any case, her father would bail her out as usual if she went to him with a trembling lip and admitted she'd got herself into a bit of a pickle again. She shook the full skirt and filed out with the others.

It was hot. The air filled at once with the laughter and wails of post-mortem. Champagne was cracked open and the end-of-term annihilation began. Isabella wandered off across the marketplace to where she had chained her bike. I don't feel part of it, she thought. Camilla's law exams had finished two days earlier, so she had already spent forty-eight hours drunk. She would be waiting for Isabella with a whoop and a wine-glass. Isabella had seldom felt less like partying. And all because of Barney. She had turned the encounter in Latimer into a light-hearted romp for Camilla, and the two of them had giggled and shrieked over the story. But Isabella had been unable to edit out of her mind the memory of Barney standing and shaking his head at her. In *disappointment*. That's what was so awful. He didn't find her outrageous and irresistible. He was disappointed in her.

She searched along the railings for her bike. As the days passed she had gradually realized that she'd give anything to have him think well of her. Even *behave* well, for God's sake. There was no denying it. She was in love with him. There was also no escaping that it wasn't mutual. He'd never made the slightest attempt to contact her. It was all so humiliating. She would rather *die* than let him know what she felt. If she bumped into him she was going to pretend that it was a huge joke, and he was only about number eight or nine on her list of intended scalps.

At last she spotted her bike against the crowded railings. God, I hate it when people park their bikes on top of mine. She struggled to untangle the pedals and handlebars. Some thoughtless, selfish bastard. 'Some *man*,' she muttered, seizing the crossbar and tugging it away from hers. Both bikes crashed to the ground and lay on the pavement with a wheel whizzing round.

'*Shit!*' She aimed a kick, then stopped. They were chained together! She looked up, and there was Barney.

'Barney!' She remembered belatedly that he must never know how she felt. 'Unlock your bloody bike, will you?'

'No.'

'Yes.'

'Only if you have lunch with me.'

'What? But I – you –'

'In Latimer. Not very exciting, I'm afraid.' She gave in and smiled. Why bother to pretend the sun shone from anywhere other than out of his gorgeous backside?

'I'd love to.' He was smiling back into her upturned face. The busy marketplace surged on around them.

'How was it?' he asked.

'How was what?'

'Your exam.'

'Oh! Terrible.'

People were tutting and trying to get past them and the fallen bikes. He bent and unlocked his chain. 'Stop looking at me like that, Isabella.'

'Why?'

'Because you're only going to be disappointed.'

Her smile wavered. 'I am?'

'Yes. I happen to know it's only corned-beef salad.' Her smile burst out again and she bent to pick up her bike. 'Nice dress, by the way,' he said. For a second she thought he was looking down the front of it, but he couldn't have been, of course. They began to cycle to Latimer. The warm breeze tugged Isabella's skirt and lifted her hair from her face. She might have been flying. They stopped and waited at the red lights. Isabella couldn't help blurting out: 'I thought I wasn't ever going to see you again.'

'Why not?'

'Well . . . I thought you were kind of mad . . .'

He turned and looked at her. 'Mad? At you? Isabella!'

Her heart was racing. His eyes, his voice, his smile – endless possibilities hinted at, then instantly denied. 'I bet you're magnificent when you're angry.'

'Mm. I think you're safe. I have a very, very long fuse, Isabella.'

'I *know* you have, Barney. Although size isn't meant to be important, of course.'

His lips twitched. 'And it burns very, very slowly.'

'Good. I like a bit of staying-power in a man.'

He lost the battle against smiling. 'You're impossible.'

A car horn honked impatiently behind them and they set off again, laughing.

'How old are you, Barney?'

'Twenty-seven.'

'I'll be twenty next month,' she supplied, when he failed to ask. They turned into Latimer Hall Road. A woodpecker thrummed deep in a walled garden as they drew up outside the college. The sound seemed to echo for joy in the woods.

Isabella felt uncharacteristically self-conscious as they entered the dining hall and joined the lunch queue. Perhaps it was the throng of chomping vicars-designate, or the po-faced clerics staring down at her from the portraits on the walls. She began to wish that her dress had something by way of a back to it. Barney, as he stood behind her waiting for his corned-beef salad, could have trailed a finger down each vertebra of her tanned spine. She felt as though the whole room was glancing at her in disapproval. At any moment someone might block her path like a guard outside an Italian cathedral and tell her to cover herself. There was nothing for it but to brazen it out. She turned and smiled up at Barney over her shoulder.

'You're not a vegetarian, are you?' he asked.

'God, no.' She flared her nostrils at him. 'I need my meat.'

His lips twitched again. 'Isabella, if you don't behave, I'll turn the fire hose on you.' He gave her a push, and she scuttled to catch up with the rest of the queue.

They collected their salad and sat down. Barney introduced

her to the men already sitting at the table. She saw at once that they could only be priests in the making: nice, but drippy. Still, they were dealing out copious amounts of interest and attention, asking her all about herself and how she knew Barney. He was sitting opposite her, watching. Before long she began to feel like Scarlett O'Hara at the barbecue. She fluttered her eyelashes at him – Why, fiddle-dee-dee, Ashley Wilkes! – and finished her salad in a welter of male admiration.

'And where do you worship?' asked the man on her left, proffering the fruit bowl.

'Where do I what?' She took an apple and began to polish it on the front of her dress. 'Oh, church, you mean. I'm afraid I'm a bit of a pagan, really. I don't go unless it's a wedding.'

A series of glances were exchanged around her like a coded message. After a moment she deciphered it. They thought Barney was trying to convert her. Hah! Was that why he was being so friendly all of a sudden? She looked at him and he raised an eyebrow.

'Barney's trying to convert me,' she said, deciding on a pre-emptive strike. 'Without much success, so far, I'd have to say. Which makes us quits, because I'm trying to –' FIRE HOSE! said Barney's fulminating glare. '– I'm just trying to understand it all. You know, God and everything.' Whoops! She looked around to see if anyone had noticed. Her words seemed to have provoked an unnerving professional silence. They waited respectfully for more, and to her horror she found herself starting to witter about the Ten Commandments, and her granny dying, and what are we all here for, anyway?

'And what about all the suffering in the world? If there is a God, how come he lets wars and famines happen?' But it had begun to feel as though there was one, after all. One who liked her enormously and was terribly interested in her, but who didn't approve of her one little bit. He was looking out at her through their eyes. She sank her teeth defiantly into the apple as they explained the concept of free will to her.

After the meal Isabella was pressed to join them in a game of croquet on the lawn. She intercepted a not-quite-Christian stare from one of the women nearby and was therefore about to accept when she remembered Camilla. She'll still be waiting in college for me, thought Isabella guiltily.

'I'd love to, but I've got to go and get pissed. *Drunk*, I should say,' she amended, catching Barney's eye. 'Well, not drunk as *such*. Just a couple of glasses. You know, end of exams and all that. Everyone does it . . .' she heard herself pleading. I can't believe I'm doing this. I don't have to explain myself to a bunch of sanctimonious celibate gits. 'Well, 'bye, everyone. It's been nice meeting you.' She waggled her fingers at them and set off. Barney fell silently into step beside her like the wrath of God.

'Thanks for lunch,' she said, as they reached her bike. 'Can I come again next term?'

'No.' He smiled at her stricken expression. 'I'm afraid I won't be here.'

'But – Why won't you?'

'I'm getting ordained. I'll be a curate in darkest Hertfordshire by then.' It felt like a slap in the face.

'Well . . . congratulations, or whatever.' I'll never see him again. She was sucking her hair and trying to blink back the tears. 'Can I come with you and be your concubine?'

'No.'

'Why not? They had concubines in the Bible. Oh, please. I'll cook for you. I'll iron your cassock, even.'

'Surplice.'

'Surplus to what?'

'No, *surplice*. The white nightie thing. That's the one you iron. Cassocks you just dry-clean and hang up.'

'Bugger the laundry,' she said impatiently. 'I *love* you, Barney.'

'Mm. You said.'

'Yes, but now I really mean it.' She could have shaken him in frustration. 'It's true. I'd do *anything* for you, Barney!'

'Really?'

'Truly.'

There was a thoughtful pause. 'How about a blow-job?'

'*What?*' She stepped back in shock. 'Did you say – Barney, do you have any idea what that means?'

44

'Why? What does it mean?'

'I don't believe this!' She felt herself getting redder by the second. 'It means . . . well, oral sex, for God's sake.'

'It does?'

'Yes. Oh!' He laughed as she made to punch him. 'Bastard. You aren't supposed to have *heard* of things like that, let alone know what they mean.'

'Why not?'

'Well, you're practically a vicar.' He was grinning at her. Isabella was by no means as experienced as she would have liked everyone to believe. She pushed her hair back from her hot face and aimed for a casual tone. 'And, besides, it's a disgusting practice – like picking someone else's nose.'

He considered this. 'More fun, though.'

There was a short silence. Her bluff had been well and truly called, and she cast about for a cool exit line. None suggested itself. 'Well, I'm late. I'd better go.' She undid her padlock.

'Did you find a partner for that ball, by the way?'

'Oh, no problem.' She made an airy gesture and was about to get on her bike.

'And will you behave yourself?'

'What's it to you?' He waited. His patient silence goaded her into saying, 'I doubt it. I expect I'll get pissed. Or laid. Both, probably. They tend to go together.'

He shook his head. 'You're worth more than that, Isabella.'

'Fuck you!' she exploded. 'No, I mean it. *Fuck you.* Don't you dare tell me how to behave! Who the hell do you think you are?' He walked off without a word. Oh, no! she wailed inwardly. 'Barney. Look, Barney, I'm sorry.' He disappeared back into the archway. She let her bike crash to the ground and chased after him.

'Now what?' he asked, when she tugged at his arm.

'I don't mean to be like this. Honestly. It just sort of happens . . .' The sentence tailed off miserably.

'Some things are like good wine, Isabella. They improve with keeping.'

'What about Beaujolais nouveau? You drink that the minute you get your hands on it,' she pointed out.

He was trying not to smile again. 'True. But I'm a claret man. I prefer something a bit more mature.'

'Oh, *thanks*. You'll wait for me to grow up, will you?'

He touched her lips briefly with a finger and smiled. 'Well, you never know.'

She watched him walk back down the long path and join the others playing croquet. The woodpecker's drum sounded hollow as she cycled away.

CHAPTER 5

It was Thursday afternoon again. Annie looked out of her window. There was a yellowish tinge to the clouds and she wondered whether it was going to snow. On her desk lay the notes for an essay. The navel-gazing session had been cancelled in favour of *King Lear*, but Annie was not about to waste the gift of two hours on the Shape of Modern Liturgy.

It was the evening of the ball. Isabella and Camilla were standing in front of the big mirror in Camilla's room wearing identical slinky dresses. This was deliberate, of course. The only difference was the colour. Camilla, being blonde, was in black, while the dark-haired Isabella wore white. As they pouted and busied themselves with their make-up, Isabella couldn't help feeling she'd got the short straw. Camilla was already tall and slim enough without the benefit of black. White could be so fat-making. Isabella scrutinized her own slim form for bulges. Still, it set off that exam-revision tan she had worked so hard on. Camilla began applying some lipstick. Isabella had just re-counted an edited version of her lunch with Barney.

'All that play and still no score,' marvelled Camilla. 'Here, put some of this on.' She handed Isabella the lipstick.

'Slut red. I like it.' There was a silence as Isabella painted her lips scarlet, and tried to muster the right casual note to tell Camilla the whole story. 'He asked me for a blow-job, actually.'

'Yeah?' Camilla was pulling on her long black gloves, unmoved by this revelation. 'They all do, sooner or later.'

'Sure,' mumbled Isabella, as she blotted her mouth on a tissue.

They did? 'But he makes this great thing about being celibate.'

'Well?'

'Well, what?'

'Did you oblige?'

'No–oo. Gravel drive, you know? Plays hell with a girl's knees.' She tossed the screwed-up tissue towards the bin and hoped she wasn't blushing. But when she slid a glance at Camilla's reflection she met an amused stare.

'Let's face it, child, you've never done it.'

Isabella grimaced. 'Nah. Never fancied it.'

Camilla laughed and put a long black cigarette into her predictably long black holder. 'Send him round to me.'

'Over my dead body.' There was a hostile silence; then Isabella abandoned pride in favour of gleaning a little information. 'It's just that . . . I mean, what do you *do* exactly, when – when – you know?'

'Spit or swallow, little one,' drawled Camilla, lighting her cigarette.

Annie shut the book with a guilty giggle. I can't write that! The scene had been inspired by an occasion when she and Isobel had shared a mirror as they prepared for the college ball. Annie owned no make-up and was borrowing some of Isobel's. The colours were all wrong for her freckled skin, and she could never apply make-up without feeling like a six-year-old raiding Mother's dressing table. Not that Mrs Brown ever wore it. It was sinful. The only woman in the Bible who wore make-up was Jezebel, and we all know what sort of woman *she* was. The Brown girls were forbidden to touch the stuff. Annie accepted this meekly, and to that day found bright lipstick faintly shocking. Damn rebelled, though. Annie could still remember the long bitter eyeshadow wars that raged throughout her adolescence.

Isobel had worked in the mirror with cool efficiency. Annie watched her sidelong as she blended exactly the right amount of blusher into her hollowed cheeks. The pinnacle of Annie's cosmetic ambitions had always been to apply mascara without getting a black line across the bridge of her nose when doing the left eye. She'd never mastered the professional backhanded method Isobel was so casually employing. Annie stared at her reflection. Her brown eyes looked rounder than ever – like a startled marmoset. The scene Annie had just written was her revenge on Isobel. She could always repent and cross it out later.

It was just that Isobel was so frostily perfect. Her dark blue silk dress had been simple but stunning. Annie had given up trying to look conventionally beautiful, much to her mother's disgust. You look like something the cat's brought in, Anne. Why don't you wear something smart for once? You've got plenty of nice things just hanging there in your wardrobe. If you're not going to wear them you should take them down to Oxfam. And look at your hair. You've really let yourself go.

Annie had ditched her teacher's image along with the job. All those polite skirts and V-necked pullovers. Beige and grey, like her life had been. These days her only sartorial rule was to wear what she wanted, regardless of what it looked like and whether other people thought it was appropriate. Her clothes came from charity shops and jumble sales, or from dark little shops reeking of patchouli. All her skirt hems drooped. Her sweaters were vast and had unravelled cuffs. Nothing went with anything else. Army surplus with sequinned velvet. Tramp's coats with silk stockings. Perhaps it would have worked if Annie hadn't lacked that special ingredient – self-belief, perhaps? – which synthesized random garments into a fashion statement. Most of the time she knew she just looked odd. Edward called it her Orphan Annie look and it annoyed him almost as much as Ingram's hair. Ted had teenage daughters and found it normal. He had only commented on her clothes once. She remembered him saying, after looking thoughtfully at her most wildly unravelled pullover, 'Don't go near any working machinery while you're wearing that, will you?'

Her choice of outfit for the ball had been a little black cocktail dress. Late fifties or early sixties, low cut and exquisitely tailored – four pounds from Save the Children. When she had tried it on in the shop it had seemed quirky and slightly risqué; but standing beside Isobel's dark blue silk, Big Mistake seemed nearer the mark. Whatever was Edward going to say?

Annie was going to the ball with him because he was trying to escape the attentions of an eager undergraduate who had – through no fault of his – got hold of totally the wrong end of totally the wrong stick. Annie could be counted on not to misconstrue his gallantry. *Thanks*, darling. Annie had tugged futilely at the front of her dress to make it plunge less, suddenly fearing that Edward would prefer whoomfy taffeta to exquisite tailoring and quirky *décolletage*. Oh, no! His feet coming along the corridor. A knock. She opened the door and he took two clear steps back, astounded.

'Gosh, Annie. *Curves*.'

She wrung her hands, looking at his dinner suit. 'Is it too awful? I don't want to let you down.'

'Turn round.' She obeyed. 'I *say*, Miss Brown. Those aren't stockings, are they?'

'Oh, no! They don't show, do they?' She tried to wriggle them up, but it proved impossible without hoisting her skirt. 'Oh, help. What am I going to do? I should have bought tights, only I hate wearing them.'

'I could lend you some,' offered Isobel politely, coming to the door with the little evening bag that matched her dress.

'No, no!' protested Edward. 'She wouldn't *dream* of troubling you.' And to Annie's amazement, he swept her up in his arms and made off with her down the corridor like a caveman. Isobel stared after them in fastidious disapproval. I may be gone some time, Annie wanted to call to her, but had not dared. She was saving the line for her novel.

From that moment on Annie had her work cut out. It was all she could do to prevent Libby from knocking Edward flat, sitting on his chest and licking his face. He was flirting outrageously. He pulled Annie onto his knee and fed her strawberries, letting her run her hand through his short brown hair. But he misbehaved so impeccably that there was never any real danger of her misunderstanding him. She was a super Christian girl, but she was not the future Mrs Edward Hunter. Annie was aware that he had had a little conversation with himself: Q. Do I want this woman to be the Mother of my Children? A. No. *Sadly*. Therefore, no entanglements. But poor old Libby couldn't grasp this.

After it was all over Annie lay awake till dawn. The taste of strawberries, his strong arms round her. It was so long since anything like this had happened to her, since she had been kissed. Edward's goodnight kisses had been enthusiastic but chaste – mwah! mmm-wah! – planted one on each cheek, just brushing the corner of her mouth. And then to round things off – mmwah! – a firm kiss on the lips. His Imperial Leather soap, his hard smooth chin. Libby howled from her cold kennel outside.

Heigh ho.

Well, what am I going to wear tonight? She decided on her long green crushed-velvet dress. It had come from a Scouts' jumble sale and she suspected that it had once been yellow, only someone had tried to dye it blue. She loved the gentle mottled effect that had been achieved. That dress looks like an old dish-rag, Anne.

Would it be warm enough, though? she wondered. The fabric was panne, light as a bird's feather. It was the kind of thing she'd worn in her teens when she had been a tempestuous Pre-Raphaelite poet with clouds of raven hair every night as she fell asleep. Maybe she could wear her baggy chenille sweater over the top. It was dark blue-green. Rookwing. Annie was as colour-conscious as Dr Mowbray. It came from all those hours she had spent as a child poring over her mother's wool catalogues, running her fingertip over the yarn samples and drinking in jade, moss, aquamarine, twilight. Colour had flooded her parched imagination.

Mrs Brown's choice in clothes and interior design had been governed by the twin principles of economy and serviceability. Colour schemes were a silly extravagance. Their home was a battleground where ugly browns slugged it out with orange and maroon. Annie and Damn were mocked at school for their strange clothes. One day, when her parents were out, Damn had thrown the ghastly curtains, carpet and bedspread out of her bedroom onto the landing and painted the walls, furniture and floorboards white. White sheets for curtains and bed cover, white pleated filepaper for a lampshade.

Annie had accepted the violent swirls and dinginess with an outward submissiveness, but in her heart she treasured up all the gems of the New Jerusalem, turning them over and over and watching them flash. Jasper, sapphire, chalcedony. Sardius and chrysolite. Jacinth. Amethyst. Damn would have found the Holy City incredibly tacky, but Annie's soul was ravished by colour. No wonder she had been drawn to Anglicanism with all its jewelled windows and winking brass.

After a moment her thoughts returned to the rookwing sweater folded in her chest of drawers. It was new and expensive – one of her rare Isabella-type purchases. 'Chenille comes from the French for caterpillar,' read the accompanying rhetoric on the label, 'because that is exactly what it is like.' *Exactly what it is like.* Annie was enchanted by the notion that her sweater could be weaving a cocoon for itself in the dark of the drawer, and might one day burst out and flutter away across the university on petticoat wings. She looked at the dull sky out of the window and saw the first flakes of snow whirl past.

The cathedral clock struck the quarter hour. There had been a time when the sound had quivered in her very marrow. She had fallen in love with the City at first sight, with its steep riverbanks and towering cathedral. Even the cold air had seemed to teem with promise when she came up on interview. Now it oppressed her. The streets and buildings had a mad claustrophobic intensity. They were dwarfed by the cathedral, belted in by the tight loop of river. Annie longed for the wide fields and huge sky of Cambridge. Each time she travelled north again after the vacation her heart sank when the cathedral ap-peared. It rose up out of the horizon like a shark's fin above the waves, full of silent menace, making her feel that God was out to get her. If ever she strayed above her ankles into the sinful tide – VOOM!

Anyway, she thought, shaking off such ideas, tonight would be fun. *King Lear* was not everyone's idea of fun, of course, but they couldn't know what it meant to her to go to the theatre without fifty teenage girls. She'd be able to enjoy the play for once with-out fearing that someone would get lost, or drunk during the interval, or put on too much make-up on the coach beforehand, or wave at lorry drivers out of the rear window. And Edward would be coming, which would be nice. He had consented to join them since the group was actually *doing* something for once.

And they would be joined by Edward's doctor friend William, whose cottage Annie had once stayed in with Ted and his family.

Annie had been curious to meet William Penn-Eddis for a long time. His cottage had been so fearsomely well furnished and decorated that even Damn would have found nothing to shudder at. It was not full of other people's discarded three-piece suites and divans, as Annie had anticipated and, indeed, would have found quite reasonable. Everything was discreetly new. There were no frills or horsebrassy knick-knackery, and no colour to speak of. It made Annie want to toss a crimson silk cushion aggressively onto the ivory sofa. Whoops! There goes my glass of burgundy onto the oatmeal carpet. All in all, the place seemed to be crying out for an axe murder to be committed in it.

Annie smiled. She knew a great deal about Dr Penn-Eddis, considering she had never met him. Edward prayed for him regularly in their Coverdale prayer meeting. William had once been a keen Christian of the same hearty evangelical Boys' Public School Camp kind as Edward, but he had gone off the rails. Annie knew all this because Edward's prayers were always superbly informative, tactfully filling God in on the biographical details of the person being prayed for. Annie pictured the archangel Gabriel riffling through a card index and trying to locate the relevant soul for God while Edward was saying, 'And we pray for Hugh, an old Etonian, now working as a missionary in Uganda . . .'

'Hugh Duncan. Got him!' Gabriel would say, plucking the card out triumphantly and handing it over. 'Born in Amersham, Bucks, nineteen fifty-two.'

William, Annie had gleaned, was a Cambridge man, the oldest son of a vicar in North Oxford. He was very bright, could have done anything, and was now working as a GP in Bishopside. (A nearby north-eastern town where, as God was no doubt aware, reluctant Coverdale students were sent by the college to gain Urban Experience.)

Edward's affection for his friend seemed to be composed in equal parts of hero-worship and exasperation. Annie thought she could account for this. Not only was William thirty-seven, four years older than Edward, he was the one who had 'brought Edward to faith'. And, if this was not enough, he had also rescued Edward from drowning at camp that same summer. Edward had therefore been saved body and soul by William Penn-Eddis, and Annie winced to think how devastating it must have been for Edward when his mentor later renounced the Christian faith. William fascinated her so much as a concept that she wasn't sure she wanted to meet the real thing and be disappointed. She tried to guess what he looked like, but her imagination could only suggest a picture of Edward with a stethoscope round his neck, barking, 'Antibiotics? Nonsense! Cold shower and a quick run round the rugger field – soon sort you out.'

What's going on? Annie demanded suddenly. I give myself permission to work on my novel, and what do I find? I sit here thinking about clothes and men, for heaven's sake. She reread the mirror scene, hand poised to strike out the rude bits.

Isabella sat on the edge of her bed. It was three p.m. the day after the ball and she had just woken up. Her head ached, but it wasn't a full-blown hangover since she'd only got three-quarters drunk, not paralytic. She hadn't got laid, either; although, if she was honest, that had less to do with self-control than that her partner had passed out face-down in a lavender bush while throwing up. She had always found Luke sexy in a dark, smutty, two-days'-growth-of-beard kind of a way; but as she tried to haul him out of the herbaceous border his charm suddenly eluded her. The mingled smells of vomit and crushed lavender did not add up to irresistibility and, on a callous impulse, she let him lie. There then followed a brief window of sobriety in which she wandered around watching everyone else's antics. The spectacle disgusted her so much that she downed a couple more glasses of champagne to obliterate it.

Now, as she sat in her room with a throbbing head, she began to see what Barney meant by preferring something a little more mature. In that brief clear-eyed period she had witnessed Camilla not as a cool cynical beauty but as a silly drunken slag. Is that how I look to Barney? She winced at the probable reply and went to have a shower.

Camilla was still dead to the world when Isabella tapped softly on her door. Was that two sets of snores, even? She hurried away, embarrassed. She decided to go out and buy a new dress to cheer herself up. *Want* and *need* were synonymous in Isabella's vocabulary, so she had no difficulty in justifying the enterprise to herself. Before long, however, she began to sense the presence of Barney's disappointed face looming above the lingerie like Banquo's ghost in every shop she entered. Bugger off, she told him. I'll do as I please. Her eye fell on a cream straw hat with deep red silk roses on it and she knew at once that she *had* to have it. Wasn't it just *perfect* for her new silk dress? It would be a sin not to buy it. She tried it on. The hat *insisted* on being bought. She took it off and looked at the price. Over a hundred pounds! Barney shook his head. Oh, please! she wheedled. He turned to leave. Oh, all right, all *right!* She put down the hat and stomped out of the shop.

After a while her spirits rose. She had done the right thing, for once. Furthermore, she had saved a hundred quid and could therefore spend up to that amount on something else with a clear conscience.

It was in the next shop that she saw The Dress. Long and tight and black, split almost to the hip-bone up each thigh with nothing but latticework down the sides. Yes! She tried it on and bought it at once. It was a dream and, amazingly, it wasn't expensive! Well, not *that* expensive. Cheaper than the hat, anyway. Oh, *no-oo*. By the time she got home she was writhing with guilt.

Tim was coming out of the college chapel as she was skulking back to her room. The carrier bag seemed to smoulder as it hung from her hand.

'How's the hunt going?' he called.

'Hah!' She remembered her blithe wager earlier in the term. Supposing he demanded the money at the end of the week?

He crossed over to her. 'What's wrong, Isabella?'

For a moment she was determined to bluff her way out, but the wonderful concerned look in his eyes was her undoing. 'He doesn't *like* me, even!' she wailed. 'He thinks I'm a silly immature drunken slag!'

Tim took her arm. 'Come and tell me all about it.'

She let him lead her to his study and make her more of his excellent coffee. After a couple of gentle questions she found herself blurting out the whole humiliating saga. 'I don't know what's happening to me,' she concluded. 'I used to think I was OK but now I feel like a turd. And I've gone and spent loads of money on this stupid dress and I'm broke.' She plucked at the bag. 'I'll have to take it back and pretend it doesn't fit.'

'Let me see.'

'No. You'll hate it.'

'Go on.' She pulled it out. 'Isa-*bella*! You're not playing fair. Give the man a chance.'

She felt herself smirking. 'Worried about your fifty quid all of a sudden?' Tim was watching her thoughtfully, head on one side. Was he getting professional again? She shoved the dress back into the bag and fiddled with her coffee spoon. He seemed to be waiting for something.

'I just feel like someone's setting me an exam,' she burst out at last. 'Only I don't know what it's in so I can't revise for it.'

'And you think you're going to fail?'

She nodded miserably, weaving the spoon in and out of her fingers. She waited for him to start preaching to her, but he just sat there in friendly silence. The spoon pinged suddenly out of her rigid fingers and flew across the room. 'Well?' she snapped. 'Aren't you supposed to convert me, or something? That's your job, isn't it?'

'I've always seen it as God's job, actually,' he said. 'He's so much better at it.'

'What are you paid to do, you lazy bugger?' This is getting heav-*y* thought Isabella. She'd never met anyone who talked like this about God. As if he knew him socially, for crying out loud. 'Well, you can at least have a word in God's ear for me, then.'

'Certainly. What shall I say?'

'Tell him I want Barney.'

'I'll mention it.'

'Good.' Isabella thought for a bit. God might not be particularly sold on the concept of fornication. 'Let's revise that. Tell him I want to *marry* Barney. Please,' she added, wondering how

56

one addressed God. Rather like a college principal, she imagined.

'Anything else while I'm at it?' asked Tim. 'I can't interest you in Redemption? Remission of Sin? Eternal Life?'

'You sound like a bloody sales rep.'

He laughed. 'That's what I am, I suppose. More coffee?' She shook her head and stood up. He rose politely too, and went with her to the door. 'Well, *nil desperandum*, Isabella.'

She made herself grin. 'Nah. I'll keep my pecker up. Better still, someone else's.' She flourished the dress. 'Thanks, Tim.'

She got back to her room and stared at the wreckage. Dropped towels, unmade bed, dead flowers, dirty clothes, wine bottles, coffee mugs. Oh, sort yourself *out*, woman! she thought. She was about to start when Camilla came groaning to the door.

'We've got that sodding garden party in John's now,' she said. 'And I *hurt*. What's that?' she asked, suddenly alert. 'New dress? I thought you were broke.' She fished it out and held it up to herself. 'You whore. You'll be walking through a thicket of hard-ons if you wear that. Can I borrow it?'

'On your bike, you cheap scrubber.'

Annie's biro paused as she tried to think of a neat end to the scene. The clock chimed again. Help! She leapt up and began to change hurriedly into her velvet dress. She peered out of the window while she dragged a brush through her hair. Snow was falling thickly. Would the roads be blocked? She pulled on her sweater and boots then, grabbing a coat and beret, she hurried down the stairs, heart pounding, to meet the others in the hallway.

CHAPTER 6

She arrived breathless to find them waiting.

'Muriel and Ingram have gone to get their cars,' said Dave. 'We thought we'd risk it.'

They all looked doubtfully out of the door at the falling snow.

'Annie, you can't go to the theatre in jackboots,' said Edward, catching sight of her feet.

'Don't be so rude, Edward,' Isobel intervened. People were always defending Annie like this, as though she were a child, or a foreign guest who couldn't be expected to know about such things. 'She's very sensible. It's snowing.' Isobel was wearing court shoes.

Ted peered down at Annie's feet with a kind of professional interest. 'Ah! Now those are a fashion item, Edward. My girls wear them.'

'Look like jackboots to me.'

'*Edward!*' rapped out Isobel, in her headmistress voice.

A car horn tooted and they wrapped themselves up and went out onto the street. The cold air struck Annie's cheeks and there was the muffled hush of snow that she had always loved. The group dithered (You; No, no *you*, please; No, honestly, I don't mind whose car I go in) before Edward lost patience and sorted them out.

Annie found herself with him and Dave in Muriel's rattly old Mini. Ingram had a new car, but even the prospect of a warm journey would not have compensated for half an hour of him lecturing them on the Bard. Muriel was a cautious driver. She was peering anxiously through the windscreen as the wipers wumped to and fro shoving the snow aside. Annie could see her lips moving silently, and decided she must either be praying or reciting bits of the Highway Code to herself. Edward was in the passenger seat, and spent the whole journey twisted round and talking to Dave about Saturday's rugby international. Annie leant her head back and huddled up in her fleabag coat. The snow raced past her in a blur and her mind sped off to find Isabella.

'Are these totally obscene?' Isabella asked Camilla the following morning. She had just been cutting down a pair of jeans to make shorts.

'Bend over,' said Camilla, through a mouthful of croissant. Isabella touched her toes obediently. 'Hmm. Another half-inch and they would be.' Isabella reached for the scissors.

Half an hour later she was heading for Latimer Hall in the cropped shorts and a skimpy T-shirt. In her mind she was going over the details of her ball statement, in case Barney interrogated her. Hell, she hadn't got laid, had she? She'd hardly got drunk, even. I mean, give me a break. But with each step the story sounded dodgier.

She was so deep in thought that it was a while before she realized she was being kerb-crawled by some wanker in an open-topped sports car. She gave him the finger without turning. The red car continued to creep along beside her.

'Like a ride, little girl?' She whipped round.

'Barney!' He was leaning across and opening the door for her with a grin. She climbed in, twittering with excitement. 'Vicars aren't supposed to drive flash-git motors,' she said reprovingly .

'But I'm not a vicar,' he protested. He pulled out and off they went. The wind rushed through her hair. Somewhere in her mind the Hallelujah Chorus struck up.

'Is this really your car, Barney?'

'Yep.'

She laughed in glee. 'This is fu –' Whoops! 'F – f – fun.' Fucking fantastic! They were speeding out of Cambridge. 'And vicars aren't supposed to drive like this, either! Where are you taking me, Barney?'

They slowed at a roundabout.

'To a land full of hills and winding lanes.'

'Yeah?'

'Where I can do a lot of unnecessary gear changing.' He went down from second to first, knuckles grazing her right thigh. A shock thrilled through her. Well, Barnaby Hardstaff! This is more like it. She nudged his hand with her knee and waited. He made no move.

'Make the most of it,' she told him. 'In another month you'll be ferrying old ladies to church in this car.'

'I'd need a winch,' he replied. 'I'll have to sell it, and buy something sensible, I'm afraid.'

'You can't!'

'Sorry.' He had both hands firmly on the wheel again as though the thought of old ladies had brought him back to his senses. Damn the Church, thought Isabella resentfully. 'But in the meantime . . .' he said. They hit the open road and the engine roared.

'*Hallelujah!*' Isabella whooped, as they seared past rape fields under the blazing June sun. Barney –

The fields gave way to dark snowy streets. Muriel parked and they got out. The snow swirled yellow in the floodlights that shone near the monument. They made their way through the slush to the theatre. Annie strode confidently in her jackboots, trying not to smirk each time Edward skidded in his brogues.

He noticed. 'Get that look off your face, Brown!'

They reached the foyer and met up with Ingram and the others in the mass of damp theatre-goers. Snatches of bright conversation were sometimes audible in the rumble of chat.

'Can't see William,' came Edward's voice over the noise. Libby gave a little whine and twitched in her sleep at the mention of his name, but Annie decided to let her lie. No point having her bounding about slavering only to be disappointed. She searched the crowd, trying to guess which Barbour-clad man would turn out to be the good doctor. Her imagination came up with a picture of Edward flexing his hands in a pair of surgical gloves: 'Right. Clothes off and on the couch. Be with you in two ticks.'

'Happy, darling?' he asked irritably.

'Yes, thank you,' she replied. 'Darling.'

'I hope you're going to behave yourself,' he boomed. Several heads turned to watch the entertainment.

'Of course, Edward.' Hmm. Even if she wasn't a couple of drawers too far down the social tallboy for him, she could never marry a man whose pillow-talk would be audible all over the parish on a still night. Annie became aware that a dark-haired man had drawn close and was standing at Edward's elbow.

Edward turned. 'William!'

They shook hands and Edward began introducing him to the group. Annie looked him over sneakily while names were being exchanged. Quite tall. Lean, with a thin face. He looked pale beside the rubicund Edward. His hair was cut very short in that aggressive all-right-so-I'm-thinning-out style she rather admired. A wide mouth and straight scowling eyebrows made him plain to the point of ugliness. Oh, well. Libby stayed curled in her basket. She liked his clothes, though. Not at all like a doctor. Long black coat, tatty jeans and a baggy old dark green sweater. And best of all – jackboots. She looked up at his face again.

'And this is Annie,' concluded Edward, as the loudspeaker announced that the performance was about to begin.

William glanced at her and nodded. Her heart jumped with something like shock. Those eyes! He had already looked away, and she knew he hadn't bothered to register her name, but her heart continued to thump. Eyes like a hungry panther. *Walkies, Libby. Walkies!*

The group began to move towards the stairs. Just as well he was a GP not a surgeon. Annie could imagine passing out with a combination of lust and fear if she encountered those pale hazel-green eyes over a surgical mask. He was a few steps ahead of her, talking to Edward, but although Edward's voice was as stupendously audible as ever, she couldn't catch what William was saying. She watched his profile. He had a slightly aquiline nose and high cheekbones. By now they had reached their seats. Edward ushered Annie in first. Ingram followed, and Annie became profoundly absorbed in her programme. She couldn't block out his voice, though, as he lectured anyone whose eyes involuntarily strayed his way on the socio-political hinterland to *Lear*. Before long the lights dimmed and the murmur of conversation dwindled.

The beginning was spoiled for Annie by the fidgety presence of Miss Brown, who kept taking notes ready for discussion in class tomorrow. She ejected her with a struggle and settled back to enjoy herself. What would it have been like at the original opening night of *King Lear*? You wouldn't know that the first half was leading inexorably up to the putting-out of Gloucester's eyes. It was horrible enough when you knew it was coming. Annie sat tense. She hated anything to do with eyes. When, eventually, the scene arrived, Regan leant forward and watched the process with an unblinking prurience. Were there really people who were turned on by that kind of thing, Annie wondered, as the applause died away.

'Who'd like an ice-cream?' Edward's cheerful voice saw off all such thoughts.

They played No, no, let me, No, please, for a moment or two until Edward extracted the information he needed and clambered out to join the queue. Ingram also disappeared, thank goodness. Piddle Trenthide, she thought, wishing Ted was near enough for her to whisper it to him. Isobel began to engage William in polite chat and Annie moved a few seats closer, hoping to eavesdrop. Before she heard anything Ingram reappeared, brimming with some purpose.

'There's a woman in the corridor who appears to have fainted.' This was aimed at William. He glanced at Ingram, but said nothing. After a moment Ingram ventured, 'I thought possibly as a doctor . . .?'

'I'm off duty.' These were the first words Annie had heard him utter and they caused a little frisson to go round the Coverdale group. He seemed to sense it. 'She'll come round,' he added. This hardly improved the situation, and Isobel and Muriel were obliged to step in, as women will, and try to take the sharp edges off the conversation.

'I expect it's the heat,' said Isobel. 'Or that last scene.' They all shuddered and laughed in sympathy.

'Is someone with her?' asked Muriel. Ingram nodded. 'Oh,

then I'm sure she's all right. They'd be asking for an ambulance if they were at all worried.'

'It's so terribly hot in here,' repeated Isobel.

Ingram opened and shut his mouth and everyone tried to think of something to say. After the temperate climate of Coverdale, where everyone was primed to go the extra mile and do anything for the least of the brethren, William's attitude was like a bracing east wind. Or a breath of fresh air, thought Annie disloyally. She could see that Ingram felt he'd been made to look a fool. The atmosphere was so awkward, despite Isobel's and Muriel's efforts, that even Edward noticed it when he clambered back, fists full of ice-cream.

'What's going on?'

'Someone's fainted,' said Muriel soothingly.

Ingram pursed his lips to imply he was too generous to rat on Dr Doolittle lounging callously in his seat.

Edward obviously knew William well enough to sum up the situation at once. 'Well?' he barked at him.

'Well, what?'

'Go and do something.'

'You go and do something. Airways, breathing, circulation. Check them.' Edward glared. 'Basic first aid.'

'I'll go,' said Ingram.

'Perhaps I'd better,' said Muriel. 'I was a nurse.'

'I'm nearer,' said Ingram. No no; Yes, yes; Please, I insist. Annie caught William rolling his eyes. Not a man to waste his time on such games. His glance flicked her way and she began peeling the paper from her ice-cream with close concentration, trying not to smile. Ingram and Muriel went off together.

'Hah. I'm glad you're not my GP,' said Edward. William looked as though this was mutual. 'Bet no one dares call you out.' Annie thought she saw a gleam of amusement.

'Let's say they think twice.'

'Well, so they should,' remarked Isobel. 'I'm sure people make totally unreasonable demands on their doctors.' Libby bared her fangs and let out a territorial snarl.

'By the way, Edward,' said William, not taking up Isobel's comment, 'I was going to tell you this – one for your sermon

63

illustration file.' The group's attention focused on him. Ted and Dave leant forward to hear better. 'I was on call on New Year's Eve,' he was saying, 'pissed off because I was at a party and I couldn't drink anything.' He would have to have a sexy voice like that, thought Annie, clinging to Libby's collar for grim death. Deep, with a husky edge. But perhaps it was just the end of a cold. 'My bleep went off – predictably – at about quarter to midnight. Sick child. It didn't sound too serious, and I was just reassuring the mother when I heard the husband in the background say, "Tell that lazy bugger to get off his arse." And I thought, *Right*. I went. The child was fine – slight temperature, maybe – so I gave them a real bollocking for wasting my time.' He paused. They waited. 'I was just getting back into my car when I knocked my party hat off.'

Edward's laugh rang out. 'Serves you right, Penn–Eddis.'

'Yeah.' William grinned. 'Thought you'd like it.'

Annie stared, bewitched. She had never seen such a totally ravishing, transforming smile. Oh no! *Libby! Libby! Come back! Here, girl!* His eyes were on her again and this time she caught a raised eyebrow before she plunged back into her ice-cream. The conversation turned to sermon illustrations generally, and several anecdotes were swapped. Annie sat observing William covertly. His accent was nowhere near as plummy as Edward's, but she suspected that both his voice and his clothes were deliberately *déclassé*. Ingram and Muriel reappeared at this point with the news that the woman had come round.

'What if she'd had a heart-attack, though?' said Edward, preempting any smugness on his friend's part. 'Eh?'

'Then I'd probably have gone.'

'Forgive me,' said Ingram, 'but you didn't actually *know* she hadn't.' Little Snidebury-in-the-Dress-Circle. William didn't reply, but retreated into his earlier hauteur. No. I wouldn't dare call him out for anything less than pneumonia. But then I'd probably get a bollocking for not calling him earlier. She was grinning into the last mouthful of ice-cream when he leant across and snapped his fingers under her nose. She jumped and looked up into those eyes.

'Some problem?'

'No, no. I was just . . . Nothing,' she mumbled.

'William!' protested Edward. 'She wasn't doing anything!'

'She was laughing at me.'

'Nonsense. She was just laughing. She's always laughing, aren't you, Annie?' He patted her shoulder and she smiled up at him. 'Don't bully her.' She stole another glance at William and saw he was not fooled. Libby flew back with a yelp, tail between legs. Fortunately the lights began to dim and they all took their places again.

Annie spent the rest of the performance struggling to concentrate. Miss Brown kept fixing her with stern glares, but Miss Brown had always been weak on discipline. Eventually the lights came on and they were gathering their things and heading towards the exit.

'What did you make of that, Annie?' murmured Ingram.

She pretended to think. 'A performance that will remain with me for a long time,' she replied.

'Would you like to "unpack" that a little?' He picked out the word by making two little bunny ear gestures with his fingers, so that she knew he was being ironic.

'I think I'll need time to sort through my reactions first, Ingram. To ponder.'

'Of course. How wise.' He began to give his own reactions without any attempt at pondering. The crowds streamed down the stairs. Annie could just see Edward and William a flight below.

'Why don't we head back to your place for coffee, William?' came Edward's voice. They were just turning a corner and Annie glimpsed William's expression. He looked as if he could think of several reasons why not. By the time they had all gathered – with Ingram still in mid-disquisition – William appeared to have allowed himself to be persuaded. They went out into the snow again.

'Right. William, you go with Ingram,' ordered Edward. 'And we –'

'No,' interrupted William. 'I'd better go in the other car so that I can give directions. You follow us,' he said to Ingram.

'All righty,' replied Ingram.

Annie trudged through the snow with Muriel. Edward came

65

skidding along behind them with his friend. After a moment she heard him point out, as though he had been toiling with the problem, 'You could have gone in the other car and given directions.'

'What, with that cunt drivelling on about the Elizabethan *Weltanschauung*?' Annie flinched in shock. Muriel seemed to be pretending she hadn't heard.

'*Will* you watch that foul mouth of yours, Penn-Eddis?' barked Edward. 'I don't see why my friends should have to put up with that kind of language.' Annie and Muriel glanced at each other. Edward knew he wasn't supposed to protest that there were Ladies Present, but both could tell that this was what he meant.

'Well, you invited them, not me.'

Annie winced.

'Oh dear,' whispered Muriel. 'Perhaps we should . . .' Think up some excuse. We'd better be pressing on. The snow. Another time, maybe . . . But it was beyond the social guile of either of them.

They reached the car and got in with William in the front. Muriel started the engine and they set off.

'There's Ingram now,' said Edward. The other car began to follow them.

'What a wankmobile,' said William.

Edward chuckled. There was clearly some male prejudice against spoilers which had passed Annie by. 'You're just jealous, Penn-Eddis.'

'It wouldn't last five minutes in Bishopside,' remarked William. 'Take the next left. So where were you a nurse, then?' And he began to talk quite civilly to Muriel about midwifery and hospitals. Before long they lapsed into silence. The snow was still falling as they crossed the river. Annie glimpsed lights reflected in the water and the outline of the other bridges. William turned to Edward. 'Well, Teddy. Looks like the Government's pissing on the last embers of the welfare state, doesn't it?' This was definitely a red rag.

The bull swished his horns. 'I'm not going to argue with you, Penn-Eddis.'

'Thought you wouldn't.'

'What's that supposed to mean?'

'That you realize your position's untenable.'

'It is not!' A few more expert picador-like gibes had Edward rampaging into the political bullring after William's blood. Not that he stood a chance. William had one of those analytical minds that terrified Annie by dealing casually in frameworks. Edward was undaunted, however, and made up in volume and belligerence what he lacked in macroeconomic theory. Annie stopped trying to understand and began counting the blasphemies and obscenities instead. If we had a swearbox we could solve the Church of England's financial problems in one evening flat, she thought. Even Edward let fly with a bloody and a couple of bullshits. Muriel's lips were moving silently again.

Annie watched the snow gathering at the window edge then peeling away. She set Miss Brown a little assignment: Criticize the following phrase, paying attention both to content and context, 'That cunt drivelling on about the Elizabethan *Weltanschauung*'. Miss Brown recoiled from the task, but Annie was firm. It was shocking because it was so off-hand. It begged the question, what did the man say when he was actually annoyed about something? It was also unpleasant because it had a human subject (that is, Charles Ingram Wallis), which put it into a different league from 'Sod this' or 'Bloody weather'. Yes, decided Miss Brown. It was the undisguised contempt of another human being that was so offensive, not the C-word itself. Wrong, thought Annie. It was the D-word. Drivelling. That's what I don't like. Dribbling. Drooling. Here was a man who despised women and their drivelling cunts. I'm glad he's not my GP. When it came to undermining female self-esteem, there was nothing quite like a contemptuous sneer on the lips of a man wielding a speculum.

'Left here,' said William. 'Park anywhere.'

They pulled up and got out. Ingram drew up in the wank-mobile.

'You'd better bring that onto the yard,' said William, as Ingram emerged. 'If you want to see it again, that is.'

Ingram seemed to take this as a veiled compliment on his car, and made a large gesture like a Christian who knows better than to store up for himself treasure on earth. 'We won't be long.'

'All the same.'

'Don't you think you're being a *leetle* alarmist, William?' asked Ingram.

'Suit yourself.'

They waited on the doorstep while William went in and turned off the burglar alarm. Annie hated the things. If she had one she'd be for ever setting it off and annoying the neighbours. A moment later they were all in William's sitting room trying to decide between tea and coffee (no, really, I don't mind, whichever's easier).

Annie looked round the room. The house was a medium-sized Victorian middle-of-terrace, which surprised her since she'd always assumed that GPs lived in big houses in polite areas. The room had the subdued creams and taupes she'd expected after seeing his cottage; and there was a lot of valuable-looking dark wood furniture. She guessed it would turn out to have come from his grandparents' place. He looked like the sort of man who would raise an eyebrow at the concept of *buying* antiques. She created a new category for him: Posh Socialist. Her eyes continued to skim around. She caught Isobel's doing the same. Like two female bower-birds assessing the worth of a potential mate by looking over the nest he has woven. Annie felt herself smiling at the idea.

'Have you had time to ponder yet?' came Ingram's voice at her side.

'Not really.' Annie got to her feet. 'Sorry. I must just find the . . .' One more moment of Ingram and she'd be screaming like a runaway train. She hovered in the hallway. William was in the kitchen. Supposing she . . . Why not? An Isabella-like impulse seized her, and whistling for Libby she went to find him.

He was leaning against the sink reading his post. He looked up – eek! those eyes again! – when she came in.

'I wondered if you needed a hand.' He scanned the mugs and coffee-maker satirically. Milk jug, teapot, strainer. 'Yes. Well, obviously you've got it all under control,' she mumbled, cursing

Isabella. 'So I'll . . .' He had returned to his letter. She shrugged and began to tiptoe away.

'By all means hide here if you want to.'

'I wasn't . . .'

He raised an eyebrow and her protest withered on the stem. Help. Am I that transparent? He was deep in his letter again and she dithered, wondering whether he was expecting her to stay. Should she pick up a medical journal from the table and pretend to browse?

'So,' he said suddenly, folding up the letter and putting it aside. 'What do you do, then?'

'Annie,' she prompted, on a mischievous impulse, seeing he had forgotten her name.

'*Annie*,' he repeated nastily. 'Well? What do you do?' He folded his arms. It was perfectly obvious that he didn't want to be talking to her. Some vestigial courtesy must be grumbling away in his conscience like an appendix.

'Um, well, the same as the rest of them.' He stared. 'You know. Training for the ministry.'

'You're kidding.'

'No.'

'Good God. How old are you?'

'Thirty-one.'

'What! Come here.' He beckoned. In her surprise she obeyed. 'Look up.' He put a finger under her chin and tilted her face towards the light. It was obviously a piece of medical observation for him, but for Annie it felt alarmingly like the prelude to a kiss. She stared up at his beautiful wide sulky mouth and her lips parted in a helpless gasp. GET DOWN, GIRL! William withdrew his hand and stared frigidly, as though she were a small child who had belched at the dinner table. She blushed. *You horrible horrible dog. I'll have you spayed*.

'You look about fifteen.'

'I know.' There was a silence. She began counting the silver teaspoons in a desperate bid not to laugh.

'So how will you arrange it?' he asked at last. 'Will you have neighbouring parishes?' She looked up in surprise. 'You and Edward.'

'Edward? Ah. Oh. I think you must be assuming we're –
we're –'

'And you're not?'

'No. I'm just, um, a friend of his.' Now he looked surprised,
not to say faintly annoyed, as though she had been deliberately
misleading him. He began pouring the coffee. 'Sorry,' she said.

'What do you mean, *sorry*?'

'To put you to the trouble of having to talk to me.' He paused
and looked at her. She'd seen this expression before on other
faces: is this girl just gauche, or was that malicious?

'Well, fuck you, honey.' Annie blinked in shock. He handed
her a tray. 'Take these through.' She carried them to the sitting
room, her hands trembling so much that the mugs rattled. Don't
you go dropping them, Anne Brown! cried her mother in alarm.
He followed her down the hall with another tray.

The conversation and coffee drinking went on around her.
She tried to compose herself. She was used to getting away with
saying rude things to people without them quite realizing.
Her mousy looks and diffident manner were a perfect disguise.
She was not at all used to people seeing through her and saying, 'Fuck you, honey.' Isobel was engaging him in polite chat
again. Her colour was heightened, and while not precisely mel-
lowed by his attention, she was certainly wearing her dignity
at a more rakish angle. Before long she lost him to a rugby
conversation, which had been started by Edward on the other
side of the room. Annie saw her court shoe begin tapping
silently on the carpet. Muriel, who had been peeping anxiously
between the curtains for some time, said, 'I wonder if we
ought to make a move? It's still snowing.' They all found their
coats and began edging their way out of the door with Edward
still talking loudly about England's chances against France on
Saturday.

Their thanks and goodbyes were interrupted suddenly by a
cry from Ingram. 'Hey! What do you think you're doing?'

There was a burst of shouting and running. Annie stood bewildered. Edward and William took off through the snow after
Ingram.

'What's happening?' asked Dave. The wankmobile. A car door

slammed. Tyres squealed, an engine roared off along the street, cornered violently and sped off.

'Any damage?' came William's voice.

'They've broken the lock.' This was Ingram.

'Looks like someone was trying to steal Ingram's car,' said Ted, who had ventured further out to look.

Ingram came back with William and Edward, visibly shaken. Treasure on earth, after all.

'Use my phone,' William was saying.

Everyone began asking questions at once.

'They got away in another car,' said Edward. 'Must have pinched it earlier. Damn lucky we disturbed them.'

'Another five minutes,' quavered Ingram.

'Try five seconds,' said William, busy dialling for him. 'The little sods can be in with the engine running while I'm still getting my keys out.'

'But they looked like ten-year-olds!' protested Edward.

'They probably were. Here you are.' William handed the receiver to Ingram.

'I should have listened.'

'Yeah. Well. Fact of life round here.' William laid a hand briefly on his shoulder. Annie saw in surprise that this was genuine compassion, when he might have been forgiven a little well-bred smirk.

'Yes? Hello? I want to report an attempted car theft.'

The rest of them drew away and, while Ingram talked, continued to murmur in shocked tones, saying how sorry they were, as though by being privileged themselves they were personally responsible for the crime levels in Bishopside.

Later, when they were heading back to college, Annie leant her head back again and tried to summon Isabella. Blazing sun. Rape fields. Barney –

'Your friend seems a pleasant young man,' remarked Muriel.

'If you edit the language out,' said Edward.

'Oh, it's just a habit some young doctors fall into,' replied Muriel. 'You get used to it.'

A pleasant young man? What about a foul-mouthed misogynist? An arrogant bastard? But the image of his hand laid kindly on

Ingram's shoulder returned to challenge her. Hmm. She left Barney and Isabella to journey endlessly out of Cambridge while she thought about William instead.

CHAPTER 7

'Yes,' said Barney, after a long pause, as though agreeing with her, 'that's definitely the nicest pair of legs I've ever had in my car.' He'd seen her admiring them.

As ever with Isabella, a reproof – even a mild one – acted as a goad. She draped a leg over the gear stick and across his lap. At once his hand was on her knee, sliding up her thigh. It stopped half-way. She sat frozen in surprise for the next mile.

Eventually he cleared his throat. 'I've got a problem, Isabella.'

'A big one?'

He ignored this. 'I've just been wondering what on earth I'm going to put on the insurance claim form if I crash.' He patted her thigh. 'Shift.'

After a moment she complied. He was quite capable of turning round and driving back to Cambridge. The road was skirting along the foot of the Chilterns. She sighed. 'It's so beautiful.'

'Mm,' he said. 'We could go for a walk, if you like.'

'I'd love to.' A short silence. 'I'm on the pill, by the way.'

'I said WALK.'

'Sorry sorry sorry!' She'd been meaning to let this piece of information fall for a while now, just in case he ever found himself holding back for want of a condom. He struck the steering wheel angrily with both hands. She giggled. 'Hee hee. You've been thinking about it.'

'And you never think about anything else.'

'How dare you!' She stretched her legs out and admired them afresh. 'My mind wanders to other matters occasionally.' He turned off the main road slightly too fast. They roared up a steep hill.

'Listen very carefully,' he said. 'I'm going to park the car. We're going to get out and walk to the top of that hill. We'll stop and enjoy the view, then we're going to walk straight back to the car again.'

'OK,' she agreed cheerfully.

'Don't push me, Isabella.'

'As if.' She saw his lips twitch.

He parked the car and they got out. A lark was singing in the sudden silence. They began to climb the hill. The short grass was slippery and Isabella's soles had no grip. Barney took her hand and they climbed in silence past may trees heavy with blossom. Grass and nodding harebells tickled Isabella's bare legs. The sun was so hot that she could feel it scorching her head along the parting. Not a cloud in the sky. No rough winds to shake the darling buds. What bliss to be climbing like this, she thought, higher and higher into the blue, with Barney's strong hand to hold her if she slipped.

They were at the top. A breeze stirred as Isabella gazed round at the fields and farms and villages stretching off into infinity.

'A view over three counties,' said Barney. 'See that spire over there?'

'Where?' she asked, spotting it immediately. His hand was on her shoulder, head bent down beside hers. A hint of Imperial Leather. She followed the line of his pointing finger. If she turned just slightly her lips would brush his cheek.

'There. See that clump of trees? Just beyond it.'

She acted dumb for as long as she dared. 'Oh, *there*. I see it.'

He straightened up. 'That's where I'll be curate.'

'Yeah? Will you take me to see it?'

'Later.' He sat down. She remained standing. The tiny spire looked like a toy church in a model village. So that's where he'll be working. It all felt a bit like a game. She turned and he patted the ground beside him.

'You're sure you trust me, Vicar?'

'No. I'm just finding those shorts a bit distracting.'

She sat next to him. 'Guess I got a bit scissor-happy.'

'You're impossible.' She could smell the wild thyme. The lark was still filling the sky with its song. They sat rapt in the paradise of one another's gaze.

'You love me,' said Barney for her as she opened her lips.

'Sod you.'

He lay back, chuckling, hands behind his head. The sun was gleaming on his golden hair. She slid down beside him, propping herself up on one elbow. For a while she contented herself with watching him as he lay with his eyes closed, but before long his self-containment began to provoke her. She tickled his face with a feathery grass. He waved it away like a fly several times before he saw what she was doing.

'Don't spoil it, Isabella.' He shut his eyes again and she stuck her tongue out. Sanctimonious git. But maybe he was right. Just enjoy what you've got, she told herself. Don't jeopardize it by being greedy.

She listened to the lark and watched his beautiful mouth. It's enough. I'm happy. These sentiments sustained her for some four or five minutes. Bugger this for a game of tin soldiers, she thought suddenly. She placed a hand on his chest. He made no move. She slid it down and felt his stomach muscles tense.

'Isabella, you lay one finger on my tackle and we're going straight back to Cambridge.' Her hand paused. He meant it. Then a happy alternative occurred to her. She slid her leg across him. For one glorious moment she felt the imprint of an erection burnt into her inner thigh, then he tumbled her roughly away and stood up.

'Right. Back to Cambridge.' He set off down the hill.

'Wait! Barney, I'm sorry. I won't do it again. Promise.' But he strode on. She scrambled up and slithered after him. 'Please, Barney. Don't be mean. I'll behave.' Her feet shot out from under her and she sat down hard on a thistle. Her screech brought him back.

He stood shaking his head at her. 'Isabella, what am I supposed to do with you?'

'Fuck me!' she yelled, losing the last shred of control. 'Fuck me! Fuck me, you stupid bastard!' Her voice carried away across three counties. He turned and started walking again. She wrenched off a shoe and hurled it at him. Some instinct warned him, and he glanced round and caught it just before it struck him on the head. She hopped her way between the thistles, cursing him. Eventually he relented enough to hand back her shoe. The moment she was within range she slapped his face.

'What are you? Impotent or something?' She aimed another slap at him, but he picked her up and slung her over his shoulder. She struggled and sobbed and pummelled him all the way back to the car. 'I hate you, I hate you!' He tipped her unceremoniously over the side and got into the driver's seat. The engine started and he headed back to Cambridge without a word.

For the first few miles Isabella, conscious that she had nothing left to lose, called him every name she could think of. After five miles she had run out of ideas. He drove on in quiet resignation as her curses gave way to violent tears. She covered her face and wailed with complete abandon for the next ten miles, like a two-year-old who has started crying, forgotten why, and doesn't know how to stop. Cambridge began to appear on the signposts. She fell silent from exhaustion, shaken by the occasional stormy sob. Gradually she admitted how appallingly she had behaved. It was way, way beyond apology. Her head began to throb. She felt sick. After another five miles she had forgotten everything in the all-consuming knowledge that she was about to throw up. I'm going to die. Sweat stood out on her face. She yawned and yawned.

'Barney, I'm going to be sick!'

He pulled over at once. She got out and threw up horribly into the grass verge, dimly aware he was rubbing her back and saying kind things. 'Oh, God!' She puked again. They were beside a rape field. The dirty honey smell of the flowers filled her nostrils. Lorries were rumbling past. Eventually she straightened up, trembling.

'All done?' She nodded. Her head throbbed viciously. 'It's probably the sun.' She got back in. He was pulling the car roof up. 'Are you all right to go on? I'll get you a drink at the next garage.' His hand rested briefly on her arm and they set off again. Isabella had no energy for anything but staying alive.

At last she was in her room. He had gone. She collapsed on the bed and fell asleep, too wretched to care if she never saw him again.

By the next morning she cared very much indeed. She remembered in dismay that he'd been going to take her to see his church. He'd started to grow fond of her, and now she'd wrecked it all beyond repair. She cringed at every fresh memory. He'd think she always threw embarrassing tantrums when she was thwarted. No sane man would want such a silly spoilt bitch. How could she explain that he was the only one who had ever made her act like that? It would sound as though she was trying to blame him. And how could she, when she remembered how patiently he had put up with her dreadful behaviour? Oh, Barney! It was all my fault. I must write to him. Even if he never speaks to me again, I owe him an apology.

She sat down at her desk in her dressing gown and scribbled *Dear Barney, I can't begin to say how sorry I am*, then screwed up the page. Ten minutes later the bin was full of crumpled pages and she was in tears. She looked round in despair. The room was like her life – a total, unmitigated, disastrous mess. She stood up and vowed to mend her ways. *I'll go and have a shower and then I'll tidy everything up.*

She came back along the corridor, fresh and clean and ready for a new beginning, and there he was.

'Barney!' She stopped in scarlet mortification. He smiled his wonderful smile, and she flung herself at him and sobbed into his shirt. 'Oh, Barney! I'm so sorry!'

'That's all right.'

'How can you say that? I –'

'Um . . . Could we go in?' He was trying to extricate himself without dislodging her towel. She pushed open the door.

'Oh, God. It's a real pigsty. I'm sorry.'

'I've got sisters.' He picked his way through the discarded knickers and Tampax boxes to the chair and sat down.

'Coffee?' She caught sight of a suspender belt dangling from the desk lamp inches from his head. How the hell had that got there? She filled the kettle quickly.

'Feeling better this morning?' he asked.

'Barney, don't be nice to me. I don't deserve it.'

'I've told you it's OK.'

'You can't just *forgive* me.'

'I'd be in big trouble if I didn't.' She was about to ask who with, when she spotted God loitering on the edge of the conversation. She blushed and muttered something about getting dressed.

'Of course,' he said politely. He turned the chair round, picked up a book, and sat with his back to her apparently absorbed in Jane Austen. Isabella hesitated. She'd expected him to retreat hastily from the room. Well, suit yourself. She dropped the towel and waited. He turned a page. She shrugged and hunted around for clean underwear and an uncrumpled dress. Each time she glanced up he was deep in *Emma*. It wasn't until she was fully dressed and approaching the mirror over the desk that she noticed he could have been watching her reflection the whole time. He met her accusing stare with a bewildered look.

'What?' She was wrong. He was too chaste to ogle. But then the glimmer in his eyes set her wondering again.

After a discreet sniff at the milk carton she made them black coffee. They drank in silence. Isabella was still feeling too raw to vamp him, but her small-talk had got a little rusty after all this time.

'So,' she began, 'you've got sisters, then?'

'Three.'

'Older or younger?'

'Older.'

'You're the only boy?' He nodded. No wonder he was proof against wheedling and hysterics.

'What about you?' he asked.

'Just an older sister.'

'And is she very, very well behaved?'

'Horribly.' They grinned at one another.

'Are you doing anything tomorrow night?'

Her heart leapt, and she mentally stood up three different people. 'No. Why?'

'I wondered if you'd like to come to the Latimer ball?'

'Would I!' She hugged herself in glee.

'Don't get too excited, Isabella. It's a very small, tame affair.'

'I can't believe you're asking me after yesterday, Barney.'

'Nor can I, frankly.'

'I promise I'll behave. I'll wear a demure smock with a Peter Pan collar, or something.'

'That sounds lovely.'

'Unless you'd rather I wore something tight and black and sexy?'

'Mm. Much rather.'

'Barnaby! I'm surprised at you! What will everyone think?'

'They'll think, Hardstaff, you jammy bugger.' He got to his feet, smiling at her shocked expression. 'I'll pick you up at quarter to eight, provided . . .' He paused, having just caught sight of the suspender belt. She saw him eye it thoughtfully as though he knew he'd seen one before but couldn't remember off-hand what it was. '. . . provided you promise not to seduce me.'

'We-ell . . . So long as I don't have to stop you if you try to seduce me.'

'I *think* I can handle that.'

'Yeah. I'd noticed.' She sighed. 'So what are the rules, then?'

'Clothes on and hands off.' With that he was gone.

'So, Annie,' said Dr Tuckerman, 'where does the shoe pinch?' Before she could answer, his phone rang. He apologized and cantered away to answer it, leaving her sitting in his kitchen. They should have been in his office in college. Would Annie mind awfully coming to the house instead? Oh, good show! We can have some of Megs's barm bread. Megs was out and they were expecting a man to come and service the Aga. Or woman, added Dr Tuckerman. Or woman. He was always so conscientious about inclusive language that Annie thought of him as Dr Tuckerperson. She was waiting for the day when he forgot himself in the Creed: 'By the power of the Holy Spirit he became incarnate of the Virgin Mary and was made man – or woman, of course, or woman.'

Annie stared round the kitchen at the examples of small Tuckerpeople artwork. Bits of egg carton stuck onto cornflake packets. Gummy collages of pasta and string. She reflected that she did mind being there, actually. Perhaps it was because the house reminded her of her own parsimonious upbringing. A cupboard door was open and Annie could see that it was full of cardboard boxes labelled *Wool, Dress fabrics, Tights, Cards* and so on. Carrier bags of yoghurt cartons and silver foil hung from doorknobs. The cards were presumably old Christmas and birthday cards ready to be cut and stuck onto recycled sugar paper. But what would the tights be for? Stuffing soft toys? Annie could remember getting a blister from hacking up tights with blunt scissors when she had been in the Girls' Brigade. She'd been making a knitted sausage dog draught-excluder, only she'd never finished it. Like that pegbag.

Her eyes wandered to the dresser. A plastic bag full of used stamps hung from a hook. Just like home, except the Tuckermans' parsimony was part of an overarching ideology. Annie's mother was just plain mean. Five years after Annie had broken off her engagement her mother had still been using cut-up wedding invitations for shopping lists. Annie had remarked to Megs once that her mother even washed cling-film and reused it. 'We try not to use cling-film,' Megs had replied repressively. Meanness was even more irritating when it was globally-conscious. Annie glared at the bottles and tins waiting to be taken to the recycling point. Hadn't it occurred to them that the boldest ecological gesture they could make would be to get their tubes tied? They had four children and Megs was pregnant with the fifth. Yes, Meggers was preggers. Annie conjured up a mountain of wrapping paper as high as K2 and set Megs to iron and reuse it as penance for their environment-hostile fertility. She heard Dr Tuckerman cantering back and tried to give her thoughts a more generous turn.

'Gosh! Awfully sorry about that.' He was panting slightly as he put the kettle on the Aga. Annie and Ted had invented a comic strip called *Tubby of Tuckerman Hall*, inspired by his penchant for schoolboy slang of a bygone era. Annie could never see him without wanting to attach a speech bubble to his head: *Jam roly-poly! Oh, I say – wizard prang!* Tubs and Megs. He was a nice man. And Megs was probably nice too, conceded Annie, as Tubby cut two hunks of barm bread. It was just that she inspired an unfortunate mixture of guilt and defiance.

'So,' he asked again, as he spooned coffee into the mugs, 'where does the shoe pinch, Annie?' A crab-pink sling-back clacked its pincers in Annie's mind. Stop it! She'd made herself come and talk to the Warden about her troubles at last, and now she couldn't take it seriously.

'Um, well. That's the problem, really,' began Annie. 'I'm not sure what the, um, problem *is*, exactly. I just feel –' She broke off with a helpless gesture. 'It's not as though I doubt everything, suddenly, or . . . The Creed, I mean, or the authority of Scripture, but . . .' She fell silent.

'You started to tell me how you feel,' prompted Dr Tuckerman.

'Did I? Oh, um, well. Sort of frustrated.'

'Frustrated. Hmm. Can you say a bit more about it?'

'Well, um. Irritable. I keep wanting to swat people with a pulpit Bible.' For example, Ingram.

Dr Tuckerman laughed. 'Gosh, so do I. Know the feeling well.'

Or wanting to haul Edward into a broom cupboard and pull his trousers off. Bet you don't feel that, Tubs old fruit.

'I suppose,' said Annie, trying to get a grip, 'I suppose it amounts to a feeling that I'm in the wrong place trying to do the wrong thing. That sounds terrible.'

'No.' Tubby raised a hand. 'Important to say it.' The kettle was about to boil. He got up and began to slide it thoughtfully around on the hob to release any beads of water trapped there. One sputtered and danced away. 'Is this because there's something you'd rather be doing, do you think?'

'Not that I'm aware of,' she said, colouring slightly, in case he meant marriage and motherhood. 'I expect it's just adolescent rebellion striking rather late.' He was still staring solemnly at the kettle. 'I feel like I've spent my whole life trying to be respectable and please people. If I'm ordained I'll have to go on doing it professionally till I retire.'

'Not necessarily. Our Lord was highly unrespectable.'

'I know.' I KNOW I KNOW I KNOW. 'I just feel . . . stifled.' The kettle boiled.

'Black or white?'

If only things were.

'White, please.'

He handed her a mug and sat down. She watched his face as he clattered the spoon round in his cup. Brown curly hair gave his Billy Bunterish features a cherubic cast. A sweet man, Annie remembered Isobel saying once. Her tone had been condemning, like a woman who took good care of her teeth and only ever ate apples between meals. What sort of sweet? Annie wondered. A marshmallow? She knew herself to be something slightly vulgar and childish. A sherbet lemon, perhaps – insipid exterior, but a nasty shock of sherbet in the middle. Isobel was a Bendick's Bittermint. What was Ingram? Chewing gum – going on and on and on getting increasingly tasteless? Or one of those jelly worms. What did we use to call them? Wrigglers. And Edward –

Dr Tuckerman rapped his spoon sharply on the edge of his mug as though calling a meeting to order. 'So, what are we going to do, Annie?' His eyes peered tinily at her through his thick glasses. She shrugged. You tell me. He took his glasses off and began to massage the bridge of his nose vigorously. She was surprised to note that his eyes were, in fact, large and rather attractive. She looked away as though she had caught a private glimpse into his marriage.

'Is there any practical way I can help?' The glasses were back on.

'Um,' said Annie. 'I'm supposed to be preaching in a fortnight's time, and . . .' I feel like one of my pupils. Oh, Miss Brown, I haven't exactly managed the essay, quite. I've done the notes, though . . .

'No problem. We'll postpone it till next term.' His glasses were slipping down his nose a little and giving him a wild air.

'Thanks.' Annie took a gulp of coffee. 'I'm sure I could do it, if . . . It's just that whenever I sit down to write it, I feel like screaming.' He frowned and pushed his glasses back into place. There was a silence. Annie heard the cathedral clock chime eleven.

'This business about feeling respectable. I wonder if a change of scene might help?' Miles of white sand, a hammock slung between palms? 'Have you done your Bishopside placement yet?' *Oof! Mouldy old swizz, you rotter!* Annie shook her head. 'That might contextualize your sense of calling and ministry a bit. We can all get so frightfully ivory-towerish in Coverdale, you know. How does the idea strike you?'

Like a stake through the heart. Annie knew it was cowardly, but she dreaded the idea of Urban Experience. Bishopside, in her imagination, was a place where ten-year-olds stole cars and malevolent green-eyed GPs told you to fuck off. Suddenly Coverdale seemed infinitely rewarding and fulfilling.

'I'm due to go on the three-week placement.'

'In July. Hmm.' He was massaging the bridge of his nose again. 'Have you ruled out the possibility of spending a term in one of the college flats in Bishopside?'

YES.

'Um . . .' She began to fear that a show of reluctance would make him send her there.

'Just a thought.' Annie crossed her legs and took another gulp of coffee. 'It just strikes me that there may be a lack of *edge* here for you. This place, somehow . . .' His gesture seemed to indicate the kitchen. Annie stared around. The encroaching boxes and bags bulged with a metaphor. Wasn't her life full of the moral equivalent of empty yoghurt pots and old pairs of tights? She was helpless in the face of things she didn't want or need, but knew she oughtn't to throw out.

'Um . . .'

'Look, I'll tell you what. Why don't you take a morning to pray and wander around Bishopside and see what you think?'

'OK.' She wondered meanly whether someone was leaning on him to send more students on Urban Experience.

'The only other thing . . .' He was steering a stray peanut across the table with his fingertip. 'Would you find it helpful to talk to a female member of staff? I expect life here can be jolly frustrating for women in ways we chaps can't begin to imagine.' Annie blushed scarlet, fearing he had imagined precisely the right kind of frustration. She took another gulp. 'Why not have a hobnob with Pauline?' Annie was obliged to sit for several seconds with a mouthful of coffee to avoid choking and spraying him. She swallowed carefully.

'Good idea.' Pauline Dodds, known popularly as Pauline Corpus, taught New Testament. Annie had always warmed to her, although they had never really hobnobbed in the true sense of the word.

'Whacko!' said Tubby, with disastrous timing. Annie sat for another long moment with her last mouthful of coffee. 'More barm bread?'

She swallowed and stood up. 'Thanks, but no. It's delicious, but I'd better . . .'

'Megs soaks the dried fruit in cold tea overnight,' said Tubby. 'That's what gives it the flavour. Let me see you to the door.'

Annie glanced down the street as she was going back into college. She saw Megs heave into view, smock flapping in the headwind, and various children bobbing in her wake. As a challenge to gender-stereotyping, the little boys were dressed in clothes Annie would have hesitated to foist on a girl. 'Look at that spider's web, children!' came her voice as the door swung shut.

From Bishopside, and motherhood and recycled cold tea, *Good Lord, deliver us*, thought Annie.

CHAPTER 8

Her prayer was not answered. Or rather it was, only the answer was no. Bishopside was immovably fixed on the divine agenda. Annie woke on the morning she was due to go there and reflected that if she were a different kind of person, less dutiful, more devious, she would simply sit in a café in Bishopside for a couple of hours then report back to Tubby and say, 'Sorry, old stick. No dice.' And if she was really devious she wouldn't go to Bishopside at all. She'd go shopping in Newcastle instead. Tubby would never know.

God would know, however. It struck Annie, while she was getting dressed, that she had turned God into someone rather like her mother. Always checking up and catching out. Always prophesying disaster then saying, 'Well, I did warn you, Anne.' When Tubby and other right-on liturgists insisted on the importance of God as Mother, Annie wanted to crawl under a pew and die. God as Father was bad enough. Her own father was the opposite of what one looked for in a deity. Omni-impotent and omni-absent, even when actually in the room. The only godlike attribute he displayed was durability. From everlasting to everlasting he sat with his newspaper or accounts while his wife rabbited on.

Annie knew that she would go obediently to Bishopside and pray and wander round. God, she felt sure, would say, 'Spend a term in Bishopside', because he could see how profoundly unwilling she was. This was her Nonconformist background coming out. She had grown up in the belief that what she really deserved was to burn in hell. Anything else was a bonus. You couldn't seriously expect to be called to something you enjoyed. The benign God of Anglicanism (who declared his almighty power most chiefly in showing mercy and pity, etc.) was getting obscured behind the wrathful fumes of judgement seeping back from her childhood. She could still glimpse him staring down benevolently through the smoke, hand raised in vague blessing, like a wall painting in a burning church.

'So, today's the day, is it?' boomed Edward at breakfast.

Annie went on spreading marmalade. They all knew. She had managed to mumble something to her Coverdale group about Doubts and Working-through-various-issues. They had all been supportive and non-judgemental. She had gritted her teeth and told Edward afterwards.

'What problems?' he had demanded. 'What sort of issues? What do you mean, you don't know? How can you not know?' Non-directive counselling was not Edward's strongest suit. He pointed her to several helpful passages in the Bible and lent her a book. *Dear* Edward. She knew he was praying faithfully for her. 'We pray for Annie Brown, Lord, an ordinand in her second year at Coverdale Hall . . .' How might the prayer go on? Annie Brown, who's sadly going off the rails?

'Why don't you call in on William?' asked Edward. 'He'll show you round. Give him a ring.'

'No fear,' said Annie.

'What? What do you mean? He's not that bad.'

'I think most of us found him just a *wee* bit abrasive,' put in Ingram.

'Nonsense!' said Isobel. 'He was perfectly civil.'

'It's just his manner,' agreed Muriel.

'I'll ring him,' decided Edward.

'But I need to be on my own,' protested Annie. 'I'm supposed to be meditating.'

'Well, you can see him after you've meditated.'

'Edward, I don't think you're quite *hearing* Annie,' said Ingram. 'She's saying she doesn't want –'

'Annie can speak for herself,' snapped Edward.

'But you're not letting her,' pointed out Isobel. 'She quite clearly said she wanted to be on her own.'

'I think we should respect that, Edward,' added Ingram.

'Yes,' said Muriel. 'It's her decision.'

Annie looked despairingly across the table at Ted. His eyes twinkled at her. The others continued to argue about what she wanted and what she was trying to say until Edward finally gave his word not to phone William.

Annie walked up the steep path to the station. Tubby was right. She badly needed a close woman friend to confide in. Unfortunately Pauline Dodds wasn't quite in that category yet. Annie had enjoyed their hobnob, a mellow affair over a bottle of wine, but it was too soon for real intimacy. Pauline was in her fifties and had a calm air, as though she had reached some high plateau and could call down reassuringly, 'Actually, it evens out a little up here.' Annie admired her. She envied the short silvery hair, the Celtic earrings, the muted slate greys and duck-egg blues that Pauline wore. They had talked about the Church and college life, but despite that second glass of wine, Annie hadn't managed to say anything about lurve and wanting a man. It had all seemed a bit crass.

As she stood waiting on the platform the real reason why she had said nothing dawned on her. It was because she wanted to keep the sin option open. The thought made her blush. She would have to tell Pauline. It would act as a safeguard. Not that her life was bristling with opportunities for the kind of sin she fancied.

The train headed north. Annie found a seat and reached in her bag for her notebook and reread the last bit she had written. She felt a sudden impatience with her characters. Isabella was so dim, despite being at Cambridge. This wasn't necessarily a problem. Annie had met any number of thick undergraduates in her time there. People who got starred firsts in medicine but were clearly not the sharpest scalpel in the kidney dish when you met them socially. Perhaps she was making Isabella too much Barney's dupe? And it was a bit Mills and Boonish, all these conflicts and will-they-won't-they? scenes. The hero older and wiser, the heroine wilful and turbulent. But – cackle cackle – he was going to get his comeuppance at the Latimer ball when he tangled with Isabella in her outrageous black dress. What price your celibacy now, my friend? Annie shut her book with a smile. They were approaching Newcastle.

Her heart rose as it always did when the train crossed the Tyne. All those bridges, different levels, styles, ages, crowded into a short stretch of river. She loved the height of the buildings dropping down to the quayside, the wheeling gulls, the energy of the place.

Her heart sank again as the metro train crossed back into Bishopside. She came up from the underground station and stood looking round. She felt lonely and bewildered. Buses roared past. What am I supposed to do? She was reluctant to get out Tubby's *A – Z* in case someone asked her where she was trying to go and she couldn't answer. Children with brutal haircuts were playing in the undergrowth on a steep bank above the bus station. Why weren't they in school? Their shouts floated down to her. A large Victorian church stood on one street corner, the Co-op on another. She guessed it had been built in the sixties. What had been pulled down to make way for it? An ugly grey concrete multi-storey car-park loomed behind the other buildings.

Annie began walking towards some shops and this led her on to what she supposed must be the high street. Dirty Victorian buildings, tatty modern shop fronts. Everywhere was selling things at bargain prices. It felt like a foreign country. The people looked different. Their accent was impenetrable. She felt raw, as though every tiny brush against someone scraped an exposed nerve. More shouting. She flinched, but it was only a bantering exchange. I can't distinguish between joking and aggression. Her heart pattered fearfully as she skirted round some old filing cabinets standing on the pavement. Someone in the doorway called a friendly greeting, but she wasn't sure if it was meant for her. She smiled nervously and hurried on. How has this happened? How have I become so scared of my fellow creatures? She reminded herself that this was the North, the home of legendary friendliness.

By now she was among tower blocks and flyovers. All the shrubs and railings were full of blown litter. Walkways, subways, grey concrete, grey sky. Oh, why am I here? Annie felt like crying. Is this where you're calling me to live, God? There's nothing beautiful here. Nothing to feast the eyes on. It felt like an affront to her soul. Is this what you want, Lord? For a second an answer seemed to come. Not a yes, not a no; but a ray of light reaching down, as though in the midst of his myriad concerns God had paused and looked on her, totally absorbed for one second in Annie Brown and what she might do next. And whatever she chose, that same unwavering interest would follow her.

After a moment Annie walked on. It was disconcerting to be offered this level of responsibility; to have God imply that even if she wilfully made a bad choice, his love would still be extended. The implications of sin became graver. No longer just a fear of being caught and punished. It was a breach of trust.

She shivered and huddled in her coat. At least hell would be warm. She walked faster, hoping to get her circulation going. Before long she was lost. She had been walking without paying any attention to direction, and now she found herself in a less run-down part of town. The old terraced houses she was passing would have been worth quite a bit if they had been miraculously transported to the right part of the South East. The wind was blowing, flipping idly through the pages of a magazine dropped on the pavement. Ahead of her she saw dark figures, young men clutching at hats and running in the wind with their black coats flapping. Orthodox Jews. The scene, which had been seeming more familiar, grew alien again. Hasidim running down rainy Polish streets in a forgotten era.

She rounded a corner. Mothers with buggies, small children, old people. They were going in and out of a building, obviously a – Help. A doctors' surgery. What if it were William's? She edged closer and her fears were confirmed. *Dr W. Penn-Eddis* leapt out from among the other names on the brass plaque. Libby let out a strangled yelp and dragged Annie off along the street. *Don't act dumb. I bet you brought me here on purpose, you stupid hound!* Supposing he had seen her? But before she could congratulate herself on her narrow escape there was a voice behind her: 'What are you doing here?'

Him! She whirled round, bag clutched to chest like a shoplifter facing a store detective.

'Oh!' The eyes! Libby let out a high keening note. He was looking more like a GP today. Jacket and tie, Barbour. 'Hello.'

'What are you doing here?'

'Annie,' she couldn't resist prompting.

'I *know* your name.' Either he had another cold or his voice was always that sexy. 'What are you doing here?' he said again.

'Nothing,' she pleaded. 'I mean, just wandering around, and . . . I was sent here by the Warden of Coverdale. Um, to see if . . . There are these placements we have to do, you see, and . . .' She floundered into silence.

'Have you finished?'

'Burbling, you mean?'

The corners of his mouth twitched. ' "Wandering around." ' She remembered his ravishing smile and wondered what she would have to do to provoke one.

'Oh, yes. Um . . . probably, that is.'

'Lunch?'

'Lunch?'

'Do you want to have lunch with me?' This was said slowly and distinctly, as if to a simpleton. 'I'm on my way home now.'

'Now? Er, um, yes. Thanks.' Libby yanked at her lead, implying she'd rather raid a dustbin.

He set off along the road hardly seeming to care whether she was trotting after him or not. She tried to fall in with his long strides. Why on earth had he asked her?

'So how's Edward?'

'Edward?' she bleated like a foolish echo. 'Same as ever.' Maybe he'd forgotten that she and Edward weren't . . . Was that why he was being polite? They turned into another street, passing by privet hedges and neat front gardens. Their feet echoed. She tried to think of some suitable topic of conversation. The welfare state? GP fundholding?

'Why the Cerberus act?' he asked.

'Sorry?'

'Edward. Standing guard over you. Telling me not to bully you.' He stopped abruptly.

'He . . . he probably thinks I need protecting. Or something.'

Oh, yeah, yeah, said his expression.

Why was he just waiting like that? He gestured to a gate and she realized. They were at his house.

Annie waited in the hall while he switched the alarm off. He was wrongfooting her at every turn and she suspected he was doing it on purpose. She handed over her coat and followed him meekly to the kitchen. Some angular classical music was playing, but she couldn't identify it. He took off his jacket and tie, poured her a glass of wine, then began to make a salad bristling with things she passed over nervously at the supermarket because she couldn't pronounce their names. The violins scraped on. She sipped her wine and looked around her. A child's picture was stuck to his fridge door, a stick man with a huge smile. His hands were like two little suns with rays of fingers radiating out from the palms. *Dr William*, said the wobbly letters underneath. Her eyes moved on. She was still wondering what to say.

'Nice saucepans.'

This earned her a long hard stare. 'Are you taking the piss?'

'No, no. I really like them.' French cast iron — God's way of telling you that one day you would own an Aga.

He carried on with his preparations, working swiftly and precisely, like a surgeon on a tight schedule. There was an edgy nervousness to him. No, not nervousness. More a taut energy. *He moved like a cat*, she suggested to herself, busy fictionalizing the scene as it was unfolding. Avocados. Prosciutto. *And* he hadn't been expecting company. I'm having lunch with the kind of man who has avocados and prosciutto lying about his kitchen. He looked up before she could wipe the smirk off her face.

'What?'

'Didn't Cerberus guard the gate of Hades?' she asked, for something to say.

'So?'

'I was wondering what that made me.'

'The devil's gateway, honey,' he drawled. 'Shall we eat?'

She managed not to flip vinaigrette over the table as she helped herself to salad. Why am I letting him reduce me to a fifteen-year-old? For a while they ate in silence. Annie began to wonder if she could get away with admiring his kitchen knives.

'So tell me,' he paused, '*Annie*, why the ordained ministry?'

She was asked this all the time, but now, under his assessing misogynist's stare, her explanations sounded fatuous. She tried to describe her growing dissatisfaction with teaching.

He interrupted her, 'Running away from something you hate doesn't constitute a vocation.'

She flushed. Part of her had often feared that this was all her calling amounted to. 'There's a positive aspect, too,' she said, trying to keep the defensiveness out of her voice. 'The sense of being called. It's difficult to define.'

'Well, try.' When she didn't immediately answer, he said, 'Come on. That's your job, isn't it? To define the indefinable.'

'Give me a chance.' He waited. She was beginning to feel hounded. 'It was . . . little things. I just had a growing sense that God was calling me to be ordained.' It was feeble, but after another brief stare he let it pass. Her upper lip was starting to sweat. She continued to eat, conscious of every clank and scrape of her fork. Please don't let him spring another question while I've got watercress dangling out of my mouth.

'Why Bishopside?' he asked. 'You want to work in a UPA?' Urban Priority Area. She remembered he was a vicar's son.

'I haven't ruled it out,' she lied.

He was looking her over sardonically. She could tell he was thinking she wouldn't last five minutes, like Ingram's car. 'You honestly think you're cut out for this?'

'Well, the Bishop's selectors obviously did.' She drank some more wine. It was already going to her head.

'I asked what you think.'

'Listen, if I didn't think I was –'

'What about the isolation?' he butted in. 'Can you cope with being on your own? And the responsibility. We're not just talking about the cure of ten thousand souls. There's the finances, the church fabric, the committee meetings, all the admin involved with running a parish. What kind of management skills have you got?'

'I –'

'Or isn't that a problem for you? Faith will see you through, will it? We're talking a hell of a lot of faith, here. Faith in God, faith in the Church – that's a tall order, but never mind. Faith in yourself. Have you got what it takes?' To her horror she could feel tears welling up, ready to spill over and prove his point. 'I'm not getting at you,' he added in surprise.

'Well, I'm afraid that's what it feels like.'

There was a silence.

'Hmm. Actually I probably am, come to think of it.'

'But why?'

'Well, if you cry I'll have to comfort you, won't I? Then one thing can lead to another and oops! There we are making love.'

'*What?*' Her tears vanished, scorched clean off her burning cheeks.

He gave her the ravishing smile. 'Sorry, Ignore me. Just thinking out loud. What sort of parish are you looking for, then?'

'Well, a good incumbent is the first priority.' She eyed him nervously. 'Someone I can learn from and respect.'

'You see your curacy as the second half of your training, then?'

'Yes. Maybe I can scrape together some management skills.' She let out a little bleating laugh. Did he honestly think she'd go to bed with him just because she'd accepted lunch? Was this how people carried on in the real world? She pushed the strange leaves around her plate. 'Is this rocket?' she asked desperately.

He took her hand and kissed the palm. Her stomach plunged as though she had nearly stepped off a very high building. She pulled away. 'Look, I'd better go. I'm sorry if I've given you the wrong impression, but –'

'Don't worry. You haven't. Oh, come on, Annie. I'm sorry. Stay and let me redeem myself.' He got up to make the coffee, and she remained where she was, immobilized by the fear of looking churlish. 'Tell me about this placement.'

She hesitated. 'We all have to spend some time here,' she began rapidly. 'There are various . . . um, ways of . . . Some people spend a term living here. I'm doing the three-week course in July.' She was conscious of not being strictly honest, but she could hardly tell him why Tubby had sent her to wander around. 'Why did you choose to work in Bishopside?'

'I thought I could make a difference.' He smiled. 'My family tell me I've got a saviour complex.'

'Do you enjoy being a doctor?'

It was a pathetic little question, but he was behaving himself now and took it seriously. 'Most of the time. And then you get one of those hellish days. You'll meet it in the ministry – situations where every course of action you can take, including doing nothing at all, is wrong from someone's point of view.'

'Like?'

'Oh, referring a woman for an abortion, for instance. Personally I'm against it, except in extreme cases, and I mean extreme. But who am I considering? The foetus? My patient? My own integrity? If I don't refer her another doctor probably will, so what difference does my refusal make? The question is, how do you live honourably in the midst of compromise?'

That is the question, thought Annie, and tried in vain to think of an answer. This new thoughtfulness was far more dangerous and seductive than his earlier manner.

He shrugged. 'You do what you can professionally, then dish out plenty of off-prescription TLC. Tender loving care,' he explained, seeing her surprise.

'Ah,' said Annie, trying to sound illuminated.

He wasn't fooled, and to her astonishment a faint flush crept across his cheeks. 'Jesus. You think I'm incapable of tenderness?'

She could see him retreating. 'I . . . I don't really know you.'

'Well, that can be remedied in a matter of minutes,' he replied. 'If you'd care to step upstairs.'

'I'm sorry. I didn't mean to hurt your feelings.'

'I have some?'

She gulped down the last of her coffee and pretended to look at her watch. 'I'd better be going.'

'I'll run you to the station.'

'It's all right.' He helped her on with her coat. For a fraction of a second he was standing close behind her. Libby panted wetly in her ear. Annie glimpsed a wild new universe in which she got into bed with strange men without preamble. She fumbled her coat around her and hurried to the door. He was setting the alarm and following her out of the house.

'Just point me in the right direction. I'll walk.'

'It's raining. I'll drive you.'

94

'Shouldn't you be at work?'

'Just get in the fucking car, will you?' She obeyed, wondering if she would ever get used to his casual obscenity. Just a habit these young doctors get into. He gave her a sidelong glance as he started the engine. 'I'm free every Wednesday afternoon.'

'That's nice for you.'

'Call round, honey child,' he drawled. 'Ride my pole. Sit on my face.'

I'd quite like to jump up and down on it, thought Annie, studying her Doc Martens in furious embarrassment. 'Are you always this crude?'

He chuckled. 'Usually. Don't tell Edward. He'll have my balls.'

They drove to the station in silence. Annie's fingers gripped her bag rigidly. What if she hadn't convinced him she was serious?

'Look,' she began as he pulled up on the forecourt, 'I hope this doesn't seem like some kind of challenge, William. I won't change my mind.'

'Will.'

'I won't!'

'No, *call* me Will.' He does do it on purpose, she thought. She got out of the car.

'Thank you for lunch.'

'My pleasure. Shall I come and visit you in college?'

'No!' she cried in alarm. He was grinning as he drove off.

She walked into the station and stared blindly at the departures board. I can't believe it. What an awful, awful man. Her knees began trembling. She remembered his lips on her palm and clenched her fist. Her stomach plunged again. At least the Bishopside question was resolved. There was no way she could spend a term there now. Perhaps it was guidance. She tried to compose herself and read the train times, but they blurred before her eyes. I've just walked away from the best sex I'm ever likely to get. She sniffed back the tears. There wasn't even the consolation that God was pleased. She wasn't chaste, merely timid. If I'd been Eve, we'd still all be in Eden. Too terrified of the green-eyed snake and the wrath of God to taste the forbidden fruit.

CHAPTER 9

The train journey home did not give Annie long enough to calm herself down. She knew she wasn't ready to report back to Tubby, or face her friends and their concerned questions, so she hurried into the cathedral before going back to college. She needed the stillness and order of the place.

The cathedral was not quiet, however. Hordes of primary-school children were rehearsing for a service. Their cheerful cacophony followed her as she made her way up a side aisle and round behind the high altar. She sat down in the gloom gazing up at the rose window. I feel like an ant. Was this why the Normans built such vast cathedrals – to remind us we are finite?

> Frail children of dust
> And feeble as frail

the children were singing.

> In thee do we trust,
> Nor find thee to fail.

Annie felt her eyes filling with tears. I know that. I *know* God has never failed me. Wasn't the Cross proof enough of his love? He died for me. What more could I ask? '*There is therefore now no condemnation.*' As a teenager Annie had underlined these words in her Bible. But she had always felt that there was an invisible footnote: *Except for me.* Except for me. This was the kind of miserable despair she felt herself sliding back into when her faith wavered. As she stared up at the glowing colours in the window Annie feared that her faith was no longer just wavering. It was toppling over. She had been planning a building as huge and durable as a cathedral, but now it looked like a folly, all rainbow glass and tracery against the sky.

Annie bent her head. Tears began splashing onto her clasped hands. Part of her wanted to blame William for his casual demolition of her beliefs, but what kind of faith crumbled in the face of a few hostile questions? She squeezed her hands together. Perhaps God doesn't want me to be a priest. Maybe I've been deluded.

Well, what did I tell you, Anne? crowed her mother.

But I truly believed you were calling me, God. I –

You honestly think you're cut out for this? interrupted William's scathing voice.

You know you're not, said her mother. You may as well admit it.

I admit it, she thought. I confess that the idea of running a large parish fills me with dread. I've been trying to tell myself I'll conquer my fears as I go on, but I'm scared I won't. I'll always be incompetent. Yet what was she to make of her sense of calling? That birthday feeling, that glorious *Yes!* ringing round the soul? The parish placement she'd done in the summer had been perfect. She'd been working alongside someone she trusted and admired. Harry had been a wonderful example, and she'd felt safe with his leadership. He'd be the perfect incumbent to train curates. If only I could be a permanent curate, she thought. She would happily accept limited privileges in exchange for limited responsibility for the rest of her working life. But the priesting of women was closing that option. The Church would want its full money's worth. And Annie sensed that women who chose to remain deacons would always have a question mark hanging over them. Why weren't they priests, people would wonder. Did they oppose women's priesthood, or had they blotted their prayer books in some way? Would anyone believe that she genuinely only wanted to be second in command?

She wiped her eyes and looked back up at the window. What a feeble person I am. God deserved better – stern saints and warriors. She thought about Cuthbert, behind whose shrine she was skulking. What would he think of me? 'Get that foul unclean creature out of my church!' probably. There was a stone boundary line way down the nave at the west end of the cathedral which in medieval times women weren't allowed to cross, in case it enraged the arch-misogynist saint in his coffin. Or perhaps old Cuthbert had been quite fond of women, and his misogyny was a later invention to keep women in their place. Annie pictured the back of the cathedral packed with wimpled women, arms folded, eyes narrowed, waiting. Waiting to storm the sanctuary. She suspected that this was the fear which lurked behind all the elaborate High Church theologizing about the priesthood.

But what was she going to tell Tubby? Perhaps she could say she was considering the possibility that she was called to be a deacon, not a priest. As she turned the idea over in her mind she could almost see William's sarcastic sneer. Now that she was safe from him she burned with indignation. He was without doubt the most arrogant, unkind, crude man she had ever met. And yet there had been that tantalizing glimpse of another William, a man who was struggling to live honourably in the midst of compromise. Or had that been a ploy? He was clever enough to know that she was unlikely to hop into bed with him on impulse. She would need to be able to convince herself that her lust was not squalid. If he presented himself as a man with integrity then she might be hooked. And yet it had not seemed disingenuous. *You think I'm incapable of tenderness?* That had sounded real enough.

Annie could hear the children beginning another song. '"When a knight won his spurs . . ."' It took her back to her own schooldays, when she had spent her whole time in subterfuge of one kind or another. She had learnt to be invisible: just the right amount of industry to satisfy the teachers without rousing their interest; never too good or too bad at anything; bland enough to escape both popularity and bullying. Home was no better. She was constantly trying to evade her mother's intrusive curiosity. The Brown children weren't allowed secrets. They weren't allowed to hide away in their bedrooms on their own. What are you doing up there, Anne? Come down and sit with the family. What's that book? Who was that letter from? Where are you off to? Annie read at night by the light of the street-lamp outside her window. Her secret thoughts were written in code. She sat downstairs with the family while in her mind she rode off bareback across Andalusia, her long black hair streaming in the wind. By the time she was ten years old she had learnt to hide away anything that was precious to her – her letters, her writing, her feelings and hopes – and now the habit was so engrained she found herself without a soul in the world who knew what she was really like. Sometimes she felt lonely and misunderstood, but at least she was safe. When someone saw through her it felt like an outrage, a violation, even. It unleashed that wave of sick impotent fury she felt each time she discovered her mother had been looking through her things again. This was exactly what William made her feel with his yeah, yeah expression and cold sarcastic insight. He despised her and was bent on exposing her for the fraud she was.

And yet he wanted to go to bed with her! Her mind doubled back to this thought again. At least there was no need to confess this episode to Pauline. However much sensitivity and integrity he displayed in future she wasn't in any real danger. *Ride his pole*, indeed. She had always tried to believe GPs outgrew their medical student humour. Perhaps they never did? 'Try to relax for me, please. This won't take a moment. Just a little prick . . .'

What would it be like to be seduced by Will, though? Would his hands work her over with the same ruthless precision he had displayed with the chopping knife? Tossing her with callous speed like a green salad? 'Get that woman out of here!' quavered Cuthbert. Annie stifled a giggle as Libby's baying echoed round the cavernous vaults.

It was a miracle that she hadn't spontaneously combusted by now, considering it was eleven years since she'd had sex. *Ow-ow-ooww-oo!* howled Libby. Eleven *years. Eleven.* It had been with her fiancé Graham. They should have waited till they were married, of course. They had intended to but one thing had led proverbially to another on a handful of occasions, and there they were. Each time she had been filled with disgust and guilt, but somehow she'd gone on and on, craving more and always more disgusted. Graham was weak and had simply followed her lead. A pliable man, malleable and ductile like something in a third-form chemistry experiment. He was as passive as her father, and to her horror his passivity began to drive her to cruelty. Graham was turning her into her mother. Sometimes she had visions of herself as she would have been had she married him: trapped with several children in an unwholesome marriage, riddled with spite and dressed in floral prints. It put her present worries into perspective.

She roused herself and started back to college. The cathedral clock chimed three as she hurried along the street. Coverdale seemed empty. Wednesday afternoon was traditionally given over to sport. Edward would be cycling up and down the towpath roaring at the college eight. Ingram would be flouncing around in his fencing class, his pale hair tied back with a velvet ribbon. Apparently he was good at it, but to Annie it was just another Ingram-type pose. 'The pox of such antic, lisping, affecting fantasticoes!' For Annie there was only one sport: the art of coarse novel writing. And very coarse it was going to be, too. She sat at her desk with a smile and reached for her notebook.

Isabella stood in front of her mirror scrutinizing herself in the black dress. A strange feeling crept over her. After a moment she recognized it: it was a qualm. A qualm, for God's sake! She was nervous about wearing a dress like this to a theological college. She was even more nervous about Barney's reaction. After all, she had promised to behave, and trying to behave in this outfit would be like attempting to stick to the speed limit in a Ferrari. From the front it looked acceptable, but the side view was hairraising. Split thigh-high and held together by straining latticework. It would be obvious even to a rookie that she wasn't wearing underwear. She was about to riffle through her wardrobe for something more suitable when she heard Barney's footsteps coming along the corridor. There was a knock at the door. Oh, Gawd. She opened it. There he was in his dress suit. He kissed her cheek.

'Is this dress all right?' she asked, arms clamped to sides.

'Looks fine to me. Turn round.' She obliged him with the full horror of the side view. He closed his eyes and leant his forehead despairingly against the door frame.

'You did say . . .' Her voice trailed off.

He shook his head briskly, like a dog coming up out of water. 'I did. Never mind. We can tell everyone you thought it was a tarts and vicars party.'

'You cheeky sod!' she pouted.

'I think we'd better run through those ground rules one more time.'

'Hands on, clothes off?'

'Mmm. Something like that.' He put his arms round her.

'I just want you to know, Barney, that this lipstick is totally smudge-proof.'

'Thank you, Isabella.'

'You see, I can't help noticing that you've never kissed me.'

'Haven't I?' He looked faintly surprised, as though he was almost sure he had.

'I'm talking about *real* kissing, not a brotherly peck.'

'Ah,' he said uncertainly. My God – he doesn't know what I'm talking about! Then she saw his lips twitch. She pushed him out of the door and they set off for the ball.

It took Isabella approximately ten seconds to reassure herself that hers was the most outrageous dress in the place. She observed a fine series of double-takes as she passed through the crowds. People called greetings to Barney as he found her a drink and led her to the marquee on the lawn. After a while, however, she began to imagine that they were casting him looks of sympathy, or pity, even. Normally this would have provoked her to act up, get drunk and bellydance in the flower beds, but she was held back by her promise to behave. She grew more miserable with each song the band played. Her jaws ached with the effort of keeping a bright smile on her face.

'What's wrong, Isabella?'

'It's this dress. Everyone's staring. They all hate me!'

'No, no!' he protested, drawing her into his arms. 'Only the women do. The men all hate me.'

'It's not funny, Barney. I'll end up misbehaving again, and you'll get mad.'

He drew her a little closer. 'I will?'

And that was licence enough. She drank too much and danced sinuously, explicitly, downright disgracefully, waiting all the time for Barney's disapproving frown. It never came. He seemed to be enjoying himself. Was it possible that these strange celibate creatures knew how to have a good time? All around her they seemed to be doing just that. She could see frumpy women and fat men blossoming when in another setting they would be disparaged and wilt. What a wonderful generous atmosphere, she thought drunkenly, as they queued up to collect their food. So warm. So accepting. And so deliciously easy to shine in.

When they got back to the marquee with their plates and glasses, all the tables were crowded. A group began waving and calling. 'Over here, Horny!'

Isabella turned to Barney open-mouthed. '*Horny?*'

'My nickname.' He shrugged apologetically.

She gave a shriek. 'But why?'

'I've *no* idea.' He steered her towards the table where people were shifting to make room.

'It's OK. I'll sit on his knee.' She pushed him down into a chair and sat astride him. The latticework took the strain. Someone ruffled Barney's hair.

'You all right under there, Horny?'

'Yes, thanks.'

Isabella began feeding him strawberries. Was this the man who had driven her back to Cambridge in disgrace? Everyone laughed.

'Look at him,' said someone else. 'He's not bothered, is he?'

He did look unflatteringly calm, thought Isabella. 'He's not interested in sex,' she remarked. 'He's a hard man.'

'Not that hard,' they warned her.

'You're not sitting where I'm sitting,' she said sweetly. Whoops! Overstepped the mark. She popped another strawberry in Barney's mouth to silence him, but he pushed her from his lap and stood up.

'Excuse us a moment,' he said grimly.

'I may be gone some time,' called Isabella, as he led her firmly out of the marquee. They were out under the stars. She glanced at his face. Oh, God. He's really pissed off. 'I'm sorry. I'll be good.'

'Now where have I heard that before?'

'I'm sorry! Please don't take me home, Barney.'

But he carried on walking. She'd lost her sense of direction. Where was he leading her? Up the garden path. She stumbled and giggled. It really was some kind of garden, tucked away behind a hedge. The party sounds continued behind them. ' "Ain't misbehavin',"' sang the band. Suddenly it dawned on Isabella that they were about to. Her stomach plunged like a mad roller-coaster. Surely his cast-iron self-control wasn't going to give way?

He picked her up abruptly. She yelped and found herself standing on a garden bench facing him. His hands were on her thighs, sliding higher, gripping her bare rump. He was kissing her through the holes in her dress, lips climbing like a plant up a trellis, inching over hip, past waist to breast, then down the other side. She could hear herself moaning, 'Oh, my God, Barney,' as she gripped his hair in her trembling fingers. He was shaking too, panting. Another five seconds he'd be hauling her down and backing her up against some convenient tree. In a sober instant she found that she couldn't bear to see him reduced to this. It felt like killing something. She cradled his head in her arms. What am I going to do? she wondered in panic. He'll go ape-shit if I change my mind now. Help! He was pulling her from the bench.

'I need a pee, Barney!' she squeaked in desperation.

His lips were at her throat. 'Can't it wait?'

'No. I'll burst. Tell me where the loos are. I'll come straight back.' There was an awful pause. Then he released her. They walked in silence back to the college. Isabella dared not look at him.

She hid in the cubicle, unable to believe what he'd been about to do; even less able to believe she'd stopped him. After all the effort I've put into seducing him! What if he cut up rough and called her a prick-tease?

When she finally emerged he was looking stunned. They wandered back to the marquee and began dancing in a slightly restrained way, apologizing if they accidentally brushed against one another. A slow number struck up. They hesitated a moment then drew closer together. A chaste four inches of air separated them. Damn, realized Isabella. I forgot to have a pee, after all that. She stifled a giggle. The song ended. They stepped away from one another, stranded in the brief silence.

'Last dance,' announced the loudspeaker.

The floor became crowded. Barney drew her closer this time. She experienced the warm glow of the virtuous. Her head rested on his chest. I'm in heaven. But all too quickly it was over and they were walking back to her college.

With every clip of her silly shoes on the pavement Isabella felt resentment mounting. Why didn't I just let him get on with it? Shit, shit, shit! He'd taken fright. All she'd get now was a chaste peck on the cheek. She fought her ignoble impulses. Just for once she wouldn't ruin everything. They entered her college. She'd been expecting him to say goodbye at the gate, but here he was seeing her to her room. An interesting idea struck her. Had her sudden about–turn whetted his appetite? Maybe he was a predator and spurned what was offered him on a plate. He wanted the thrill of the chase, did he? Hmm. They were outside her door.

'Well, thanks again, Barney.'

'You're welcome.' He seemed to be lingering. Isabella bit her tongue to prevent herself inviting him in for coffee. Playing hard to get was not in her usual repertoire. She stood on tiptoe and gave him that chaste little peck.

'I won't ask you in . . .'

'Mmm.'

'I'll just say goodnight, then . . .'

'Goodnight.'

All at once the tension was too much. Fuck hard-to-get! It wasn't working. Isabella pulled him to her, sank her teeth into his neck and clung on like a limpet.

'Get off! Ow! Isabella, get off me!' He tried to wrench her away. In the end she let go. He stood rubbing his neck. 'Have you left a mark?'

'Yep. But don't worry. God will know you didn't score. That's what counts. Who cares what the rest of them think?'

His cheeks were flushed. 'You just made a *big* mistake.' He turned on his heel and left.

In her room Isabella screeched with rage and hurled a mug against the wall. Why do I always, always have to do that? She cursed her stupidity and flung herself sobbing onto the bed.

Annie glared at the page. Do as I tell you! she commanded. But her characters were clearly not going to be ordered about. Her valiant attempt to get Barney's trousers off for Isabella had been thwarted – astonishingly by Isabella herself. Annie guessed it was her own disappointment at seeing Barney reduced to a lusting fool that had made her intervene. Besides, there were the practicalities to consider. No self-respecting evangelical ordinand would roger his ball partner in the Principal's garden to the strains of *Ain't Misbehavin'*. No matter how great the temptation. Even if they were married. 'Ah, Principal,' pump pump, 'I don't believe you've met my wife . . .'

Tim the chaplain was returning to his flat. He glanced across the dark quad and saw a big man in a dress suit stride angrily towards the main gate. Barney? He was about to call his name when the figure hesitated, wheeled round and began walking back the way he had come. The footsteps echoed. After a moment they stopped again. There was a brief silence, then the figure turned once more, muttering, 'Bloody bloody bloody . . .' Tim stood listening as the footsteps walked out of the college and faded off along the street. It occurred to him that his fifty pounds had just had a very narrow escape. He smiled and went up to his flat.

CHAPTER 10

Atonement. From the Middle English *at one*-ment. Reconciled. In harmony. Annie scratched her head with her biro. Her desk was piled with books and notes for her essay on The Cross. It was Thursday afternoon again, an hour before her Coverdale group was to meet. That morning she had been for a chat with Tubby about Bishopside and had confessed her fear of parish life. Tubby had listened, affirmed and fed her chunks of Megs's flapjack. ('She makes it with blackstrap molasses, you know.') Annie had left feeling absolved. She promised herself a fresh start, and this was why she was working on her doctrine essay, and not sending Isabella round to apologize to Barney yet again.

As always, it was a question of finding a structure for what she was trying to say. A framework. Frameworks were not her natural medium. They provoked the kind of sweaty panic she felt when trying to fold up a map or erect a deck chair. Edward had no difficulty in this department. His essays, though a little pedestrian, always had a clear logical argument to them. So did his sermons. In fine evangelical style they had three alliterating points. 'There are three things I'd like to say about this passage,' he would boom from the pulpit, 'Prayer, Praise and Perseverance.' It was what Ted and Annie called the Bible, Brogues and Barbour school of preaching. Edward's theology could be folded out briskly like a portable clothes-airer ready to support any biblical text or doctrinal theme. If only I could get a grip on Scripture like that, thought Annie. Nice neat rows of socks and pants. When she read the Bible or thought about atonement she felt as though she was wrestling with seventeen double bed sheets. Her framework creaked and collapsed under the weight.

Before she could pursue this image any further she heard the clump of brogues advancing down the corridor.

'Come in,' she called.

'Well? How did it go yesterday?' asked Edward, pushing a bunch of carnations into her hands. 'Thought you needed cheering up.'

'Oh, Edward, thanks.' He leant down to let her kiss his cheek. Mwah! She put the flowers in a vase. They were white, frilled with red at the edges. Chaste with a spice of passion?

'Now what?' he demanded, seeing her smile as she went to fill the vase at the sink.

'Nothing. They're beautiful.'

'How was Bishopside?'

'Well, it's given me plenty to think about.' She could feel herself blushing slightly. It would be natural to tell him about meeting William, but she found herself overcome by guilty furtiveness. There was no time to analyse this.

Edward was asking, 'What? What do you mean? What did it give you to think about?'

She started to tell him about the possibility of remaining a deacon.

He gave a nod of approval. 'Good girl.'

'That's very patronizing, Edward.'

'Well, you know what I think about women vicars.'

'Yes, I do.'

'I'm not bothered about women priests, but a woman shouldn't have charge of a parish. Not biblical.'

'I said *yes*. I *know* what you think.'

'There are lots of super girls who'd make excellent curates or parish assistants, but I can't think of a single one who'd make a good vicar.' They argued pointlessly for a while, stamping up and down the familiar battle lines, until Edward dropped the subject and asked whether she was going on holiday with Ted again that Easter. She nodded. 'Thought I might gatecrash on my way down from Scotland. If Ted and Mrs Watts don't mind, of course.'

'I'm sure their daughters will be delighted,' remarked Annie.

Edward groaned. 'I'll count on you to protect me, Annie.'

'Shall I pretend to be your girlfriend and beat them off with a rolled-up newspaper?'

'Gosh, Annie. That would be wonderful. Do we have to pretend, though?'

She smiled, used to this kind of gallant banter. She wondered occasionally what he'd do if she took him up on it. Would etiquette demand that he went out and shot himself?

'Maybe I should drag William along. They could pester him instead.'

Annie jumped, fearing that Edward knew about her lunch and was testing her reactions. His face seemed as guileless as ever.

'Perhaps they wouldn't fancy him,' she ventured.

'Oh, come off it, Annie. He's always got women chasing after him. I don't know why you've taken against him,' he added irritably.

'He's a misogynist.' She was waiting for a suitable slot in the conversation to say, By the way, I had lunch with him yesterday.

'Oh, rubbish. He is not a misogynist.'

'That's how he comes across.' Each second that passed gave the lunch another layer of significance.

'He's had his share of problems,' conceded Edward. 'You know. Girl trouble. He's a bit uptight about relationships.'

'Mm.' Somehow it was too late to come clean.

'He's a good man. I know he can be a bit abrupt.'

She clasped her hands together, aware that she was making Edward into a complete fool. Here he was, defending the good character of the man who only yesterday had invited her to sit on his face. 'It's just me, I expect,' she said.

'You'd like him if you knew him better.'

'Yes. I'm sure I would.' Help. Her reluctance was making him bloody-minded. He'd start throwing them together with evangelistic zeal, determined that she should value his foul-mouthed, bullying friend. The only way to stop him would be to tell him the truth, but she knew he'd be furious. She wouldn't be able to stop him going round to sort William out. And then William would be furious with her for telling tales. Annie had always been terrified of causing trouble.

After Edward had gone she began to wonder. Am I sure I'm not just trying to keep my options open? She tried examining her motives and decided that she honestly thought she was harbouring no intention of going to bed with William. Or, at any rate, she honestly thought that she honestly thought it. She didn't even like the man. But how could she say what treacherous motives lurked in her unconscious?

The rest of the Coverdale group would be arriving in a few minutes. Annie began to pray. Lord, you know I'm trying to please you, to do what's right. I'm trying not to be devious, as far as I can tell. But even as she prayed she could sense a defiant writhing in the depths. Help me. You've got to help me! But she could hear footsteps and voices approaching her room and she was forced to postpone her prayer.

Cambridge term ended. Tim waived his right to Isabella's fifty pounds. She stayed up a few more days to take in the last round of parties, but it all seemed trivial and empty. She resisted any urge to go crawling round to Latimer to apologize to Barney. Now where have I heard that before? he might quip. Besides, sod it all, he'd hardly been a gilded saint himself. It was down to *her* that he was still *celibato intacta*, or whatever the phrase was. *He* could bloody well do the grovelling for once.

Four miserable days passed. He was obviously not coming. She began to fear that she'd never see him again. She should at least call to say goodbye. The inconclusiveness of their non-affair was unbearable. A clean break was called for. She'd call round and say All the Best.

She stopped at the pigeon-holes for her post. There were a couple of snotty letters from the bank and the credit-card people. KINDLY RECTIFY THIS SITUATION IMMEDIATELY. Kindly bollocks, thought Isabella, shredding the letters and dropping them in the bin. There was another letter, which her mother had forwarded from home. The handwriting was unfamiliar, but it felt promisingly like a wedding invitation. She opened it as she walked to her bike. *Barnaby Hardstaff* leapt out. He's getting married! Wait – *Please pray for Barnaby Hardstaff who will be ordained deacon* . . . Thank God for that! There was a note with it: *Darling*

Isabella . . . darling! – *Are you still talking to me? If so, would you like to come to my ordination?* Details followed. *Love Barney.* Kiss kiss. What! Not a word of apology. The bastard thinks he just has to click his fingers and I'll come running! she thought, as she pedalled furiously to Latimer Hall. Darling Isabella, love Barney! And he'd got hold of her home address from somewhere.

It was late afternoon. The shadows were lengthening and the air was full of the scent of mock orange and lilac. Her tyres skidded to a halt on Latimer drive. She hurried through the archway. People were milling about on the lawn. Jackets and ties, pretty dresses. Some event must be under way. There was Barney. She was about to dart across to him when she saw he was laughing with a tall attractive woman. The woman laid a hand on his arm, and he gave her the smile Isabella had thought he reserved especially for her. So that's it, she thought with a curious detachment. Ah, well. She turned to slip away, but someone recognized her.

'He's over there.'

Barney turned and saw her. There was nothing to do but summon some hasty dignity and go to him.

'Isabella! I thought you'd gone.'

'No.' Brave smile. 'I'm off tomorrow. Thought I'd pop in and say goodbye.'

'This is Mary.'

Even braver smile. 'Hi, Mary.'

'Hello, Isabella. I've been longing to meet you,' said Mary, as though she and Barney had shared a lot of cosy chats about poor funny old Isabella. 'I'm Tim's sister. Your chaplain, Tim.'

'Oh!'

'I've known Barney since he was a spotty adolescent.' The two exchanged a comfy going-back-years smile. 'I hear you wore a terribly naughty dress to the ball and looked stunning.' Isabella laughed gaily, ha ha!, wondering how Mary could be so apparently generous.

'Barney totally disapproved,' she said.

Barney waggled his eyebrows.

'Barney, you're impossible!' chided Mary. 'You mustn't let him get away with it, Isabella. He'll turn into one of those prim, pompous clerics.' Ha ha! they all laughed gaily. 'Tim thinks you're *won*derful,' went on Mary.

'Really?' Mary was smiling at her. This was something of a first for Isabella. Really nice women like Mary usually lost some of their niceness when they met her. She must be very secure about Barney indeed.

'Well, anyway,' said Isabella, 'I can see you're all busy. I'll say goodbye. All the best, Barney.' She set off with a trembling lip.

There was a murmur and Barney fell into step beside her. Perhaps Mary had said, 'She's upset. Go with her, darling.'

'I sent you an ember card,' said Barney, as they reached Isabella's bike.

'A what?'

'A card saying I'm getting ordained.'

'Oh, I got it. Thanks.' Mary would have known what an ember card was.

'So you'll come?'

'Look, Barney, I'd really love to, and all that, but I'd better not.'

'Why not?'

'It's been great fun this term, but I can see that I've been kidding myself. I mean, shit, you're going to be a vicar, for God's sake. You won't want someone like me hanging around.' He was listening in a compassionate pastoral sort of way that made her want to burst into tears. 'Mary's very nice.'

'Yes.'

She couldn't gauge anything from this response. 'She's the sort of woman you need,' she persisted, trying to smoke him out. 'I mean, she's *good*.'

'Mm. The thing is I prefer bad girls, Isabella.'

'You do?'

'And you,' he said, 'are without a shadow of a doubt the worst girl I've ever met.'

'Oh, Barney!' She flung herself at him. He grunted like a rugby player hit by a flying tackle. 'Nobody's ever said that to me before.'

He chuckled. 'I can't think why not.'

She wrapped her arms tight round his neck. 'I love you.'

'Come to my ordination, then.'

'OK.' There was still a mark on his neck. She touched it with a guilty finger. 'Sorry about that.'

'Mm. A little hint, Isabella.' She scowled. He was going to say something prim, pompous and clerical. 'Keep the hickeys below the dog-collar line.' The chapel bell began to chime. 'I'll have to go. It's the leavers' service.'

'Is Mary staying with you?'

'With Tim.'

'She fancies the pants off you.'

'Men and women do have *other* ways of relating, Isabella,' he said, in a slightly nettled way. Aha. He knows she's in love with him.

'I hope you're kind to her, Barney.' He began unwinding her arms from his neck. 'You'll have to be kind to all those pathetic women parishioners when they fall for you.' He pushed her away, muttering something which might conceivably have been oh, piss off. 'I'll see you on your Big Day, then. Shall I meet you outside the cathedral, or something?'

'I'm afraid not. You won't see me till we all process in down the aisle. I'll be the one in the long black dress.' The chapel bell stopped ringing. 'Goodbye, Isabella.'

'Don't I get a proper kiss?' He leant and kissed her cheek. 'That wasn't a proper one!'

'It was extremely proper.'

She stuck two fingers up at his retreating back then cycled off, giddy with excitement.

That seemed like a satisfactory breaking-off point. Annie put down her biro and looked at her watch. The rest of her Coverdale group would already be in the college bar. She checked how much money she had in her purse and set off to join them.

Bars and pubs always made her nervous in the way she imagined church intimidated non-churchgoers. Would everyone stare as she walked in? What if she sat in someone else's place? Supposing there were unwritten rules she was transgressing? Growing up in a strict teetotal household had left Annie incapable of walking confidently into a bar and ordering a drink. She didn't like beer. Spirits felt somehow too grown-up – she could imagine people thinking, She looks a bit young to be drinking whisky. She usually settled for fruit juice. And, to crown it all, there was the ordeal of buying a round. If you only ever drank orange juice, would people really expect you to take a turn? How would you remember seven different drinks, how could you carry them all, and had you got enough money to pay for them? Perhaps God, in his infinite mercy, would call her to work in a Muslim country.

The college bar was in the cellar. She went down the steps into the smoky, crowded room. Her group was squashed round a table in the corner. Edward was with them. Good. She began to make her way between people. He caught sight of her and got to his feet. She froze. William was there.

'Have a seat, Annie,' Edward was ordering her. The group squeezed up. She cast William a pleading look, but he stared blankly as though they had never met. Edward gestured for her to sit. 'William, you remember Annie?' She sat beside him.

'Should I?' he drawled.

'You met at the theatre.'

'Oh, yes.' His tone was bored.

Annie forced herself to smile. Edward was hovering, waiting for her to launch into bright chatter, but she could think of nothing to say. William turned and resumed his conversation with Isobel.

'What would you like to drink?' asked Edward.

'Grapefruit juice, please.' She was left fiddling with a beermat, trying to look composed. She'd never understood before how wounding a well-administered snub could be.

' "Shop assistant required. Must be flexible," ' said Ted, leaning across the table. He'd been watching her over his ale.

' "All tights and stockings down," ' she replied, hoping he had noticed nothing. Ted was an expert in the fluctuations in female happiness. He'd probably witnessed his daughters making themselves endlessly unhappy over unfeeling men. Edward returned with her drink. She supposed she should be grateful that William had told him nothing. Perhaps he was covering for her? Had he foreseen how awful it would be for her if Edward suddenly demanded, 'Why didn't you tell me you'd had lunch with William? Eh? Well?' She sipped her grapefruit juice.

Edward sat down and Annie was crushed up closer against William. She could hear Isobel talking about opera. William was being *perfectly civil*. Annie glanced and saw a faint glow on Isobel's cheeks. Then Ingram cast in his two-pennyworth about Verdi, and William withdrew from the conversation. Annie stared down at her glass. The ice began to clink as her hand trembled. Was William watching her? They were thigh to thigh.

'Annie was in Bishopside yesterday,' remarked Edward.

'Was she?' It was said in the same snubbingly casual tone. He wasn't covering for her. He was punishing her for rejecting him. Edward was clearly itching to knock their heads together. William deflected him, 'So how do you rate England's chances, then, Teddy?'

Annie sat for the next five minutes with a fierce rugby controversy raging over the top of her head. Before long the argument deteriorated into the bollocks, bullshit! stage, and Annie decided she would rather spend her time with Barney and Isabella. She finished her drink and took a sneaky look at her watch. Nearly ten.

'Another drink?' asked William.

Annie jumped. 'Me? Um –' Help! 'Oh, er, no thanks. I'd better be –'

'So soon, honey?' he drawled.

She flushed and tried to get to her feet.

'Don't be ridiculous,' said Edward. 'You've only just got here.' He pulled her firmly back. 'Another grapefruit juice, William.'

'*No*. Thank you.' She peeled Edward's hand off her arm. 'I've got to go.' She knew he'd be angry with her, but she found, for once, that she didn't care. ' 'Bye everyone.'

She got back to her room and pulled out her notebook. Edward would probably pursue her to remonstrate. All she'd have to say was, 'Actually, I'm not feeling too good,' and he'd back off full of remorse. 'Gosh, Annie, I'm sorry. Why didn't you say so? Can I get you anything?' But . . . but *sod* it! Annie never swore, but this time nothing else would quite do. Who wants to spend an evening sandwiched between two squabbling rugby fans? Not to mention William's hateful behaviour. Had he really come all that way just to put her in her place?

Hold it! she told herself. Don't start crying. What if Edward comes? She opened her notebook and reread the last scene. Coverdale vanished and she was back in Cambridge.

When Isabella –

There was a knock at the door. Annie's pen hovered. She'd been so absorbed she hadn't heard Edward's brogues bearing down on her. She hid the book.

'Come in.'

It was William.

'Hi, honey child.'

She scrambled to her feet. 'What – w – w – You can't –'

He closed the door and crossed to the desk where she stood wringing her hands. 'Why didn't you tell Edward you'd seen me? I damn nearly landed you in it.'

'You told me not to!'

He was too close. She shrank back and sat on the desk edge.

'So I'm a misogynist?'

'I –'

'Edward's very upset you don't like me, Annie.'

'It's not –'

'Give me another chance. Please. Saturday afternoon. We can walk on the beach in the rain. Or find some quiet teashop with an open fire. Then go out for dinner in the evening. Whatever you like.' She shook her head. 'Oh, come on, Annie. You owe it to Edward.' She stood opening and shutting her mouth at his audacity. 'I'll pick you up at the station at about two, OK?'

'No.' He was giving her that irresistible smile. '*No*. I'm not –' She broke off. The sound of brogues echoed in the corridor. Edward! She made a guilty move.

'Ssh!' said William. The footsteps paused. A knock. Annie opened her mouth to call him in, but William laid a finger on her lips. Her heart thumped. The silence was endless. His finger-tip on her parted lips. The radiator ticking. Her breath coming fast, then suddenly his mouth on hers. Her hand which had reached out to push him away clutched him instead. At last the footsteps clumped off the way they had come.

'I thought I wasn't imagining it,' he said, kissing her again, more slowly this time, working his tongue deep into her mouth. She was whimpering inside, shocked that it could be so horribly arousing. She would end up letting him stay. Then abruptly he released her. 'See you on Saturday?' She nodded, looking at the floor in shame. 'Yes?'

'Yes.' She had stranded herself on the side of sin. There could be no other answer.

'Good. I'll pick you up at two. Look at me.' He tilted her chin up and studied her expression. 'Come on, it's not the end of the world, honey.'

But as his soft footsteps faded away, she felt that it was.

CHAPTER II

'"Almighty and most merciful Father, we have erred and strayed from thy ways like lost sheep, we have followed too much the devices and desires of our own hearts, we have offended against thy holy laws . . ."'

Annie knelt in her pew in Coverdale chapel as the general confession rumbled briskly along. It was Lent, the term when they used the Book of Common Prayer.

'". . . That we may ever hereafter live a godly, righteous and sober life . . ."'

Tubby absolved them genially. '"Pardon and remission of all your sins, time for amendment of life . . ."' Time for amendment. There was still time. She didn't have to visit William tomorrow. The Lord's Prayer, then a clattering as they all stood for the responses. The Venite. Help! Help me, Lord. The service swept past her like scenery past a train window. Psalm, lessons, Creed, collects. The final hymn.

> Forty days and forty nights
> > Thou wast fasting in the wild.
> Forty days and forty nights
> > Tempted, and yet undefiled.

Oh, let me be undefiled! But she could tell she had already made her decision.

The service was over and they all went out into the cold foggy morning. Annie shivered and pulled her hands up into the sleeves of her ragged sweater.

'It's like a bloody working museum,' boomed Edward, who was not a fan of the prayer book.

The old Beauty-of-the-Language argument was proposed by Ingram. Ted, who was something of a Hot Prot, raised a theological point about the Alternative Service Book including material that Cranmer had got rid of. It was shaping up to be a full-blown liturgical debate over breakfast.

'You're very quiet this morning,' said Edward as they sat down.

I wish you would be, thought Annie. Everyone seemed to be listening.

'What got into you in the bar last night?' he demanded.

'Leave her alone, Edward,' said Isobel.

'I called round,' went on Edward relentlessly. 'Where were you?'

'I wasn't feeling too good.'

Ted flicked her a glance, then went back to the letter he was reading.

Annie blushed. Well, I wasn't.

'Gosh, Annie. I'm sorry,' said Edward. 'What's the matter?'

'Perhaps a *leetle* sensitivity, Edward?' suggested Ingram, possibly taking her blush to indicate Women's Matters.

'All right, all right.'

Annie made herself spoon cornflakes into her mouth. Come on. Chew. Swallow. She had been kept awake most of the night by Libby clanking her chain and baying like a werewolf. Her stomach still felt clenched in a fierce grip. Chew. Swallow. She realized Ted had spoken to her.

'Sorry?'

'Look at this. Penny sent it.' Penny was his wife. He handed over a church magazine with an item underlined.

Vic Huggins, organist and evangelist, also played. He uses his organ to open doors to non-believers who would not otherwise hear the gospel.

Annie whooped and passed the article round. Edward laughed till the tears rolled down his face.

'Like a jemmy, do you suppose?' asked Annie.

'Or a battering ram,' suggested Ted. Edward bellowed again.

'Honestly, Edward,' said Isobel. 'You're like a smutty school-boy.' Her rebuke took in the rest of the group as well. They fell silent. She clattered her plate and bowl together primly and left the room.

'Or a credit card,' said Ted. Annie could still hear Edward guffawing as she climbed the stairs to her room.

I'm cutting myself off from them, she thought. They were good people, on the whole, despite their occasional bickering and hobby-horse riding. They cared about what happened to her and how her soul was faring. She was risking their friendship for the sake of a man who cared nothing for her – apart from how quickly he could persuade her onto her back. If only he had a little more kindness or generosity she might be able to justify it to herself.

Her room seemed unnaturally still. As she gazed, the furniture took on a new clarity, as though it were coming into focus for the first time. The desk with its books and notes, the bed, the Indian cushions with their scraps of mirror, the Blake print of Michael binding Satan. There will be no justification, she thought. I won't twist the Bible round and tell myself that God approves. '*He who sows to his flesh will from the flesh reap corruption.*' Did she dare set herself against God? Her style was not defiant. She was more at home with evasions and invisibility. Perhaps God wouldn't notice. His mind must be full of Bosnian refugees and Aids victims. What would it matter to him if Annie Brown misspent her Saturday afternoons? She felt a pang. It did matter.

Isabella walked with the crowds towards the cathedral. She was so very suitably clad for the occasion that there was practically a hint of satire about her hat and gloves and her (ai-yai-yai) horribly expensive linen suit. Still, it was a timeless classic. A suit like that wouldn't date. I mean, it was practically an investment, for God's sake.

The crowds swelled. As she stood queuing outside the vast door Isabella wondered what the service would be like. She tried to remind herself that the purpose of the day was to ordain Barney *et al*, not to provide a stage for Isabella Deane. She was the sort of woman who chafed at weddings because she couldn't hog the limelight.

She made her way eventually into the cathedral with the throng. The vast building rumbled with the sound of feet and voices. The organ was playing thoughtful muted chords. Isabella sensed the excitement in the air and marvelled. It was church, after all. She didn't associate religion with that kind of happy anticipation. Perhaps she hadn't grasped just how big Barney's big day actually was.

An elderly man in a cassocky thing stepped forward as she hesitated in the nave. She half expected him to ask, 'Bride or groom?'

'A friend of mine's getting ordained and I don't know where I'm supposed to sit.' She flashed her nicest smile.

He was unmoved. 'Deacon or priest?'

How the hell should I know? Then she remembered the ember card. 'Deacon, I think.' Was that faint disdain on his lips at her ignorance?

'What name?'

She was on the point of giving her own name, when she realized what he meant. 'Hardstaff.'

She followed him as he trundled off up the aisle. Shit, I should go to church more often then I wouldn't feel like a complete twat. They reached a row of chairs and Isabella could see *Hardstaff* pinned to the end seat. She turned to thank the man, but he was already trundling away. The row was practically full. She hesitated again, rebuking herself for imagining she was the only person he had invited. His family – this must be his family, of course. A youngish woman caught sight of her hovering.

'Isabella?'

'Yes.'

'Hey, listen everybody. It's Isabella. Barney's girlfriend.' Girlfriend! Isabella hardly had time for a shocked blush before she was being greeted, introduced and exclaimed over. Barney had told them all about her. They had marked Midlands accents. It occurred to her that she knew nothing about them, not even where they lived or what they did. She cursed herself for not finding out more, but how was she supposed to know she'd be billed as Barney's girlfriend? Was that what he thought? She blushed all over again.

His three sisters were handsome blondes with bluff, moustached husbands. The children had been left with relatives. Barney's father was almost bald. (Oh, no! Had Camilla been right about Barney's hairline?) His mother was silent. In that, Isabella feared she could read contempt. She found herself sitting next to her in the seat nearest the aisle. Before she could say something to banish that derisive curl on Mrs Hardstaff's lips the organ began to play more assertively. The chatter hushed, then a booming sound swept up the cathedral like a tidal wave as everyone rose to their feet.

Isabella fumbled with her order of service and was forced to peel off her gloves. They lay in limp supplication on the hymnbook rest in front of her.

> All my hope on God is founded.
> He doth still my trust renew.
> Me through change and chance he guideth,
> Only good and only true.

She didn't know the hymn. The procession was making its way up the aisle. She gave up trying to anticipate the tune and turned to stare. First came a beadle-y figure with a stave of some sort, then the choir. The unfamiliar tune went by in blasts: treble, treble, alto, tenor (mmm, nice), bass. Then some fancy clerics. Canons? she wondered. Two types: tall and cadaverous or round and Friar Tuck-like. Oh, and a woman. And, after her, the Bishop. Hey, not bad. He had a naughty twinkle in his eye. What glorious robes. That fabric would make wonderful drawing-room curtains. He was smiling and looking at people, unlike the clergy who followed. She resisted a childish urge to stick out a foot. It was the way they were gliding, hands folded piously, as though they were travelling up the aisle on a conveyor belt. Here came some younger ones. Maybe they were going to get ordained. Yes, there was Barney, his face sweetly serious as he sang the hymn. He caught sight of her and broke into a wide grin. Another second and he was gone.

The hymn ended and the procession arrived at the front.

'The Lord be with you,' said a polite disembodied voice from a speaker on a nearby pillar. Isabella craned her neck. The Bishop.

'And also with you,' rumbled the congregation.

Then the Bishop said a prayer. Everyone sat for a reading. Isabella's mind wandered to the subject of bishops in general. This one was a pleasant surprise. The ones you usually saw on television were either wintry or unctuous. They waved their hands around and chopped the air while they spoke. They wore horrible glasses with heavy black tops to the frames. Surely in this image-conscious age the Church should have an Episcopal Eyewear Advisory Committee? And a good haircut should be compulsory. No more draping of bald patches. Closet slapheads must be outed.

Whoops! Everyone was standing again. A psalm, followed by another reading. Isabella began to get bored. The sermon was a wash-out. The PA system seemed to have taken against the preacher's voice and bestowed on him a sharp British Rail announcement echo. A reference to a *wireless operator* was distinguishable, but little else.

They stood for the Creed. After a few sentences Isabella began to mumble. Then she fell silent. She couldn't in honesty say she believed in all this. She gazed up at the vaults and felt tiny, like some kind of insect that had scuttled in. Perhaps God would simply sweep her back out again. A nasty sense of unworthiness crept over her. No right-minded deity would give her the time of day. What was she, after all? Just a silly undergraduate who thought about nothing but sex, and squandered wicked sums on clothes when two-thirds of the world went to bed hungry. She bowed her head and looked down at her empty pleading gloves.

If there's anyone there, then I'm sorry. I want to be different. I want to be . . . good. Worthy. She broke off. The words seemed clumsy. She couldn't express the longing she felt. But as she stood helpless a voice seemed to speak:

You're accepted.

Her heart jumped. Me? How could she be? She felt so completely unacceptable. But the words wouldn't go away. *You're accepted.* Then Isabella felt a wild yelp of jubilation welling up inside her. She bit her lips. Yodelling for joy was probably not the done thing in cathedrals. The Creed ended and everyone sat down. She felt as though she had looked at the finals results board and seen her name up among the firsts when she knew she should have failed. I don't believe it. I've gone and got myself converted.

Annie looked at what she had written. She had planned to put so much more into this chapter, to produce a conversion scene that would move the reader to tears of repentance. But how can I? How can I sit there writing about grace and conversion when I'm planning to fly in the face of God's law? A Bible verse rose up to accuse her: *The works of the flesh are plain: fornication, impurity, licentiousness . . . Those who do such things will never enter the kingdom of God*. I'll finish it later, she promised. I'll come back to it when I'm in a better frame of mind.

The final hymn ended and the cathedral began to hum with excited chatter. New priests and deacons were reunited with friends and family. Everyone was pressing towards the exits. Isabella stood on tiptoe, hoping to catch sight of Barney.
'There he is,' called a sister. 'Yoohoo! Barney-boy!' He was waving from the steps near the door in a black shirt and dog-collar. Eventually they reached him. Isabella stood on the side-lines while he was hugged and congratulated and slapped on the back.
'Well, well, well. Not bad, son. Not bad at all, eh?' said his father, rubbing his hands together. 'You'll have to behave your-self from now on. There'll be no more –' A hiss from his wife silenced him.
'When do you get a purple shirt, then?' asked a brother-in-law.
'When pigs fly,' said a sister. 'Look at you, Barney! You've got dandruff. And your hair's falling out.' She flapped at his shoulders.
'Leave the poor bugger alone,' his father protested.
Barney pushed his sisters aside and reached Isabella.
'Thank you for coming.'

He kissed her cheek and she stifled a giggle. It felt odd to be kissed by a man in a dog-collar. She couldn't quite take him seriously. It was like seeing a well-known actor miscast in a bad film. 'You look like something off *The Thornbirds*,' she said.

'Except he's not good-looking,' said his sisters.

Isabella frowned. They treated him like a little brother who must be squashed and kept in his place. They were nearing the Bishop now as he stood greeting people just outside the cathedral.

'Hello, Barnaby,' he said, as they shook hands. Barney's family were all introduced. Isabella felt overlooked.

'And this is Isabella,' he said at last, not adding 'my girlfriend', or even 'a friend of mine from Cambridge'.

'Hello. I'm his concubine,' said Isabella, shaking the Bishop's hand and giving him a dazzling smile. Barney covered his face in despair. 'I think you're wonderful, by the way. Not at all like a bishop.'

'Er, thank you,' replied the Bishop.

Isabella felt Barney grip her elbow and steer her away. ''Bye,' she called.

The Bishop smiled and turned to the next group.

'Well,' said Barney as they walked off. 'There go my chances of an early preferment.'

'Are you mad at me?' He smiled down at her. The bells were pealing, the sound tumbling joyfully down around them. Before Barney could reply he was told to hurry it up by an impatient sister.

What a weird day, thought Isabella in the train on the way home. Strange to see Barney in two new lights: as a clergyman and as a member of the Hardstaff family. If only they'd had more time together. She wasn't used to sharing him like this. He'd had dozens of people to talk to over lunch. The afternoon sped by, and in no time it was Evensong. After that there had been a bunfight in the church hall with Barney endlessly circulating and being charming to grey-haired women in nylon jersey dresses. A horrible sense of foreboding seized her: if she married Barney then this could be the first of many such occasions for her. Her eyes rested in dismay on the vicar's wife with her pageboy hair-cut and fifteen-year-old Laura Ashley smock. I'd have to kill myself! She clutched her plate of quiche and crisps. Barney caught her eye across the crowd in front of the urn and smiled. Why couldn't you be a merchant banker, for God's sake? Or a farmer, even, like your father.

'I'm just running Isabella to the station,' Barney had said, when it was finally all over.

'Oh, yes?' said his father, eyebrows waggling. His wife cuffed him. 'I've said nothing!' he protested.

'I think God spoke to me in the cathedral,' said Isabella, as they drove off in Barney's new and disappointingly staid car. 'Do you think that's possible?'

'What did he say?' She explained. 'Yes. Sounds like God.'

'I think I might have been . . . converted. Or something.' It occurred to her that he might expect some evidence, some altera-tion in her behaviour. She glanced back through the day and saw herself vamping the Bishop and despising the vicar's wife. Hmm. Barney took one of her hands in his and kissed it.

'Good.' They drove the rest of the way in silence.

'I know I'm not perfect,' she gabbled on the platform, 'but I'll change. I'll –'

'Don't worry about it.' he said. 'It's God's job not yours. And it's a slow process. A lifetime's work.'

'Really?'

He grinned. 'Well, he's been working on me for about eight years and I'm still a bastard.'

'You aren't! I won't let you say that.' The train was approaching.

'Isabella, you've got no idea.'

'Yes I have. I'm a world expert on men. I know a bastard when I see one.'

But he only smiled and shook his head at her.

CHAPTER 12

Annie stared at the page. Christus Victor. Penal substitution. Redeemer. Messiah. Second Adam. She sketched some arrows between these ideas, hoping that this would trick the long-awaited essay framework into appearing. The Bridge Illustration drifted into her mind. GOD and MAN divided by SIN. All the fault of WOMAN, of course. Eve and the fruit of the tree. Annie reached for a book and turned to a passage she had marked earlier, where one of the early fathers roundly blamed Eve (and, by association, all women) for the death of Christ. 'You are the devil's gateway,' she read. That sounded familiar. She remembered with a jolt of surprise that it was what William had called her. A different man – Ingram, say – would have added casually, 'Tertullian, by the way.' William hadn't cared that his erudition went unremarked, or that she might think he was expressing his own misogynist views.

She'd be seeing him in a couple of hours. The passage of time always amazed her. Here she was standing on one bank looking across. That evening she'd be on the other side looking back. What would it be like, that icy tide in between? Did Eve circle round the tree, eyeing the fruit, knowing it was inevitable that one day her hand would reach out, her lips taste, and that she would *know* at last?

The train crossed the Tyne and drew into Newcastle. Annie clamped her arms tightly round herself. She hadn't felt this sick with nerves since her Cambridge interview when she was eighteen. She wanted to curl up under the seat and stay on the train till Edinburgh. Why hadn't she rung him and said she'd changed her mind?

He wasn't on the platform. A dozen fears fluttered about in her head. What if he'd changed his mind? What if she'd got the wrong day or time? People surged past her. An announcement echoed. She would have to wait. But for how long? She began crossing the footbridge. What if he never came? But then she caught sight of him on the concourse. For a few seconds she was able to watch him from above. He made a dramatic impression in his long black coat, scowling, shifting impatiently from foot to foot, glancing at his watch. It dawned on her that he might be as nervous as she was. She hurried down.

'Annie!' His face lit up. 'You came.'

'Well, I said I would.'

'You could have stood me up. Something tells me I deserved it.'

'A little voice inside you?' she asked. 'We call it "conscience" in the trade.'

He gave her a nasty look. 'I won't ask what state your conscience is in.' She blushed. 'Come on.' She had to trot to keep up with him as he headed for the car-park. 'Have you eaten?'

'I tried to.'

'Nervous?'

'Terrified.'

He tossed his keys into the air and caught them with a grin. 'Where shall we go?'

'Um . . .'

He unlocked the door for her and she got in. 'The moors? The coast? Say something. Choose.'

'Whichever's easiest.'

'Right. The coast.' He slammed the door. She cringed down into her coat, knowing her feebleness provoked him.

'Look,' she tried, 'sorry I'm being –'

'Stop apologizing,' he interrupted.

'Sorr –' Help! She clamped her mouth shut.

He started the car and pulled out of the station. It was raining heavily. She glanced at his profile as he drove, but couldn't decide whether he was angry or amused. His fingers drummed on the steering wheel. Before long they were out of Newcastle and heading for the coast. The weather worsened. Annie watched as the windscreen wipers thrashed backwards and forwards. Dared she talk about the weather? She was starting to giggle.

'Just look at it,' she said.

'Mm. Don't you love it?' She glanced again, doubted, and said nothing. 'Well? Do you love it, yes or no, for God's sake?'

'The rain?'

'Yes, of course the *rain*.' His tone accused her of smuttiness. She looked out of her window to hide a smile. Would they ever achieve a straightforward conversation? The rain slashed across the window as she gazed out.

'Um. . . No. I don't. Didn't you mention a tea-shop with an open fire?'

'Too late.' His fingers drummed on the steering wheel in time with the rain.

'Do you love it?'

He flared his nostrils at her. 'God, yes.'

She bit her lips. He's mad, she decided. There's no point trying to understand or placate him. What if – daring thought – she was just herself, like the agony aunts in women's magazines always recommended? *Just be yourself*. It had always struck her as dangerous advice. He was whistling through his teeth, something jaunty and baroque-sounding. I bet he's itching to put the radio on. Edward would be chemically bonded to the television by now.

'Do listen to the rugby, if you want to,' she said.

He chuckled. 'Kick-off's not till three.' He smothered a yawn. 'Sorry. Two a.m. call out last night. Always buggers me up.'

'Anything serious?'

'Yeah. She should've gone straight to Casualty really, but she wanted to see me because I'm so kind and understanding.' He slid her a look. 'Hard to credit, hmm?'

'Er . . . what was wrong with her?'

'Broken nose. Concussion. Classic symptoms of a congenital tendency to walk into doorframes.'

'Is that congenital?' asked Annie, in surprise.

'No. Well, only in the sense that women with violent fathers tend to pick violent partners.' He saw her puzzled expression. 'Her man beat her up.'

'Oh! Will she leave him?'

'No. The flat's in her name. Everything's in the woman's name in that bit of town. All the benefits, and so on. They've got the power. The men just run around doing the shagging.'

'And the beating up.'

'Yes – because they're emasculated. Don't think I'm condoning it,' he added. 'It's what the system does to people.'

'She could throw him out,' said Annie, hoping to avert a political tirade.

'Another woman would take him in. Look. There's the sea.'

Annie stared at the grey stripe low on the horizon. She was depressed by Will's bleak view of society. He parked the car. The rain spattered on the windscreen in the silence. They got out and she heard the waves booming on the shore. Cold rain lashed her face.

'Come on!' he shouted, above the wind. They ran hand in hand down the steps and staggered across the sand. He was laughing out loud.

He really does love it. 'You're mad!' The wind tossed her words away.

He flung his arms wide and shouted, 'Yes! Yes! Yes!'

Another wave crashed in and he sprinted to meet it. She watched him down at the water's edge conducting the storm. For a moment it looked as though he really was calling up wave after wave, a demon impresario with the elements at his bidding, his long black coat swirling in the wind. She envied him his total abandon. He was gesturing her to join him. She went as far as she dared. A wave raced at her and she danced out of its path.

'I'll get wet.' He strode towards her. The sea was foaming round his feet. 'No!'

But he reached out and pulled her to him. Icy water seeped into her boots. He began kissing her. Cold lips, hot tongue. She clung to him, feeling the shore sliding under her and the sea booming in her head. Another wave surged in, drenching them to their knees. Annie screamed. He dragged her higher up the beach, laughing. The sea chased them.

'Yes! It's coming in, Annie.'

'I know!' she wailed. 'Now I see why the Northumbrian saints used to stand in it to mortify the flesh.' He was kissing her again, salt on his lips, icy hand undoing her jeans. She squealed.

'Stand still.'

'Someone will see!' A sea gull screamed on the wind. 'Does it feel weird doing this without gloves on, Doctor?' she asked. 'O-oh ah!'

'Stop thinking and start feeling.'

But I'm feeling too much already. She tried to fight it back but it rose as swiftly as the tide. 'At least kiss me,' she pleaded.

He laughed. 'I want to watch your face.'

She was burning up like a heretic saint, martyred on his icy fingers. Help! Think about something else. Seven times table. Seven sevens are . . . Am I the first woman in history trying to fake not having an orgasm? Forty-nine!

'Mm-*ah*!'

'Bloody hell. I've hardly started.'

'Sorry.' They stared at one another in surprise.

'Are you always like this?' He sounded almost annoyed.

'No. Not . . . It's you, not me.' Some expression flickered in his green eyes. She shivered. Her feet ached with cold.

'My God, Annie. What are we standing here for? Let's get back.' He grabbed her hand and ran with her to the car.

They drove in silence. Annie hugged herself and shuddered. Whatever must he think of me? And they were speeding to his house for more. Underwear doubts assailed her. Her knickers had looked all right in Coverdale, but how would they seem against his (doubtless) pure white Egyptian cotton sheets? Then a worse thought occurred.

'Um . . . I'm not on the pill, or anything . . .'

'Actually, honey child, down here on planet Earth we all use condoms these days.'

They lapsed back into silence. Annie began to wish they would crash or that the Second Coming would take place before they got back to Bishopside.

'What's wrong?' he asked.

'I'm still nervous.'

'*You're* nervous. What about me, for Christ's sake? You're only the instrument. I'm supposed to be the maestro.'

Well, if his bowing was on a par with his fingerwork she could look forward to a virtuoso performance.

'Are you laughing at me?' he asked.

By the time they reached his house a fatal awkwardness seemed to have descended. They took off their wet jeans and bundled them into the washing machine. Annie giggled at the absurdity of bare legs in the kitchen and was almost relieved when he led her upstairs to his bedroom. They undressed and began kissing. This is hopeless, she thought, after a while. We should have done it on the beach. His confidence seemed to have abandoned him. She reached down timidly to caress him. He thrust her aside, sat up and to her dismay began to call down a string of vile medical curses on his impotent flesh.

'Don't, Will.' She placed a hand on his arm, but he flung it off again. 'It's OK.'

'It's not OK!' he raged.

A nursery rhyme flitted improperly through her mind. *My master's lost his fiddling stick, and doesn't know what to do!* She giggled. There was a horrible silence. She stared into his wild eyes, appalled at what she had done. He grabbed his dressing gown and stormed out of the room.

Oh, no! Annie sat frozen in dismay. She hadn't really been laughing at him. It was nerves. She sat on the bed dithering, knowing she must go and apologize yet terrified of his anger. Go on, she urged herself. It was unforgivable to laugh at such a moment. The poor man. She wrapped a blanket round herself and crept after him.

He was sitting in the kitchen pale with rage. Another giggle trembled in her.

'Look, Will, I'm really sorry. Couldn't we try again? Please? It doesn't matter if –'

'Don't you patronize me,' he spat.

She flinched. Her eyes filled with tears. 'I'm sorry. Can't I . . . um, do anything to – to . . .'

He sat biting his lip. Gradually his expression grew less wild.

'You could always kiss it better,' he muttered. For a moment she didn't catch his meaning.

'Oh! I . . .' She hesitated.

He was waiting, raw from his recent humiliation, poised to take further offence. Now wasn't the time to say she'd never done this before.

The tiles were cold under her knees. She felt him pulse to life between her shrinking lips. The washing machine was still threshing away. She was trying not to gag and offend him. Rain spattered against the window. He groaned and his hands began to stroke her hair. Perhaps one day she might grow to like it, this strange mixture of power and vulnerability, of tenderness and disgust. He was whimpering her name. Then he was hauling her off him.

'Lie down,' he whispered urgently. Her back cringed against the cold tiles. He parted her legs. She clung to him and waited.

'Jesus fucking *Christ!*'

'Will!'

'I can't do it!' he sobbed. 'I can't do it!' He wrenched away from her. His face was distorted with rage, hatred. 'It's you. You're unfuckable. I need a woman, not some giggling fucking schoolgirl. Get out. Get your clothes and get *out!*'

She listened to his footsteps pounding up the stairs.

God stood there like her mother spitting in triumph. Well, you got what was coming to you, Anne Brown. I just hope you've learnt your lesson.

She got up off the floor and wrapped the blanket tightly round her, clutching it under her chin. Tears streamed down her cheeks. The machine began its spin cycle. I can't go till it's finished. She sat huddled in the blanket like an accident victim beside a road, waiting, trembling. He hates me. I should never never have come here. At last the machine came to a stop. She tried to pull her jeans out but they were tangled with his. Her fingers were too weak to free them. A sob escaped. He was upstairs having a shower. She could hear the water running.

She sat down again and clutched the blanket. Her mind reached out to God, pleading, but he turned away. I'm busy. It's your own fault, Anne. You've got to realize I've got better things to do with my time than run around after you . . . On and on went the voice.

I shouldn't have laughed.

She could hear him coming back. Her hand tried desperately to smooth her hair.

'Your clothes,' he said.

'Thanks.' She took the bundle from him. He wouldn't even look at her, just bent and turned the washing-machine dial. The drying cycle began. Annie heard the soft clatter of jeans rivets against the drum.

He picked up a bottle of whisky and left the room. A moment later she heard the television. Rugby. Crowds roaring, *Swing Low, Sweet Chariot*, the commentator's voice rising and falling. Ordinary Saturday noises. Washing machine, rain on the window, sport on the television.

She made herself get dressed. The jeans tumbled round and round. She was watching herself staring at them. *It will end. It will end.* She hadn't known a man's face could look like that. She had never been hated before.

I should never have laughed at him. Time crept by. *You're unfuckable. Unfuckable.*

There was a soft slump and final rattle as the machine stopped. Silence. 'But the linesman's flag is up . . .' She fought her jeans free of his and pulled them on, feeling the buttons burning her stomach. For a moment she stood looking around as though there was something else she had come with but mislaid. Her coat was in the hall. He heard her and came out of the sitting room.

'I'm just going.'

He shrugged. They stood. Behind him she glimpsed the television. The rugby was over. Players were being carried shoulder high through the crowds, but she couldn't tell who had won. The whisky fumes on his breath reached her, and among them another smell, something from her childhood. She couldn't identify it.

They hesitated, neither seeming to know how they should part. Then she heard her voice foolishly thanking him.

'*Thanks?* For what?' She cowered back from him. 'Oh, just fuck off, Annie.'

133

As she hurried through the rainy streets towards the station she remembered what that smell had been. Johnson's baby shampoo. She started crying again.

CHAPTER 13

The ten days of term that remained were among the worst of Annie's life. The numb shock wore off to expose an ache of misery. She felt too bruised and sick for other people's company, their laughter, jokes and worried looks. And yet to be alone was worse. If only she could get her mother's voice out of her head she might have a chance of straightening things out with God, who was, after all, slow to anger and of infinite mercy. But whenever she tried to repent another tirade burst out. Oh, 'sorry' is all very well, Anne Brown. You should have thought about that before you went off to a strange man's house. What did you expect, I should like to know? I don't know why you thought you'd be any good at sex. You're not much good at anything, are you? You can't blame him, you know.

Her appetite dwindled and she couldn't sleep properly. The growing anxiety of her friends forced her to invent a mild but lingering bout of flu. This provoked a great deal of concerned advice, and one day at breakfast, when for the fifth time Edward had ordered her to go to the doctor's, she could stand no more. They had stared after her in surprise as she rushed out of the dining room almost in tears. She tried to take refuge in her novel, but her characters and their lives seemed unbearably trivial.

She made herself go over every detail of that awful afternoon. How could she have been so stupid, so cruel as to laugh? Of course he was furious. Any man would be. No wonder he hated her. There was nobody she could confide in. No one to advise her whether to apologize, or to steer well clear of him. Oh, if only I knew what to do! Sometimes she wondered if he would make some move, but then his horrible words would burst afresh into her mind. You're unfuckable. And his expression as he said it. She had never really fallen out with anyone before. She'd always been too placating and timid to bear being even vaguely at odds with someone. And now this awful crushing mortifying . . . Her only hope was that she would gradually get over it.

The days passed. She made herself carry on with her routines for the sake of her friends. Chapel, meals, study, sleep. Her world seemed dead. There was no Libby bounding along at her heels. Occasionally she caught sight of her reflection in windows and saw how gaunt she was looking. No wonder they were all worried about her. They had tackled her one after another in their different ways. If she hadn't felt so wretched she might have been amused by their different tactics. Ted seemed to be holding back, but in the end even he came knocking on her door.

'It's not crossing the sea that makes a missionary,' was his opening remark. Annie stared. 'But . . .?' he prompted. The penny dropped.

'But seeing the cross.' She felt herself smile for the first time in days. A new Ted Watts game. 'The heart of the human problem is . . .?'

'The problem of the human heart. That's an old one, Annie. Come on. Let's go out for a wander. It's a lovely mild evening.'

They walked arm in arm down across the old bridge. Annie heard a blackbird singing and noticed that the buds were swelling.

'Soon be spring,' said Ted.

'Mm.' The evidence was there, yet she didn't have the heart to believe it. They began walking along the riverbank with Ted steering round the muddy puddles because of his open-toed sandals. Before long they came to a bench with a view of the cathedral rising up above the trees on the steep bank and reflected in the river below. They sat and listened to the rushing of the weir. Annie wondered if Ted's tactic was simply to allow her the chance to confide if she wanted to. This had been Isobel's approach over a polite cup of lapsang earlier in the week.

'Well, well,' he said at last. 'One day we'll be dead and it'll all

136

be over. That's what I generally tell my girls when they're making themselves miserable over some heartless male.'

Annie's heart jolted. Was this just a shot in the dark or did he know something? 'And what do they generally reply?'

' "Push off, you horrible old man." '

Annie felt herself smile again. They didn't know how lucky they were, having a father like Ted. She pushed her hands up the opposite sleeves of her coat and gripped her wrists. If only she had a big cuddly dad she could fling herself at. Daddy, he was horrible to me and I want to die! Annie watched the water rolling over the edge in a glassy curl, then surging and frothing below.

'You can tell me to push off, too, if you like,' he offered.

'Oh, Ted.' Her hands gripped tighter. 'It's just that . . . There's really nothing to say.'

'I suppose there isn't,' he agreed. 'Apart from the usual truisms, like there being plenty more salmon in the loch.'

Heavens – does he think it's Edward? 'I expect salmon's a bit posh for me,' she said, to encourage this idea.

'Well, unless it's tinned salmon in a white bap with salad cream,' said Ted. He gave her a friendly hug and she leant her head against his shoulder. The light was fading. A tear slid down her cheek and grew cold.

'Do you still want to come on holiday with us?' he asked, after a moment.

To William's cottage. She felt another tremor of fear that Ted knew more than he was saying. 'If that's all right with you.'

'Of course. I wasn't sure you were up to a week with the Watts family.'

'Well, I coped last year.'

'So you did.' There was another silence. Annie watched the water. 'Edward said he might look in.'

'Yes.'

'Penny and the girls call him Edward "Crunch" Hunter, because you can hear the hearts breaking as he enters a room.'

Annie laughed out loud, perhaps a little too spontaneously for one of Edward's supposed victims.

After another small pause Ted added casually, 'He was talking about bringing that doctor friend of his.'

'Yes. He said.' He knows. There was a long silence. The water rushed on and on. Ted was warning her and giving her the chance to pull out of the holiday. Oh, why don't you just tell him? she urged herself. But he probably thought she was suffering from unrequited love. The squalid truth would shock him. She couldn't bear the thought of him drawing back in disapproval. The cathedral clock chimed and they roused themselves.

When they arrived in college the stairs were shuddering as Edward came crashing down three at a time. He bounded up to them.

'Taking a break from my sermon prep,' he boomed. 'Evangelistic talk on the Ten Lepers. Can't seem to get enough oomph into it.' Annie saw his eyes darting between her and Ted, wondering if there had been some important breakthrough on the Annie front.

'Well, Edward,' said Ted, 'I'm afraid that if you can't put fire into your sermon . . .'

You'd better put your sermon into the fire, thought Annie with a giggle.

Edward's face lit up. 'That sounds like the old Annie.' He crushed her briefly into his guernsey. 'Why don't we all head for the bar?'

Annie woke the next day feeling that her misery had eased a fraction. Perhaps she would never understand why things had gone so disastrously wrong with William. After moving so long in Christian circles where people aspired to forgiveness, the lack of reconciliation was hard to endure. But she would have to learn to live with it. At least she had friends who cared about her.

She was considering this as she leafed through the post in the B pigeon-hole. This was always a potentially amusing occupation, as there was also an Anthony Brown training at Coverdale. All kinds of jolly mix-ups could occur when things arrived addressed to A. Brown. Here, for instance, was a challenge. It was probably for Anthony, as Annie didn't recognize the writing. And what appalling writing it was. Someone – a desperate postman, perhaps – had written 'try Coverdale Hall' beside the scrawled address. Was that a Mr or a Ms? Impossible to tell. The postmark was smudged. She put it back. Anthony would probably recognize it at a glance as a note from a senile uncle, or something. Unless – She snatched the letter back and peered again at the postmark. Did it say Bishopside? Doctors were famed for their atrocious handwriting. Oh, whatever shall I do? The crime of violating Anthony's mail could not possibly outweigh the risk of him intercepting a letter from William. She tucked the letter up her sleeve and fled back to her room. She could always apologize later.

It contained a single sheet. She stared in dismay, unable to read a word of it. Come on, Miss Brown. You were a teacher. You're good at deciphering scrawls. But no overdue third-form essay written on the school bus compared with this. The signature began with a W, but beyond that, nothing was definite. Even the date was illegible. A hasty jagged script with the pen never leaving the paper. It looked like the cardiograph of a mad spider. She squinted and held it at arm's length. Dear A-scribble. It was hopeless. She let out a laughing sob and pushed the letter into her desk drawer before she burst into tears. It might say anything from 'Sorry. Please get in touch', to 'Fuck off out of my life for ever'.

'Dad, you've blocked off the double word score!' cried Hayley.

'Sorry,' said Ted. He rearranged the letters on a different bit of the board. Annie and the rest of the Watts family craned round. FLAIMO. They were playing neological Scrabble on the fourth evening of their holiday. 'It's an upper-class lawn-mower,' explained Ted. Annie stared at her letters, then added PLONG to the board.

'That's the sound you get when you play a piano with a fork,' she said. Beside her Ted's younger daughter was humming thoughtfully as she fiddled with her tiles. Suddenly a great shout went up from the others.

'Ten p! Ten p!'

'I wasn't!' protested Lisa.

'Yes, you were!' said Penny, rattling a British and Foreign

Bible Society collecting box at her. '"Take Time to be Holy."
We all heard you.'

'Hah!' said Lisa. She posted a coin into the slot. The Watts
family levied fines not only for profanity but also for piety. That
week there were particular penalties for singing hymns from
Sankey and Moody's *Sacred Songs and Solos*. Unfortunately for
Annie these were familiar from her chapel childhood and she
had paid a small fortune into the Sankey box. The tunes had an
infuriating habit of lodging themselves in her brain for days at a
time. *Take time to be holy, speak oft with thy Lord!*

The holiday had gone a long way towards restoring her peace
of mind. Perhaps it was the combination of lunatic Watts company and breathtaking scenery. When the game of Scrabble was
over and the others were absorbed in different occupations,
Annie got out her notebook to see if she was equal to Barney
and Isabella yet.

She read over the passage about Barney's ordination and Isabella's conversion and sighed. It seemed glib, and she had meant
it to be so moving. To hear God's voice saying, *You're accepted*, she
thought. What could surpass the joy? 'That sweet "well done" in
judgement hour', as the hymn put it. Her eyes filled with tears.
She had been starved of approval all her life, and longed to hear
her Maker saying, '*Well done, good and faithful servant.*' It wouldn't
happen. She was nothing but a failure. Even her little attempt at
fornication had failed. And there was Isabella, silly worldly
Isabella, skipping with a wiggle of her hips into salvation. The
novel was too lightweight. Barney was supposed to be a good
solid evangelical – a bit like Edward, perhaps – but he seemed to
be coming out as a complete pagan. In her mind she had all the
details of his spiritual life worked out. She knew how he prayed,
how he agonized over Isabella and their relationship, but none of
this had made it on to the page. It was a bit of a busman's holiday,
writing about faith. She feared it was horribly telling that she
could write more easily about sex than spirituality. Well, perhaps
she could come back to it and weave it in later.

While she was pondering this Ted's daughters were playing
some game which involved looking things up in the dictionary
and hooting with laughter. They were speaking rapidly in their

own private and very complicated pig Latin. Even Ted and Penny admitted they were baffled by it. Annie watched them as they giggled and flung their long shiny hair back off their faces. She had taught plenty of nice fifteen- and sixteen-year-olds like them. It was pleasant to be a companion rather than (groan) Miss Brown.

'Grasshopper!' wailed Lisa. They were weeping with laughter.

'We're doing this for you, Annie,' gasped Hayley. 'Just wait. You'll love it.' Annie smiled and returned to her notebook. Suddenly she had no stomach for her characters and their easy lives. She put the book aside and sat gazing blankly at the chimney breast until, at length, she was distracted by Hayley who was waving a sheet of paper at her.

'Hey, Annie, look at this.'

'No, you've got to explain first,' pointed out Lisa.

'Oh, right. OK. It's a poem,' said Hayley. 'I think you'll recognize it.'

'Only we took all the nouns out and looked them up in the dictionary,' said Lisa.

'Then we counted on ten entries and found the next noun and put that into the poem instead. Here.' Annie took the sheet.

'Read it out loud,' suggested Penny. Ted looked up from his book. Annie cleared her throat and began:

The Tightrope by William Blancmange

Tightrope, tightrope, burning bright,
In the foretaste of the nightgown,
What immortal handcart or eyeful
Could frame thy fearful sympathy?

In what distant defamations or skylarks
Burnt the firebomb of thine eyefuls?
On what wingdings dare he aspire?
What the handcart dare seize the firebomb?

And what shove and what Artemis
Could twist the singers of thy heart failure?
And when thy heart failure began to beat
What dread handcart and what dread felafel?

What the hammer toe? What the chainprinter?
In what furrier was thy brake fluid?
What the aorist? What dread grasshopper
Dare its deadly tertiary bursaries clasp?

When the starlets threw down their spearwort,
And watered heavy breathers with their tearooms
Did he smile his worker to see?
Did he who made the Lambeth Conference make thee?

Tightrope, tightrope, burning bright . . .

When the laughter died down Annie folded the sheet and
slipped it into her notebook. As she did so William's letter slid
out. She replaced it hastily, resolving to hide it somewhere better
in case Edward called and caught sight of it. Why's William
writing to you, eh? Well? She yawned and stretched. 'I think I
might go for a little walk.'

It was getting dark and the others weren't inclined to leave the
fireside. Annie put on her coat and slipped the letter into the
pocket. When she reached the streetlight at the end of the lane
she paused, pulled out the letter once again and squinted at it.
She had pored over it frequently, if only to reassure herself that it
didn't say, *Dear Anthony, just a quick note to say thank you for the
hankies. Walter.* No. It was definitely for her, but she was still
unable to decipher more than a couple of words. She folded it
again and continued to walk. It remained as a symbol of their
inability to communicate.

CHAPTER 14

The following day was bright and windy. Annie was out in the countryside with the Watts family. They were following a muddy path through a pine forest, heading for a place called the Lady Well.

'Papist nonsense,' Ted remarked.

'Go on with you, you curmudgeonly old Prot,' said Penny, giving him a shove. They walked on arm in arm. Annie fell back a little. The air was mild and the larch trees on either side already had their soft green tassels. Above her head the treetops were rushing like the sea. Hayley and Lisa were in front playing a game in which you could say anything except yes or no. Their laughter echoed in the wood.

Before long the track reached the edge of the trees and crossed a field. Annie saw Ted and Penny exchange a peck at the kissing gate. She felt a pang. When would she ever manage to have a relationship that survived till the companionable arm-in-arm stage? She picked her way through the mud and sheep dung. The Watts family were all bleating. Occasionally a sheep raised its head and stared in astonishment.

'Cutlets! Cutlets!' cried Hayley and Lisa. They were heading for a group of trees.

'Do you suppose that's it in there?' called Lisa.

'Yes,' called Ted.

'You said the Y-word!' yodelled his daughters.

The sky was clear apart from the occasional white cloud that the wind hunted swiftly along. Annie paused. Something was flapping on the barbed wire fence. When she got close she saw that it was a line of seven moles, long-dead, desiccated, the barbs driven through their snouts. She drew back in shock. Who could have done such a thing? The farmer, presumably. She walked on, hoping the animals had been dead before they were impaled there. A picture of them writhing and dancing on the wire filled her mind. It made her think of the Crucifixion. Easter was only a few days away.

The Lady Well was a large shallow rectangular pool with a Celtic cross in the middle. Trees stood on all sides. There were daffodils in the undergrowth. *Tossing their headcollars in sprightly dandruff* – another work of literature desecrated by Hayley and Lisa the night before. Annie walked round the edge of the pond. The game had revealed a deep-seated hostility to these poems she had taught.

> They flash upon the inward eyeful
> Which is the blitzkrieg of solo whist.

At the far end of the pond was a slope. Annie climbed it and sat on a bench watching the others as they tried to make out the inscription on the stone cross.

'It says Paulinus, Archbishop of York, baptized three thousand Northumbrians here on Easter Day in . . .' Ted paused.

'Six hundred and something,' said Penny. 'I'm hopeless at Roman numerals.'

'Imagine Roman maths lessons,' said Lisa.

From where Annie was sitting the cross was framed on either side by two dark yew columns planted at the water's edge. All the trees were dancing in the wind. Some of the buds were beginning to burst. A clump of daffodils nodded, yes, spring will surely come. She took her usual consolation in the fact that the seasons rolled round with no reference to Annie Brown.

This place is like a windy outdoor cathedral, she thought. The tree trunks might be pillars round a watery nave, windows of sky with beech twig tracery, and the branches meeting in vaults high up above. Dear God, she found herself saying, I'm so sorry for letting you down. I've made such a mess of everything. For once her mother's voice was silent. There was nothing but the big rushing of the wind and a sense of expectation, as though the landscape were waiting for something, a crucifixion, a new birth – she wasn't sure which.

'What's that you're writing all the time?' asked Hayley, peering over Annie's shoulder. Annie closed her book. The girls had followed her after lunch up to the bedroom the three of them were sharing. Perhaps Ted and Penny had told them to be sensitive and not exclude her from their games too much.

'It's all in code,' said Lisa. 'Is it your journal?'

'Sort of,' lied Annie.

'When you're dead and famous someone will decipher it,' said Hayley. 'Like Pepys.' She wandered to the window and let out a huge sigh. 'I wish Crunch would come.'

'He's late,' said Lisa. She went to join her sister at the window. They talked about Edward, and quoted bits of their latest work 'Ode on a Grecian Urogenital System' to each other.

'Hey, there's a car coming!' exclaimed Hayley. 'It's him!' The tyres crunched down the lane and came to a standstill. Annie heard doors opening, then, unmistakably, Edward's voice. Her spirits rose. Dear old Edward.

The girls rapped on the window and waved. There was a pause, then they both wailed.

'Still a babe!'

'Eat him *alive*!' They darted out of the room.

'Mum! Dad!' Annie heard them calling as they pounded down the stairs in their Doc Martens. 'It's Crunch!'

Annie went downstairs to join them.

'Annie!' said Edward. Mwah! Mm-mwah! The girls were reeling off long sentences in their secret language. He glared at them suspiciously. 'What are you two on about?'

'Nothing!' They giggled.

'William here yet?' asked Edward. Annie froze.

'Are we expecting him?' said Penny.

'Said he was coming over this afternoon,' Edward replied. 'Paying a landlordly visit. Hoping to catch you all in.'

Ted's eyes were seeking Annie's anxiously. She looked away.

'What's he like?' demanded Lisa.

'Is he as good-looking as you?' chimed in Hayley.

'No,' said Edward frankly. 'Ugly bugger, if you ask me. Can't see why he's got women crawling all over him.'

The girls began rattling away in code again. Penny began to suggest putting on the kettle when they all heard the sound of another car approaching.

'That'll be him now,' said Edward. He went to the door. Annie wrung her hands. What am I going to do? Oh, God, he can't have realized I'm here. Ted was watching her again and she tried desperately to compose herself.

'William!' boomed Edward's voice out on the road.

The two girls were at the window. They let out a shriek.

'His eyes!'

'Oh, no! Sex on legs!'

'It's Dr Sex!'

He was in the room. Edward was making introductions. Everyone was shaking hands. 'William, you remember Annie?'

'Vaguely.'

Annie flinched and smiled blindly in his direction.

'Why don't I put the kettle on?' asked Penny again. 'Tea, everyone?' They were all in the sitting room.

'Gosh, Annie, you look dreadful,' said Edward with an untimely burst of perceptiveness. 'Are you all right?'

'I'm fine.' Her lips trembled back into a smile. Ted began at once to engage William in conversation. The girls tittered on.

'I've got a bit of a headache, that's all,' said Annie.

'Did you go to the doctor?' persisted Edward. She shook her head. 'William, persuade her.' The rest of them fell silent at Edward's commanding tone. 'She's had flu and lost loads of weight, but she refuses to see a doctor. Talk some sense into her, will you?'

'She's not my patient,' said William coldly.

This was too much for Annie. She pulled away from Edward. 'I said I'm fine. I just need some fresh air.' She rushed out of the room and grabbed her coat.

Edward pursued her. 'Where are you going?'

'Out. Leave me *alone*, Edward.' She tugged away and plunged out of the door and up the lane.

She half ran up the hill out of the village. They must all realize now, she sobbed to herself. There was a stile in the hedge. She climbed it and struggled up the grassy hill, hoping Edward wasn't following. Why had William come? What if he stalked her for the rest of her life, appearing without warning, cold and sarcastic, sending her menacing letters she couldn't read?

She reached the hilltop and flung herself down on a rocky ledge. I can't take any more of it. They were all wounding her in their different ways. Edward with his blundering concern, the girls with their banter. Even Ted with his worried glances and tactful intervention. I can't survive till tomorrow. I'll have to leave this afternoon. She wrapped her arms round her knees and sobbed bitterly.

'Jesus, Annie.' She whirled round. William. Her sobs stopped short in terror. He knelt beside her, panting from the climb. 'Oh, Christ. What have I done? This is my fault, isn't it? Look at me, Annie.' She shrank away as his hand reached out to push the hair back from her face. 'How much weight have you lost?'

'I don't know,' she stuttered.

'Can't you eat? Are you sleeping all right?' She shook her head. He tried to take her hands but she hugged them to herself. 'Look, Edward's right. Seriously, Annie. You're depressed. You should see a doctor.'

'I'll be fine,' she choked out. A skylark was singing some-where as though none of this mattered.

'I've been desperate to see you. Did you get my letter?'

'I couldn't read your writing.'

'*Fuck*. Why didn't you phone and say? Don't tell me – you couldn't read the number and I'm ex-directory. Fuck it.'

'I'm sorry I laughed at you,' she couldn't help blurting out.

'Laughed? When?' She saw him remember. 'Have you been blaming yourself all this time? Oh, Annie, for God's sake! This is my problem, not yours. Surely that was obvious?'

'I couldn't think what else I'd done to make you hate me.' She wept.

'Hate you? It's me I hate. Please don't cry like this, Annie.' His hand was on her arm. 'Christ, I'm so sorry. And don't say it's all right. That's why I couldn't bring myself to apologize at the time. I knew what you'd say.' She tried to wipe her eyes and stop

147

crying. 'The only good thing that's come out of this is that it's made me do what I should have done years ago – find a therapist.'

'Has it helped?'

'Early days.' The lark was still singing. Annie searched the sky, but it wavered through her tears and she couldn't see the bird anywhere. 'I still can't believe it. I meet this wonderful, funny, sexy woman and bang! I turn into the mad wolf-man. It's –' She saw that he was close to tears. 'This is, um, incredibly difficult to talk about.' There was a long pause. 'It's just that in the past I've been involved in a couple of . . . of . . . disastrous relationships, that seem to have left me . . . And somehow I ended up taking it out on you. Punishing you for what she –' He broke off.

'Thanks for . . . for trying to explain,' she said, after a while.

'That's what I tried to write, really. I wanted to say sorry. Sorry you had to be involved in one of the most shaming episodes of my life. And you didn't read a bloody word of it.'

'I did try!' she protested. She felt in her coat pocket and brought out the crumpled letter. 'You read it to me, then.'

He unfolded it and held it at arm's length. 'Hmm. Well, that looks like my address there. And that must be the date. Let's see: "Dear Annie, I can't" – No, wait, "I'm sorry I" . . . something something . . . Jesus! What diabolical handwriting.' He handed it back. 'Haven't a clue.'

She let out a sobbing laugh. 'I hope the local pharmacist can decipher your prescriptions.'

'We're computerized these days.' There was the ravishing smile at last. She could feel herself colouring. What had he said – wonderful, funny, sexy? 'Look, it's a lot to ask, but am I forgiven, Annie?'

'Yes. Except for putting the rugby on afterwards,' she added mischievously.

'Oh, God, did I? I did. I didn't want you to hear me crying. I was completely pissed and deeply, deeply ashamed.' She wished she had said nothing. He was not a man to suffer humiliation lightly. How much had it cost his pride to get help?

'Well, these therapists are very skilled,' she ventured.

'Yeah. But why are they all women of a certain age? I mean, I

148

may as well talk to my *mother*.' His words hung in the air uncomfortably. 'Annie . . .'

The skylark was still pouring its song down on them. She felt his hand tucking her hair gently behind her ear. He was humming something she almost recognized.

'What's that tune?'

' "Maxwellton braes are bonnie, where early fa's the dew . . ." '

'You have a beautiful voice.'

He smiled and sang her the whole song.

' ". . . And for bonnie Annie Laurie, I would lay me doon and dee." '

She laced her fingers together to stop them trembling. What am I going to do? He was made up of such wild extremes – needlessly cruel, absurdly tender. But how could she be sure this man was the real Will, and that that afternoon had just been some terrible aberration? He stopped singing.

'You're completely mad, Will.'

'Afraid so. Welcome to Dundee, honey child.'

The home of the rich fruitcake? She bit her lips.

'Come on,' he said. 'Let's get back before Edward comes yomping through the fields looking for us.' They got to their feet and stood for a moment looking out across the countryside spread out below them.

'I haven't told him anything,' said Annie anxiously.

'So I gathered – when he didn't call round with his horse-whip.' He took her hand and hesitated. 'Annie –' But at that moment there was a loud hallooing from below them. They looked and saw Edward on the stile, waving.

'Sod it.' William withdrew once more into his distant manner and they made their way down the hill.

CHAPTER 15

It was the middle of the night. Annie was curled up near the sitting-room window, looking out. The cottage was quiet. Sometimes the wind murmured around the chimney pot or in the old pine tree in the garden. The fields and hills were silvery in the moonlight. She took another sip of chamomile tea. At the other side of the village the chapel clock chimed tinnily. Three o'clock. Will was asleep in the next room, having been persuaded to stay the night . . . Annie pricked up her ears. What was that? Was it panting? There was a clatter of doggy claws on the floor. *Libby! I thought you'd gone for good, girl!* Annie knew she must banish her at once to her cold kennel outside, but she hadn't the heart.

The events of the afternoon and evening chased round her brain. What had William been about to say when Edward interrupted them? Surely it had been a declaration of some sort? It was just as well that he had been prevented. It gave her time to marshal her resistance. Here was her opportunity to get it right; like Jonah, spewed up on dry land and given a second chance to denounce Nineveh. She really mustn't – *must not* – fail God a second time. And wasn't Penny right? Annie had caught the tail end of a comment she made to Ted: '. . . *serious bad news for any woman who got involved with him.*' But all the same . . . *Ow-ow-ow-ooo!* Stop it, Libby, or you'll be outside!

The man was so dangerously irresistible. Fifty pence in the Sankey box for humming 'Yield Not to Temptation.' Annie had watched him enslaving Ted's daughters. His appeal could be broken down into three component parts: 80 per cent indifference, 17 per cent rudeness and 3 per cent devastating charm. She pictured him again, kneeling on the hearth trying to light the fire, keeping up a *sotto voce* stream of profanities as the damp wood failed to light and Edward tried to take over. Hayley and Lisa sat nudging and daring one another until at last Hayley picked up the Sankey box and rattled it at him. He turned and treated them to his icy stare. They shrank back, giggling.

'Do you take Access?' he asked. He gave them his ravishing smile and calmly reeled off every obscenity Annie had ever heard. The girls screamed.

'Stop that!' barked Edward. 'I'm not standing for it!'

'It's my house,' Will pointed out.

'That won't stop me throwing you out,' said Edward, towering over him. 'You bloody apologize right now! What?' he demanded, as everyone laughed. Hayley rattled the Sankey box at him.

William apologized with wheedling insincerity. It was shameless, but the girls found it irresistible. Edward glared, but was forced to be content. Annie saw Ted and Penny exchange glances, and realized how deeply uneasy they were about Will's effect on their daughters. Later he beat everyone at Scrabble – despite an embargo on obscenities and medical terms – and scandalized the Watts family by deliberately blocking off the triple word scores.

Afterwards everyone sat reading and chatting round the fire. Hayley and Lisa had rattled away in their private language.

'What are they on about?' demanded Edward, irritated at last. Ted and Penny shrugged.

'They're speculating about my sexual orientation,' replied William, without looking up from his book. He was right, for the girls shrieked and fled from the room leaving Edward looking baffled.

Hayley and Lisa had giggled for hours under the bedclothes as they went over the day's incidents, comparing and contrasting the merits of Crunch and Dr Sex. They wept with mirth to discover that the first three and last two letters of William's surname spelt penis. Annie lay awake long after their whispering had dwindled into sleep, before creeping downstairs to make a drink. They thought she was in love with Edward. Looking back she could see why. It was Edward who had apparently driven her from the house in tears. She feared they must have tackled him about his heartlessness, because he had cornered her on her own and said, 'Gosh, Annie. I hope I . . . um, haven't been making you unhappy.'

She had shrugged. 'It's just one of those things, Edward.'

To the end of her life, Annie knew, she would be ashamed of that cowardly sentence. It sprang from relief that he hadn't guessed the truth. The image of him standing there repeating, 'Gosh, Annie,' in stricken tones made her squirm. But in self-justification she could think of several occasions in the past when he had made her very unhappy indeed.

She hugged her shabby dressing gown closer. Her feet were cold in the school hockey socks she was wearing. This must rate as the world's least glamorous nightwear ensemble, she thought. The old T-shirt that served as a nightie was that much-loved shade of grey achieved by adding a single black sock to the white load. She got up and groped around the sofa and chairs hoping to find a blanket or something. Her fingers found someone's sweater. She wrapped it round her shoulders and sat down again. It was Will's. She leant her face against the sleeve, smelling his smell in the soft wool. *How-owl!*

Well, Libby was in fine fettle. Annie could see her bounding fluidly across the fields like a red setter in a dog-food advert. Not a particularly intelligent hound, she had to admit, but one with a certain sly cunning to her stupidity. The kind of dog who would eat your shopping on the way home from Sainsbury's and then be sick all over the back seat of the car. It was good to have her around again. She sat begging, lead in mouth, and at last Annie gave in. The two of them went bounding off, over hill and down dale, until they found themselves in Derbyshire, where Barney had taken Isabella to meet his family.

'I wish you'd kept the sports car,' pouted Isabella, as he drove her from the station to his parents' farm.

Barney grinned. They were passing through what looked like a run-down ex-mining area, but at any moment Isabella was confident they would emerge into spectacular country-side.

'Nearly there,' said Barney. They went through a sprawling village. Isabella gazed in disappointment. It was all so scruffy. The urban and the rural seemed to be jumbled up together: factories, fields, terraced housing. The hills of the Peak District were visible, but depressingly distant. She saw a sign above a shop: *Hardstaff Family Butchers.*

'Oh! Is that your family?'

'Yep.' Hermione would shudder. Good God! Associating with tradesmen! But at least the farm might be picturesque. Barney got out to open a gate. They drove up a long bumpy lane until they reached an assortment of buildings and barns with corrugated aluminium roofs. The farmhouse itself couldn't have been more than forty years old. Isabella philosophically ditched her ivy-clad Georgian mental image. It didn't matter, so long as she was with Barney. He stopped the car and they got out.

It was a blazing August afternoon, but Isabella perceived at once that skimpy sundresses and high heels were not what one wore on a farm. She glanced at Barney's ancient jeans and open-necked shirt. Damn it. They went into the house and found his parents in the kitchen.

'Well, well, well. My word,' said Barney's father, coming forward rubbing his hands together. He planted a smacking kiss on Isabella's cheek. 'Yes, that'll do nicely, I'd say, son. She looks good enough to eat.'

'Go and make yourself useful,' said Barney's mother. She was peeling off her rubber gloves. 'Take Isabella's bag up to the spare room.'

'The spare room!' repeated Barney's father. 'They'll want to be together. She's not come all this way just to hold his hand. The spare room it is!' He retreated hastily before his wife's venomous glare.

Isabella found herself blushing. She handed Barney's mother the bunch of flowers she had brought.

'That's nice of you,' said Mrs Hardstaff. Her tone sounded ironic. Orange lilies suddenly seemed as frivolous as sundresses.

Mrs Hardstaff put them down on the breakfast bar. 'Now, how about a cup of tea? Turn that off, Barnaby.'

'In a minute,' said Barney, fiddling with the radio. He tuned it to the cricket. 'I want to catch the score.'

His mother reached over, but he retreated with the radio. 'You've got a guest,' she said.

'I'm just waiting for the score.' He fended off his mother.

'I don't mind,' said Isabella.

'Hmmph.' Mrs Hardstaff began to clatter cups and saucers noisily.

'And England are a hundred and twenty-seven for four on the first day of the second test here at Edgbaston . . .'

Barney turned it off and put his arms round his mother. 'Happy now?' he asked, trying to kiss her.

She pushed him away. 'Get off. You've not shaved.'

'I'm on holiday.'

'You can still make an effort.'

'Oh, I think people can please themselves on holiday,' put in Isabella, feeling it was time Barney was defended.

'He pleases himself every blessed day of the year,' said his mother. 'Go and get the milk, Barnaby.' He went. Mrs Hardstaff treated Isabella to another ironic glance. You don't know you're born, young lady.

'Well, I think you have a very sweet-natured son, Mrs Hardstaff.'

'Oh, yes. He's sweet-natured, all right.' She filled the teapot. Isabella could see she was brimming with amusement. 'Provided he gets his own way.'

At that point Mr Hardstaff reappeared and they all sat round the kitchen table drinking tea. There was a lot of talk about Grandad Hardstaff's birthday celebrations the following day – who was bringing what food, when Great-Aunty Betty was to be picked up, whether there would be enough cold chicken for everyone. By the time the discussion had turned to farming matters, Isabella was beginning to feel rather small and homesick. Barney seemed to sense this and gave her one of his beautiful smiles.

'So what've you got lined up for Isabella, then, son?' asked Mr Hardstaff. His tone implied a row of haystacks.

Barney yawned and stretched. 'I thought we might slump in front of the cricket.'

Mrs Hardstaff cuffed him.

'No, no, no. That won't do at all,' protested his father. 'She'll want to look round. I'll bet she's never been on a farm before, have you, Isabella? Yes, you show her round, son. There's that cat with a litter of kittens in the hayloft. She'll want to see them.' He took a last slurp of tea and got to his feet. 'Well, that top field wants baling. Otherwise I'd show her myself.'

His wife shot him another look and he went out chuckling.

Barney reached for the radio again, but Mrs Hardstaff was too quick for him.

'If you've nothing better to do you can go and get me a couple of chickens for tomorrow.'

'OK.' Barney stretched again and got up.

'I'll go with you,' said Isabella, suddenly desperate to escape from the farm. She caught a swiftly suppressed grin on his mother's face and paused.

'You do that, Isabella,' said Mrs Hardstaff.

Isabella followed Barney out into the yard. A red-haired man was climbing onto a tractor. He doffed an imaginary cap to Isabella and ran his eyes over her. She cast him a sunny smile.

'Hey up, Barnaby,' he said. 'One of your choir girls? Don't forget to show her the kittens.' Barney grinned, and Isabella suddenly perceived that the kittens were a family euphemism. The tractor roared then puttered off towards the fields. There was a huge cow on the other side of the fence. It had blond curly hair and a placid expression. And a ring in its nose. Isabella bent down to look at its tackle. 'Lucky cows,' she remarked, tottering after Barney, trying not to turn an ankle on the rutted yard.

He paused. There was a strange expression on his face. 'Isabella, you do realize I'm not going to the supermarket?'

'Where are you going, then?'

'To the henhouse.'

'The . . .' She stared at him aghast.

'This is a *farm*, Isabella,' he said impatiently.

'You're going to *kill some hens*?'

'Well, you eat meat, don't you?'

'Only the sort that comes on polystyrene trays covered in clingfilm.'

'Hypocrite.' So that's what his mother had been laughing at. 'Look, why don't you wait here?' He led her to a wall. 'Talk to Brenda.' Isabella peered over and saw a very large sow stretched out on her side asleep. 'Won't be long.'

He disappeared round a corner. There was some frenzied clucking and Isabella put her hands over her ears. I'm in love with a man who wrings birds' necks! Watch yourself, Brenda girl. Brenda's muddy pink sides rose and fell peacefully. Isabella liked pigs. She even liked their smell. There was something very satisfying about their straightforward appetites. After a while she heard footsteps behind her.

'All done,' said Barney.

Her eyes strayed to the things that dangled from his left hand. One of them flapped. Isabella shrieked.

'Down, girl,' he said sternly to the hens.

She looked over the wall at Brenda again. 'Why Brenda?'

'My mother's idea. After the Avon lady.'

'Do all the animals have names?'

'Not the cows. Too many of them.'

'What's the bull called?'

There was a fractional pause. 'I'm not telling you.'

'Not *Barney*!' She whooped. 'It is! You're blushing!'

'I'm not. The goat's called Betty after my great-aunt.' He held up the dead hens. 'Susan and Angela.' Isabella shrieked again. 'Only kidding.' He was smiling down at her. He looked like a stranger; a farm labourer, unshaved, shirt half open. Brenda made a happy snortling sound in her sleep.

'I like Brenda,' said Isabella. 'I feel a certain affinity to pigs, somehow.'

'Why?'

'Because I've got piggy eyes, I suppose.'

'You've got beautiful eyes.'

'And kissable lips?'

'Very.'

'Well, kiss them, then.' He leant and placed a swift peck on her lips. 'Oh, Barney. You great big innocent.' He bent down again. 'Mm-mm —' Nothing innocent about this. His tongue searched her shocked mouth. The dead birds gave a helpless flutter. Her legs began to tremble.

'Better?'

'I — I —' He gave her another long punishing kiss. She whimpered, face raw from his stubble. The stench of the pigsty filled her nostrils. At last he raised his head. Isabella stared up into his eyes. Oh-my-*Go-o-od*. He's probably five times as experienced as I am. He's just been playing with me all these months.

'Yes. Well. You seem to be getting the hang of it,' she said.

He grinned and set off back to the house, swinging the chickens casually by the legs. After a dazed moment Isabella stumbled after him in her silly shoes. She glimpsed Mrs Hardstaff in the distance, shooing a goose out of her way. Her voice floated down the yard. 'Get a move on, Isabella, you daft bird!'

Annie jumped to hear the front door opening quietly. After a moment it shut again and she heard the sound of feet going up the lane and fading in the distance. Will. The footsteps were too soft to be Edward's. So he couldn't sleep either. She shivered and leant her cheek into his sweater again. Outside the first blackbird began to whistle. Annie crept back upstairs to bed and shuddered in her cold sheets. At last she fell into a shallow sleep. She was standing in her wedding dress waiting to go up the aisle. The organ was playing. Everyone turned to stare.

'Go on!' hissed her mother.

'But I'm sure I cancelled it,' Annie tried to say. 'I don't want to!'

Somehow she was marrying Graham anyway.

CHAPTER 16

'I'll run Annie to Morpeth station,' announced Edward that afternoon. William stood up and stretched.

'Or I could drop her at Newcastle,' he said.

'Um . . . thanks.' mumbled Annie. She bent over her holdall to hide a blush.

'Is that OK, Annie?' asked Edward.

She nodded, glancing up in time to see his stricken look: I've hurt her so much she prefers to be driven by a man she dislikes.

'William! You're not leaving too, are you?' demanded Hayley and Lisa, their awe of him having worn off a little.

'Yeah. Work.'

Was he lying? Annie wondered, as he put her case in his car and they all said goodbye. She thanked the Watts family and kissed Edward – mwah!

'Be good,' said Ted, as he closed the car door for her. She had heard him utter this casual admonition to his daughters a dozen times, and hoped there wasn't a new significance to the phrase on this occasion. Will drove off.

'Thank you,' said Annie, after a while.

'Any time, honey child.'

The next few miles passed in silence. Annie pressed her hands together between her clamped knees. Perhaps he would just drop her off at the station and that would be the end of it.

'Sleep well?' he asked suddenly.

'Um . . . Not terribly.'

'Nor did I. Edward. The bugger snores like a foghorn.'

They fell silent again. She asked herself once more what he

might have been going to say on the hilltop the previous day when he took her hand. If only she had the courage to raise the subject, to tackle him as Isabella, no doubt, would have done. Libby was wheedling and pawing at her. *Get down, girl!* Annie risked a sidelong glance. Will was frowning. He began drumming his fingers on the steering wheel as though in prelude to some announcement. She held her breath, but the miles continued to go by swiftly and silently.

'Annie . . .' he began at last. Libby let out a crashing bark and bounded off for her lead. 'Is there any particular reason you have to be home today?'

'Oh! Um . . .'

'Spend the night with me, Annie.'

Libby skidded back, lead in slavering jaws.

'Oh! Goodness, um . . . I don't think I can. My mother's expecting me, and –'

'Give her a ring.' He handed her a mobile phone.

'It's just that . . . um . . . She doesn't like to be messed around.' The phone slipped a little in her sweating hand. Her words sounded like the lamest of excuses. 'She . . . Perhaps another time . . .'

He grabbed the phone back. 'Stop being so fucking nice,' he snarled. 'Just say no, for Christ's sake.'

'It's not that.' I'm thirty-one, she thought, and I'm scared of annoying my mother. 'I'll ring her.'

He handed the phone back. Her hands were trembling so much she could hardly press the buttons. She was afraid he'd snatch the phone again and snap, 'Jesus, don't force yourself!' The ringing tone sounded in her ear, then her mother's voice saying the number.

'Hello, Mum, it's Anne. Um . . . there's been a change of plan and I won't be home till tomorrow. Sorry to mess you about.'

This provoked the tirade she'd anticipated. On and on went her mother's voice: 'Oh, that's all very well . . . inconsiderate . . . could have phoned yesterday . . . your father . . . better things to do with my time . . .' Annie held the phone away from her ear to let Will hear. He glanced at her in disbelief. She knew from

long experience that any attempt to placate would simply pro-
long the outburst. There was one way to cut her off, though.

'Look, Mum, I'm sorry – this is someone else's phone bill,
so –'

'Well, I hope you offer to pay them, that's all, Anne.' There
was a click. She had gone. Annie handed the phone back to
Will.

'Is she always like that?' he asked.

'Yes.'

'God, I'm sorry. I thought you were just fobbing me off.' His
hand took hers. What on earth have I done? she thought wildly.
I've agreed to spend the night with him! She'd been so intent on
proving to herself she wasn't afraid of her mother that she'd lost
sight of the real reason for the phone call. She slid her hand away
so that he wouldn't feel her trembling. He pulled over and
stopped the car. Libby had bolted.

'Are you sure about this, Annie? Don't let me bully you.'

'It's just . . .'

'Look, I know I said some unforgivable things. I'll be a perfect
gentleman this time. Promise.' She managed a brave smile. 'Perfect, except in the crucial department,' he added bitterly.

'It doesn't matter.'

'Of course it fucking matters. If you're selling your immortal
soul for sex you need a lover who can at least get it up.'

'But you can,' she pointed out. It's a matter of keeping it
there.

'Don't you laugh at me!' His eyes were wild in his pale face.

'Well, maybe if you laughed at yourself sometimes,' she
pleaded.

'Hah!' He sat scowling and biting his lips. Annie gazed out at a
neat square of pine forest on a distant hill. It's *not funny*. How was
she to encourage him without being patronizing?

'It's just so fucking humiliating,' he muttered at last.

'For me, too,' she protested. 'Not being arousing enough to
. . . um . . .'

'Are you kidding? That was half the problem. I felt totally
outclassed. Shit, I hardly have to look at you and you come.'

'It must be your penetrating stare. I mean,' she hurried on, remembering it wasn't funny, 'it's you, not me. I'm not like it with anyone else. I'm just the instrument, remember?'

She saw an awakening flicker of lust in his eyes. He reached out and tucked her hair behind her ear, his hand lingering on her cheek, thumb brushing her mouth. She gasped his name and he slid his thumb suddenly between her parted lips. Libby shot clean out of her basket as though electrocuted.

'God, you're wanton,' he said. 'Let's get back.' He started the car.

Before long they were approaching Bishopside. Annie caught herself in the act of praying that it would be all right and felt a jolt of guilty fear.

Candlelight gleamed on the taps in the dim bathroom. Annie lay back against Will's chest, the water lapping at her chin. She took another sip of champagne and held it in her mouth. The bubbles burst against her palate like a tiny round of applause. I've gone to the dogs, she thought drunkenly. The libby-dibby dogs. Her body was still throbbing from his lovemaking. He had begun tentatively enough – a swift scale, a few arpeggios – until he mastered his stage fright. He'd worked up at last to a ruthless virtuosic cadenza, sobbing and laughing with relief in her arms as the last strains died away. And now those musician's fingers were at work again, intent on wringing one more agonized crescendo from her.

'Don't,' she pleaded. 'Will, I can't stand it. You're insatiable.'

He chuckled. 'Just born again.'

Ah, the benefits of a little gynaecological know-how. A man who wouldn't joggle her around as though she had a loose connection, or jiggle her like a bathroom door, implying, Are you going to be much longer in there? I'm getting desperate! The champagne was roaring in her head. Here it comes, she thought. Rumbling drums, mounting strings, tearing brass . . . Then the blinding white *crash!* of cymbals. *Ffffortissimo!*

The water subsided into calm. Libby lay poleaxed.

'I'm tingling,' murmured Annie.

'You were hyperventilating.'

She saw that medical expertise had its down side. 'You lied,' she accused him. 'You told Hayley and Lisa you had to work tonight.'

'Excuse me – I've worked bloody hard.'

'True.' She giggled. 'It's nice to be played by such a maestro.'

'Why, thank you, honey. Nice to get my hands on a Stradivarius.'

He raised his glass. 'A toast to my newly recovered manhood. God, it's been years, I can't tell you.' Their glasses clinked, they drank, then he turned her lips to his and drooled a cold trickle of champagne into her mouth. His fingers were at her breasts plucking idle chords. Libby quivered afresh. Not *more*!

'What nice shiny taps you have,' she remarked in desperation.

'That's Ethel for you.'

'You employ a cleaning lady? Is she a treasure?'

'Yes. Dusts the skirting-board under the radiator. Cleans the light switches. Even irons my underpants.'

'Ethel's a sick woman.'

He laughed. '*I'm* Ethel. I have a multiple personality disorder.'

'Who else have you got in there?'

'You've met the mad wolf-man.' He let out a bloodcurdling howl. 'Tamed but not domesticated by the love of a good woman. And there seems to be an Italian Calvinist with a death-wish. Very confusing. What about you?'

'Oh, Miss Brown the schoolmarm. She's the snotty one.'

'And someone who gave me a look of stark naked slavering lust the first evening I met you.'

'Oh!' She blushed. 'Libby.'

When she explained he threw his head back and laughed. 'Here, girl!' he called, clicking his fingers and whistling. 'Walkies!'

'No. Honestly, Will, I'm exhausted.'

'Hang on to those taps, Miss Brown. It's the mad wolf-man.'

He was asleep. She could hear his soft breathing beside her. The bedroom was dark apart from the faint orange glare of city lights, which shone through the crack in the curtains and fanned out across the ceiling. She listened to the night noises. The last drunken voices had gone. A helicopter hovered overhead. Wind scoured the streets. A gate banged once, twice. She could hear a siren tearing along a distant road, and far off, almost swallowed up in the night, an alarm bell was ringing on and on. She stretched out a leg cautiously in his cool sheets, hoping her restlessness wouldn't wake him. Her body was still aching and pulsing. She thought of the princess who could feel the pea through twenty mattresses and twenty feather beds. 'I don't know what it was in the bed,' the poor princess cried, 'but I'm black and blue all over!' How could he just roll away and sleep like a baby? After all that. She clenched in a sudden shudder. Her feelings bordered on disgust. Had he run through his entire repertoire? What if he'd merely dished up the hors d'oeuvres, and some vast unimaginable *plat du jour* still lay waiting for her, quivering in aspic in the sexual pantry?

She was feeling thirsty and thought of creeping to the bathroom and slurping from the tap. The taps! She saw herself on her knees clinging to them, wailing, as frantic tidal waves swamped the candles. No, she couldn't face the bathroom. Besides, she knew he was above the vulgar practice of drinking tap water.

In the end she decided to creep down to the fridge. She tiptoed naked along the dark hall and opened the kitchen door. Instantly the night was shattered by a howling siren. She shut the door in panic, but the howling continued. Will came pounding down the stairs.

'Sorry!' she cried, over the noise. He pressed some buttons and the alarm cut off in mid-howl. 'I was just getting a drink,' she bleated in the silence.

'You should've asked.'

'I didn't realize it was on. I didn't want to wake you.'

He chuckled in the dark. 'Silly cunt. Get back to bed.'

She felt a stinging slap and fled back upstairs, her pride and backside smarting. He followed her a couple of minutes later with a bottle of mineral water.

'Sorry,' he said. 'Forgot to warn you.'

He poured her some water and explained briefly how the system worked. The glass clattered against her teeth. They lay down again and he turned the light off. She listened for his quiet breathing. Would he fall straight back to sleep? Perhaps doctors could do that after those grim houseman months. She was still jittery from shock. The helicopter throbbed in the distance. I feel so lonely, she thought. All kinds of terrifying intimacy, yet I daren't reach out and hold his hand. A tear crept down her cheek. He hit me. He called me a cunt. She lay rigid in case a sniff betrayed her, not wanting to become a demanding accusing woman. Her throat ached from holding back her sobs.

De-dum de-dum. De-dum de-dum. The Intercity sped south. Annie watched the countryside slip past. Fields of winter wheat, hawthorn hedges hazed over with green, chestnut and beech speckled with unfurling leaves, pale clumps of primroses. The landscape was charged with spring. No more holding back, it seemed to say. Buds will burst, shoots will spear up from the earth, song must and will pour out of every throat. She quivered with the force of it, barely able to keep in her seat. All this is God, a voice was murmuring. If you glory in the creation what are you doing but praising the Creator? The voice of the serpent: Eat, eat. You will not die.

Why didn't she feel guilty? Was it because she hadn't grasped the enormity of what she had done? Or because guilt must lead to repentance and amendment of life and she wasn't ready for that yet? She'd woken sick with shame that morning, as though suffering from a sexual hangover. The hair of the dog – or wolf, possibly – had worked wonders. She'd been expecting to sober up on the train, but after two hours here she was as tipsy as ever. Libby had never looked sleeker. Annie shivered at the memory of Will's face between her thighs, his warm mouth, the shock of tasting herself on his lips . . . *How-oo-owl*! She felt as though someone were feeding her insides slowly through an old-fashioned mangle. Hadn't one of the saints been martyred like that – intestines wound out on a windlass? Her stomach plunged again. It struck her that lust was barely distinguishable from dread. And only a hair's breadth away from disgust. Could she really have done those things and enjoyed them? The train flashed through a wood thick with celandines. She gasped. The sun might almost have fallen and spilled out along the ground, the flowers were so bright.

The trouble with sudden passion, she thought, is that it's blinding. It plunges your lover into close-up before your eyes have a chance to focus. Will was a baffling puzzle of light and dark that she felt she would never solve. Touchy, bad-tempered, sexy, honest, funny, crude, kind, ruthless. The bits never seemed to fit together. They tumbled over one another like shapes in a kaleidoscope, worrying her with new patterns all the time. That morning had been a good example.

'Where are you taking me?' she had asked as the car turned off the A1.

'To the biggest Marks and Spencer's in the known universe.' He saw the sudden look of foreboding on her face. 'That's right. It's the night of the long knives for your knicker drawer, Miss Brown.'

'No! I couldn't possibly let you.'

'Why not?'

'I'd feel . . . humiliated.'

'Why?' He parked the car. 'It's a gift, not a payment. Wake up, Annie. I'm your lover. Lovers do this kind of thing.'

'But –'

'God, you're so ungrateful! If you don't get out of this car pretty damn quick I'll go and choose it all myself. Want to risk that?'

She trotted after him protesting until he stopped and caught her hands in his and kissed them.

'Come on. Don't be mean, Annie. Please let me. I've got no one else to spend my money on.'

She wasn't proof against such shameless wheedling, and her holdall was now bulging with new underwear. Whatever will Mother think when she goes snooping through my things?

'Well, I hope you're not going to overhaul the rest of my wardrobe,' Annie had muttered, as the assistant was folding the knickers and bras.

'You mean you hope I am?' asked Will. 'Why? Seen something you want?'

'I mean,' said Annie flushing, 'exactly what I say.'

'Like fuck you do.'

The assistant started a little. She was holding out her hand for his chargecard, which he was tapping angrily on the cash desk.

'I have to decode all this tight-arsed tact and politeness to get at what you really want.'

Annie made no reply, fearing he was quite equal to a stand-up row in the lingerie department. Ungrateful, causing a silly fuss about nothing, suggested her mother's voice.

Will paid and handed her the carrier bag.

'Thank you.'

But he wasn't placated. She hurried to keep up with him, clutching the bag in sweaty hands. They got into the car and drove off. After a couple of miles he broke the silence. 'At the risk of humiliating you further, can I take you out for lunch?'

She flinched at his sarcasm, but found the courage to say, 'Um . . . can I buy lunch?'

'No. Stop being so fucking difficult. You're on a student grant, for Christ's sake. My income's ten times yours.'

She blinked rapidly. Please don't start crying, she pleaded with herself. He'll think you're just resorting to the classic female weapon. The car turned off the main road, and before long they were out on the moors. She tried to think of something to say in case he interpreted her silence as sulking.

'Will . . .'

'Shut up, Annie.'

What am I going to do, she wondered in despair. Isabella would wind down the window and strew the new underwear across County Durham if a man treated her like this. 'That's what I think of you and your sodding money!' Annie pictured a flock of knickers whirling off like racing pigeons.

Without warning Will pulled over and got out of the car. She watched him stride angrily across the dead heather, then fling his arms wide at the sky in a cosmic *Why?* This must be the Italian Calvinist, thought Annie. His gestures seemed to have the right mixture of ferocious repression and Latin flair. She got out of the car and approached him cautiously, trying to keep the smile off her face. He rounded on her, demanding, 'Why am I doing this? Christ, can't I relate normally to a woman for once? Look, Annie, I know you're not a scheming bitch. I don't mean to treat you like one.'

'I'm sorry if I seemed ungrateful,' she ventured.

'Stop fucking apologizing!' he raged. She closed her lips tightly to stop another 'sorry' escaping. 'Jesus, do you have any idea how provocative your meekness is?' There was a pause. 'I don't believe this. You're laughing at me.'

'Only very gently.' She gazed up into his stormy eyes and after a moment was rewarded with a smile.

'Libby! Here, girl!'

'No!' She turned to run, shrieking as he felled her with a rugby tackle. 'Don't! Someone might come.'

'Both of us, I hope.'

He's like a mad March day, thought Annie, leaning her head against the headrest. She could almost feel the springy heather under her back and his deep hungry kisses. Sunshine and cloud chasing one another, wild winds, freak hailstorms. More lovely than a summer day, though far less temperate.

My word, Barney and Isabella were in for a scorching honeymoon. Annie had been wondering how to warm up the unappetizing memory of her couplings with Graham and pass it off as a banquet.

The summer vacation ended and Isabella returned to Cambridge. She started attending the church Barney had recommended. It was full of galumphing evangelicals, but she persisted nobly. He came to visit her every other week, but never repeated those passionate kisses she'd enjoyed at the farm. He held her hand and took her out for pub lunches, which were all right in their way, of course, but they were not candlelit meals in exclusive restaurants. Perhaps he had no money, Isabella reminded herself. She didn't know what a curate's stipend was, but the glimpse she'd had of his house in September suggested that there wasn't much left over for interior design.

The awfulness of his sitting room haunted her. Was she seriously considering spending the rest of her life with a man who owned a secondhand plastic sofa, which farted sighingly like a whoopee cushion on Valium every time you sat on it? And the orange and brown carpet with its pattern of exploding cabbages – had it come with the house, or did it reflect Barney's taste? To say nothing of the blown vinyl. Still, you could always regard it as a challenge. Amazing things could be done with a pot of paint and a really nice kelim.

Christmas drew near. Isabella's spirits rose at the thought of all those festive parties. Barney, however, could not be persuaded to escort her to a single one of them. No. Sir was too busy in his bloody parish. All right, so it was the silly season in the Church, but all the same. Surely he had *one* free evening between now and Christmas?

Isabella had reached the 'Well, sod you, Vicar' frame of mind when Camilla called round to tempt her to yet another party. Isabella threw on a little black number and went.

When she woke the next morning her ceiling looked odd. After a moment it dawned on her what was wrong with it. It was not her ceiling. It was not her bed, either. Oh, God – I haven't, have I? Someone grunted and wallowed beside her. Oh, God – I have!

She sat up and stared aghast at the dark head on the pillow. Her instinct was to leap out of bed and bathe and scrub and scream and cry until she'd washed it all away and made it never happen. Her head throbbed. Barney. Oh, God, Barney I'm so sorry! Tears oozed out under her gritty eyelids. I didn't even enjoy it. She had a dim recollection of lying limply and saying, 'Go away. I hate you. I want Barney,' and of – what was his name? – climbing good-naturedly aboard and rogering her anyway.

She got out of bed and searched for her clothes. He was stirring. When his face emerged at last from the pillow she recognized him. Luke. The dark smutty one she'd gone to the May ball with. At least it wasn't a complete stranger – as if that made things any better.

'You going?' he mumbled as she struggled into her dress.

'Yes.'

He groped for a cigarette and lit it. 'Who the fuck's Barney?'

'My boyfriend,' she muttered.

Luke cackled. 'The dickless parson, right?'

'He's got a bigger one than you have!' shouted Isabella.

Luke blew a smug little smoke ring. He was still smirking as she slammed the door and stumbled out into the foggy morning.

Back in her own college she stood under the shower and bawled. There was no washing this one away. How could she have been so stupid? She'd let Barney down appallingly. And herself. And God. Whatever must he be thinking?

She dressed and hurried round to the chaplain and blurted out the whole miserable tale. Tim assured her of God's forgiveness. She couldn't help noticing he was less sanguine about Barney's generosity.

'Isabella, you really must tell him,' he urged.

'I daren't,' she said. 'He'll bloody murder me!'

Tim did not demur. 'But supposing . . . um . . . he heard from a different source?'

Shit. Camilla. Isabella wouldn't put it past her. She'd developed a real dislike of Barney, for some reason. 'I'll write to him. I can't phone.'

Tim gave her a hug and she went back to her room.

The results of several hours' work read as follows:

Dear Barney
I'm afraid I've done something really stupid. I went to a party last night and got drunk and ended up in bed with someone. I'm really really sorry. You can't possibly hate me as much as I hate myself. I'll regret it for the rest of my life and I'll totally understand if you never want to see me again. I still love you, but I can hardly expect you to believe that now.

Isabella

Being a complete coward Isabella posted it second class to defer the moment when he'd read it and respond. She went in dread of him phoning or calling round unexpectedly before he'd received it, but term ended safely and she crept miserably home to her parents.

On the second evening she was at home, the rest of the family went out to see a local production of *Iolanthe*. Isabella wasn't up to Gilbert and Sullivan and stayed at home on the sofa reading a Georgette Heyer and eating chocolate Christmas-tree decorations in deep self-loathing. At about nine o'clock the doorbell rang. Isabella went to answer it.

There on the doorstep in a towering rage stood Barney.

'Ladies and gentlemen, this train will shortly be arriving in King's Cross . . .'

Annie stared out of the window, pondering again her night with Will. It had been enough to show her that he was capable of treading a very fine line; teetering, pausing, teetering again on the brink of what was bearable, yet finally coming down on the side of pleasure. She shivered and collected her things together. What if he pushed too far? Would she protest? Or collude? And finally enjoy?

The train slowed to a stop. Tubby had sent her to Bishopside to find the 'edge' that Coverdale Hall lacked. She had the feeling that this was not the edge he had in mind.

CHAPTER 17

'New underwear, I see,' said her mother, watching Annie unpack. 'I'm surprised you can afford it on your grant.'

'My fancy man bought them for me,' replied Annie, knowing that the truth was sometimes the best deception of all.

'Sarcasm is the lowest form of wit, Anne.'

Well, you're the lowest form of company! Damn had once yelled in reply. Annie continued putting things in drawers and wishing her mother would stop tutting and twitching around the room and leave her in peace.

'What did you do with the old pairs?' demanded Mrs Brown.

'I threw them away.'

'Hmph. You could've used them for dusters.'

Annie was forced to turn away and pretend to arrange her books. She had accurately predicted this conversation to Will that morning to make him laugh. It saddened her to think that the only useful function her mother served was as a source of awful anecdotes. Annie watched her furtively. She always went about with her head and neck thrust forward like an angry hen. A permanent frown had scored three vertical furrows between her eyebrows. Her grey hair was tugged back in a bun and she wore old-fashioned spectacles that looked too heavy for her face, as though she were a child borrowing Grandma's glasses and scowling in an effort to focus through them. She forked aggressively about in Annie's new underwear and snapped, 'Pretty.'

'Mm,' said Annie noncommittally. It sounded like a shorn-off condemnation: Pretty extravagant, I call it! Or was her mother attempting a conciliatory gesture? Mrs Brown closed the drawer with a thump, pecked her way across to the window and glared down at the street below.

'Your father's working late,' she said, managing to give these words an ominous ring. 'Again.'

Is your life really so small, Annie wanted to ask, that you have to wring drama from non-events like these? Why don't you do something? Go on a course, join a club, see a film? Read a book, even?

'Hmph,' said Mrs Brown again. 'Well, they've been married nearly seven years and still no sign.'

Annie saw that the conversation had rattled over some idiosyncratic set of points in her mother's mind and was now lurching towards her brother Colin and his wife. 'It's her, you know. Colin wants to start a family. But she can't bear to lose her career. Or her figure!' added Mrs Brown derisively.

'Perhaps they can't have children,' suggested Annie.

'Pah!' snorted Mrs Brown, as though conception were simply a matter of knuckling down. 'And Dawn's no better. It's all work work work with her. Not that she could fall pregnant if she wanted to. They can't, you know.'

'Actually, I don't think she's –'

'She's got that slimmers' disease.'

Annie tried again, 'No, I don't think –'

'Oh, yes, she has, Anne. I know these things.'

Annie waited miserably for her mother to point out that she, Annie, could have had three or four children by now, if only she'd married Graham.

'Still,' said her mother, as though summing up the main points of the conversation, 'I always said he wasn't right for you.'

'Mm,' said Annie, alerted by this totally new departure after eleven years of blame. There would be worse to come.

'Some of us just aren't cut out for marriage, that's all. No point shedding tears over what will never be. You're thirty-one, Anne,' she concluded heartlessly.

'Yes.'

'Well, I'd better get the potatoes on.' Mrs Brown pulled out a duster (a pre-war vest?) from her apron pocket and began fidgeting it along the mantelpiece long enough to enjoy her victory.

Annie listened to her impatient tread on the stairs. I'm her daughter. Why doesn't she wish me well? It was ridiculous to be so wounded by the words of an unhappy woman, but Mrs Brown's utterances still had all the potency of a malevolent curse for Annie. It will never be. You're not cut out for marriage, Anne. Men may sleep with you, but they'll never marry you. Will's going to use you for a couple of months, then dump you. She sat in the ugly room until the sound of her father coming home roused her.

Their evening meal was dreary. Mince, carrot and boiled potato. Mrs Brown's cooking seemed to reflect an opinion that eating was a vice to be discouraged. Annie wondered what she would say in condemnation of Will who distinguished between butter and *cooking* butter, and who did his food shopping at Italian delicatessens – or Marks and Spencer, if all else failed. Last night as he'd cooked Annie had been obliged to hide her smirks.

'Fuck. I'm out of *crème fraîche*.'

She forced down the last mouthful of slimy mince and tried to study her father objectively. He had greeted her cordially and was now eating in neutral silence as his wife stabbed away at this subject and that. How had he put up with her all these years? Had he ever loved her? Annie poured some evaporated milk over her bowl of orange jelly.

After dinner – or tea, as the Browns called it – Annie helped her mother with the dishes. Mr Brown had vanished with the newspaper.

'I'd get one tomorrow, only your father doesn't eat frozen food,' announced Mrs Brown, without warning.

'A deep freeze?' hazarded Annie.

'What do you think I mean? A lawn-mower?' This manifestation of wit's lowest form silenced Annie. She wiped the last plate and hung up the tea towel.

Mrs Brown sat down with a library book. She only ever read as an act of aggression: Oh, well, if everyone else is lazing about doing nothing then I'm going to sit here and read my book. Except she seemed to be about half-way through her novel and engrossed.

'*And* a microwave,' added her mother combatively.

'Mm.' As usual this seemed the safest response. 'Good book?'

'Not bad, I suppose.' Her mother surveyed the cover with a sneer then went back to reading. Annie was tiptoeing away when the telephone rang.

'I'll get it,' she said.

The house had only one phone – in the draughty hall to militate against long calls. There was an egg-timer beside the directory. Three minutes was all the Brown children had been permitted. Annie picked up the receiver.

'Hi, honey child.'

'Will! How . . .' Annie stopped short. Her mother would be listening.

'Last number redial. How about some aural sex?'

'What?' she clamped the earpiece hard to her head as though his words might escape and echo round the quiet hall.

'Come on. Talk dirty to me.'

'I'm afraid that's . . . that's not possible right now,' she said, trying to sound businesslike.

'Mother prowling about?'

'Yes.'

He chuckled, then began to detail with alarming anatomical frankness what he had on his mind and – more alarmingly still – in his hand.

'Um, could we discuss this later?' she bleated, as his husky voice drooled and lingered and caressed. Mrs Brown had emerged into the hall on some pretext. Annie burned as though he had stripped her bare and was violating her under her mother's gaze.

'Look, I'll . . . I'll call you back, then. 'Bye for now.' She put the receiver down on his panting with a clatter.

'Who was that?' asked Mrs Brown, pretending to straighten the coats on the pegs.

'Oh, someone from college.'

She escaped from the house a moment later. 'Just off for a walk,' she called, slamming the door before her mother could interrogate her.

You horrible sick pervert, Penn-Eddis, she muttered, as she

strode along. Had he really been lying in bed playing with himself and her old underwear? Well, at least her discarded knickers were serving a useful purpose. Mrs Brown would be gratified. Annie was struck by a wave of dreadful mirth at the thought of telling her mother this. Before long she was hooting and whinnying out loud as she hurried along the empty street.

She reached the edge of the town and followed the path out to the woods. It was dark. The moon was nearly full as it rose above the hill. A fox barked in the distance. Annie had fled up here many times over the years to lie in the low drooping branches of the chestnut tree and watch the leaves against the sky. Cows swished in the grass as she crossed the field and searched for her tree. She came to the place. It had gone. She stood for a long time staring at the stump in the moonlight. The sky above was sprinkled with stars where the leaves had been.

> When I survey the wondrous cross
> On which the Prince of Glory died.

It was Good Friday. Annie was standing beside her mother in the market place at the open-air ecumenical service. Shoppers hurried past or stopped for a moment to listen. Mrs Brown tutted at the secular world serving Mammon on Good Friday. It was a warm morning. As she sang the familiar words Annie looked up at the cherry trees that lined the graveyard behind the marketplace. Their sugared almond blossom was clustered thick against the blue sky. The hymn ended. The Salvation Army band lowered their silver instruments and the Baptist minister began reading the story of the Crucifixion. The young man who had carried the rough wooden cross now shifted it slightly where he stood in preparation for the long reading. Annie gazed at it. Graham had helped make it fifteen years earlier in school woodwork classes. Each Good Friday it was carried out of the parish church for this service.

What sort of wood had the Romans used for crosses? Annie asked herself. There must have been a brisk and grisly timber trade in first century Palestine. She pictured centurions placing orders and carpenters sawing and planing, knowing what their planks were destined for and somehow justifying it to themselves. She called her attention back guiltily to the Gospel.

'. . . And about the ninth hour Jesus cried out with a loud voice "*Eli, Eli, lama sabachthani?*" that is, "My God, my God, why hast thou forsaken me?"'

Annie gazed at the cross. Look what you've done! cried her conscience. How can you go on sinning and making a mockery of his suffering? Annie stood helpless, knowing she should repent, knowing she would not, could not. The Salvation Army band began to play softly, 'There is a green hill far away . . .'

> We do not know, we cannot tell
> What pain he suffered there.
> But we believe it was for us
> He hung and suffered there.

Your sin nailed him there. He had to die in your place, Anne. Suddenly she wanted to kick aside this idea like an empty old can. What kind of a god was incapable of forgiving without first exacting bloodthirsty justice, without requiring the death of an innocent victim? She knew she must be misunderstanding. Something deeper must be at work. All the oceans of human suffering – her own droplet in there somewhere – must be gathered up somehow in that bitter passion.

Annie began to cry and hunted around in her pocket for a tissue. Mrs Brown palmed her a handkerchief. It was frayed, but her mother had carefully ironed and folded it. Annie recognized the faded Minnie Mouse print from her childhood and the sight of it made her want to sob wildly. She blotted her eyes and joined in the last words of the hymn.

> . . . And trust in his redeeming blood
> And try his works to do.

'Let us pray,' said an unmistakably Anglican voice. The vicar led them in a few brief prayers and the service ended.

Annie walked back up the high street with her mother. The band was playing 'The Old Rugged Cross'.

'What on earth came over you, Anne?'

'Oh, um . . . I don't know, really. The Cross and everything . . .'

The Browns were a staunch Bible-believing family, but talking about religious experience was taboo.

'Let's buy some hot cross buns,' said Mrs Brown. 'He'll never know.'

They went into the baker's. Annie didn't know whether 'he' signified God or just the pastor. Mrs Brown bought two buns. 'There you are.' She thrust the paper bag into Annie's hand abruptly.

'Thanks,' choked Annie. Her mother had no vocabulary to express affection. This was the best she could do.

That afternoon Annie sat with a fat book on the atonement hoping to sort out the Cross once and for all. Her mother was washing windows and polishing them violently with old newspaper. The afternoon passed slowly. Her father came in and they had tea. (Shepherd's pie with yesterday's leftover mince followed by Arctic Roll.) The house was oppressive. Annie longed to escape, but could think up no excuse. It was just as it had always been. The only escape was mental. She sat staring at the words on the page and thinking of Will, just as she had sat with her French vocabulary at the age of thirteen and lain in Sherwood Forest under the spreading oaks with Robin Hood himself. If only she could harness the impulse and use it to rescue Barney and Isabella from their dilemma, but the stifling atmosphere of her parents' home crushed the creativity out of her.

Annie jumped. The phone was ringing. She darted to answer it, but her mother was quicker.

'Hello?' There was a pause while Mrs Brown listened. 'Why don't you phone the Samaritans?' she snapped. 'They can help perverts like you.' She put down the receiver abruptly, but not before Annie recognized a voice saying, 'Oh, *shit*.'

'Sick in the head,' said Mrs Brown. 'That's what they are, these heavy breathers. Sick.'

Annie did not trust herself to reply.

CHAPTER 18

Term started. It frightened Annie how easily she slipped into living a double life. She was a hopeless liar, but she made an extremely good hypocrite. After all, she had spent years perfecting various types of deception to foil her mother. It might all have been preparation for her affair with Will. Her friends only remarked that she was her old self again this term. Annie occasionally caught Ted staring at her thoughtfully, but he made no comment.

God knew, however. Annie was avoiding him, although she still went to chapel every day and attended her lectures and seminars. She felt like a tenant in arrears with the rent. Sooner or later there would be a knock at the door – the Landlord demanding his due. There was no way she'd be able to pay, and she couldn't stop running up bigger and bigger debts, listening fearfully all the time for that soft football. Behold, I stand at the door and knock knock knock. One night she dreamt she had died and was in hell. There were no fires or demons, just a silent, empty blackness. She couldn't move. She called out to God to help her, but knew beyond a shadow of a doubt that he was gone for ever. When she woke it took her a long time to shake off that desolate terror.

And yet the days were bright. April pressed on her window. Each unfurling leaf or rapturous bird song seemed charged with a personal intensity. It invaded every corner of her life. To her amazement she found she could study and concentrate as never before. Her creativity was restored and her notebook filled up rapidly as she cantered towards Barney and Isabella's honeymoon.

★

Barney came in and shut the door. Isabella stood wringing her hands in fear at the expression on his face.

'Can I get you a drink?'

'No.' He took her arm and steered her into the sitting room. 'Why? Why did you do it?'

'I don't know,' she whimpered. 'I was drunk.'

'Why did you get drunk? You knew what would happen.'

'I –'

'To punish me?'

'No! I've told you it was just a stupid stupid mistake.' She wept.

'Don't lie to me.'

'I'm not! I wasn't trying to punish you.' But now she came to think of it . . . 'It's just that you're so bloody undemonstrative. You're completely unromantic, Barney.' His stony-faced silence unleashed a flood of complaints she'd been suppressing all term. Pub lunches. Hand-holding. Too busy to visit her. Sanctimonious killjoy. 'And another thing!' she sobbed in conclusion. 'You never give me flowers!'

'Flowers!' he exploded. '*Flowers!*' He strode from the house slamming the door behind him. Isabella flung herself onto the sofa and sobbed bitterly.

Half an hour later the doorbell rang again. She ran to answer it.

He was back on the doorstep looking pale and wild. 'You want flowers?' He piled three heavy bouquets into her arms. 'Here are your bloody flowers. Now, you listen to me, Isabella. You're the most impossible, outrageous, maddening woman I've ever met and I'm hopelessly in love with you. Will you marry me?'

'What?' The bouquets slithered to the floor and she burst into tears. 'Yes, you idiot.'

'I was going to ask you on Valentine's Day,' he said, with something approaching a pout.

'Oh, Barney!' Before she could fling herself into his arms he handed her a little box. Vinyl sofas and swirly carpets flashed through her mind. She swiftly resolved to love the ring even if it turned out to be a nasty little solitaire. It was a moonstone surrounded by seed pearls.

'It's beautiful!' Thank God! He slid it onto her finger. 'I don't deserve you, Barney.'

'Yes, you do,' he replied grimly. 'I'm exactly what you deserve.' He kissed her so hard she winced. He still hasn't forgiven me, she thought.

'It won't happen again.'

'It'd better not! I can't make you be faithful to me,' he said, 'but I'm warning you, Isabella, I can make you very, very sorry if you're not.'

She widened her eyes. 'You'll take a belt to me?' But he refused to smile. 'I just want you to know,' she began, 'that he had the tiniest weeniest little willy I've ever seen . . .'

His lips twitched at last. 'I thought size wasn't important.'

'That's just male propaganda. Women aren't totally insensate. We know a cocktail gherkin from a cucumber.'

'Impossible,' he murmured, kissing her more gently this time. 'Completely . . . totally . . . impossible.'

'Take me to bed.'

'Is that the only way you'll be faithful to me?'

'Of course not!' She coloured in mortification. 'I just thought now we're engaged . . .'

'Can't we wait till we're married?'

Suddenly it dawned on her. 'Barney Hardstaff, you're nervous! I thought you said you weren't a virgin.'

'No, but . . .' He rubbed a hand through his curls and looked so adorably bashful that she didn't press for details.

'OK. We'll wait till we're married.'

'Will you be patient with me till I get the hang of it?'

'Idiot.' She kissed him. Mmm, it was going to be fun licking him into shape. After a while she remembered the flowers lying at their feet. She gathered them up and took them into the kitchen. 'Wherever did you get them this time of night?'

'The graveyard.'

'What?' she shrieked. 'I'm engaged to a man who robs graves!'

He smiled an angelic smile. 'I said you deserved me.'

The irony of it all wasn't lost on Annie. Barney and Isabella were on the home straight to wedded bliss as surely as she was headed for heartbreak. It was wonderful, intoxicating, but it wouldn't last. Annie knew it couldn't. The end of the affair was stamped across the beginning. This only made the hours they had together more intense. The long slow days between their meetings were shot through with sudden pangs of lust, or overlaid with hazy desire as she willed the hours past till Saturday, Wednesday, Saturday . . . The affair never lost its dangerous edge of fear. Annie felt she was queuing endlessly for some terrifying fairground ride; then suddenly she was away, crying, 'Help, stop, let me off!' until it was over and she was staggering with buckling knees back to the beginning crying, 'Again!'

If they lived together it wouldn't be like that. A few weeks would start to tame everything. She would begin to understand him. As it was, the lack of continuity meant she had no yardstick against which to measure his behaviour. There was no predicting what mood he'd be in, or what might spark a wild swing. In the background lurked the spectres of former girlfriends, the ones who had left him impotent. He never talked about them. Had they tried to trap him into marriage, perhaps? To gain control of his cheque book? To suck out his immortal soul? Whatever their goal, she was fairly certain of their methods. Anything that smacked of deviousness or emotional manipulation infuriated Will, and she tiptoed around trying to avoid these pitfalls. Unfortunately, tiptoeing also enraged him, but Annie could not help herself.

She never told him she loved him. It might be interpreted as blackmail. What if she forgot herself one mad afternoon and gasped out the terrible three words? Would he bundle her into the street and throw her clothes out after her? She knew that their relationship was an uncomplicated matter of sex as far as he was concerned. The moment he suspected she was manoeuvring him into some kind of commitment he would get rid of her.

'Do you want me to go on the pill?' she asked once.

'No, I don't trust you to remember to take it.'

'I just wondered if you found condoms a bit inconvenient . . .'

'Not half as inconvenient as an unwanted pregnancy. Forget it.'

She read this as a warning and redoubled her efforts to seem unscheming. Even compliments began to feel loaded.

'I assume you wouldn't be doing this if you didn't find me attractive,' he remarked in the end.

'Oh! Of course I . . . Am I too reticent?'

'Well, you squeal when I fuck you. I guess that counts as a compliment.'

'Don't say things like that!'

'Like what, Miss Brown? Fuck?'

'No. The . . . the other bit. I don't like to think about it. I get self-conscious.'

'You poor child. You've never made love in front of a mirror?'

'Never. I'd – No! Will, please . . .'

I don't know him at all, she thought each time they met. They had bypassed the getting-to-know-you rituals. After a few weeks she knew his body and sexual appetites intimately, but she still knew little about his background other than what she had gathered from Edward's instructive prayers. He seldom spoke of his family. Although he would talk about his work in Bishopside he rarely mentioned anything from his past. It was not that he was secretive, exactly, but there was a reserve about him that made curiosity seem crass.

'Did you really save Edward's life once?'

He scowled. 'I should have thrown the bugger back in.'

His house reiterated the message. The pale oatmeals and ivories suggested that colour would be an ostentation. He had no photographs lying about the place, no clutter, no memorabilia, nothing that seemed to be treasured for sentimental rather than aesthetic reasons. His musical taste seemed austere to her as well. He seemed to prefer discordant twentieth-century music or spiky modern jazz. She studied his house in awe as though it were a beautiful book in a foreign language. There was one room downstairs she had never been in.

'What's in there?'

'The heads of my former wives.'

Later she heard music coming from the forbidden room and followed the sound. Will was sitting at a grand piano. He paused in his playing and beckoned when he saw her hesitating in the doorway. She went and sat beside him and he played for her, indulging her with recognizable tunes. Annie was deeply ashamed of her musical philistinism. She had only ever been to one opera and that was by accident, in Stuttgart with her German penfriend. They had both been under the impression that *Onegin* was a ballet. Will cuffed her round the head when she confessed this. She pleaded her background in mitigation. His family were 'all musical', he admitted in an off-hand way, which convinced her they were all concert pianists.

Term went by. Ted introduced another game: Favourite Typos. A list went up on the noticeboard and each day new howlers were added. 'The three parsons of the Trinity'. 'The Apostles' Greed'. 'The redeeming wok of God'. In a college where most students owned a word processor but few could type properly the supply was constant. 'Go froth and multiply'. 'Give me oil in my lap, keep me burning'. And Annie's all-time favourite 'Get thee behind me, Stan'.

Exams approached. Annie had one or two papers to sit, but after the experience of Cambridge finals a decade earlier, she couldn't get worked up about them. Edward slogged dutifully. Ingram, of course, was fine-tuning the sleek engine of his intellect in preparation for his theology finals. There were volumes of Schleiermacher by his plate at lunchtime.

'What a glorious day,' said Muriel.

'What a pity we can't enjoy it properly,' said Isobel blightingly.

'Why don't we go punting this afternoon?' boomed Edward. 'Break from revision. Do us good.'

There was general assent. Annie continued to eat her apple in silence. It was Wednesday. She was supposed to be meeting Will.

'Tell you what,' went on Edward, 'I'll drag William along. He doesn't work on Wednesday afternoons.'

Excuse me, Annie pictured him saying, I work bloody hard. She finished her meal and slipped out before Edward could press-gang her into punting. Ted glanced at her and away again.

Footsteps thundered up the stairs and Edward came panting along the corridor before she could shut her door. 'You are coming with us, aren't you, Annie?'

'Um, actually I really must finish my –'

'It's William, isn't it?' Edward broke in belligerently. 'You're still being silly about him!'

'No! I . . . he's very kind. I'm . . . I have to finish my doctrine essay.'

'Then do it tonight. What's the *matter* with you, Annie?'

'Stop bullying me!'

He opened his mouth, then a stricken look crossed his face. She watched him think, Oh, no, I thought she'd got over all that.

'Gosh, Annie. I'm a brute. Sorry.'

She smiled wanly at him and hated herself as he pounded off down the corridor.

Her head lay on Will's chest.

'To think we could have been messing about on the river,' she said.

Will chuckled. 'I told him I had better ways of spending my time.' His fingers played some languid sonata up and down her spine. 'When will you tell them about us?'

'What? You're kidding! "Oh, and by the way, Will and I are having an affair."'

'So it's OK to do it but not OK to tell people.' She raised her head and stared at him to see if he was serious. 'How do you square it with God, just as a matter of interest?'

'I don't.' She leant her face against his chest once more, hearing his heartbeat. The Landlord at the door. Knock-knock. Knock-knock.

'So what's going to happen to us?'

'I don't know,' she whispered.

'Don't worry, Annie. Keep your head down, do nothing and the problem will go away.'

'That's not fair!'

He rolled her off him suddenly onto her back. 'So you're happy with just sex?'

'Delirious.' She smiled up into his eyes and saw they were cold.

'My God, the perfect woman. She asks no questions, she makes no demands, just fucks like a rabbit.'

She turned her face away.

They lay a long time in silence. This is it, she thought. The beginning of the end. It seemed hard that she should have put so much effort into being what she thought he wanted – undemanding, incurious, happy with just sex – only for him to fling these things back as faults. She saw what it was: he'd had enough and this was how he would get rid of her. She wondered numbly how many afternoons of sour little squabbles and silences she would have to get through before it was over. Or did he want her to go now?

'Shall I go?'

He sighed. 'No.' He reached for her wearily like a player returning to his instrument. What else was there, after all?

He might die. The thought struck her as she walked back to college from the station. She wouldn't be allowed to grieve. He would be someone she was supposed to know slightly, just a friend of Edward's she'd never really liked. Nobody would think to ask her to the funeral. Tears welled up without warning. Nobody would ever know that I loved him, she thought. The pretence would continue for the rest of her life. I don't even have a photograph of him. I'd have nothing to remember him by except one illegible letter and a drawer full of underwear. She saw what a fool she was. It was going to end. She would be hurt and he would not. What did I tell you, Anne Brown? gloated her mother. If you play with fire don't come crying to me when you get burnt!

She made her way to the college library and finished her essay on atonement. It was not a good essay. It felt like a cheap jigsaw. The pieces didn't fit properly but she forced them together anyway. Why did Christ die? She reread her wooden answers in a kind of despair. Once she had asked Will if he ever looked at all the pain and suffering in the world and wondered how God could let it happen. It was an old chestnut, the thing every vicar was asked.

'Do you ever look at the pain and suffering of Christ on the Cross,' he had replied, 'and wonder how God could let that happen to himself?'

As an afterthought Annie added this conversation to the end of her essay. Dr Mowbray might like it, although it was anecdotal. She stacked the pages together and went back to her room.

It was half an hour till supper-time. Annie went to her window and looked down across the Coverdale lawn to the riverbank. After supper it would be the weekly College Eucharist. She had come to dread them, receiving communion – eating and drinking judgement on herself – and hearing the terrifying words of the Bible dinning in her ears: *It is impossible to restore to repentance those who have once been enlightened . . . they crucify the Son of God on their own account and hold him up to contempt . . .*

She tried to imagine what Christ would say if she were dragged into his presence like the woman caught in adultery, half dressed, still damp with lust. Would he look at her with love and understanding? 'Neither do I condemn you. Go and sin no more.' But that was the problem. She would go on sinning till Will threw her out. Then she'd creep back to God for forgiveness. Oh, yes, like an adulterous husband ditched by his young mistress and skulking back to his wife: 'Darling, it meant nothing. You know that! I love you. Just give me another chance and I'll prove it to you. Things will be different from now on.'

You'd be a fool to have me back, she said to God. Why do you put up with me? Why do you let me treat you like this? She went to her desk and took refuge in her novel. At least here she was in control. Sins could be done and undone at the stroke of a pencil. There were no lasting implications for her characters' blunders. 'Months later, everything looked different,' she could say, tossing in repentance like a pinch of herbs. That was what she had reduced Christianity to in her novel – a dash of spice to flavour the sex.

Camilla received the news of Isabella's engagement a little frostily, although she thawed noticeably when asked to be a bridesmaid.

They chatted for an hour or so about dresses until Hermione

appeared and enquired snottily if she might be permitted to use the phone that millennium.

'See you at the party, then,' said Isabella to Camilla. 'Barney's coming, too.'

'You're kidding! You do know Luke will be there?'

'Shit.'

'Does his lordship know about that little episode?'

'I told him.'

'God – did he go ape shit?'

'Yep. Then he proposed to me.'

'Not picky about shop-soiled goods, eh?' Isabella did not respond to this remark. 'Well, see you on New Year's Eve,' said Camilla, after a tricky pause.

Ought she to warn Barney? worried Isabella as they drove to Camilla's parents' house. No. Surely she could rely on Luke's discretion. He was hardly likely to bound up to someone and announce he'd bonked their fiancée, was he? Anyway, with a bit of luck he'd be pissed and communing face down with the carpet by the time they arrived.

'Oh, by the way, Barney, I've asked Camilla to be a bridesmaid.'

'Mm.'

'Listen,' she cried, 'I don't know what you've got against her!'

'Don't you?'

'No! She's my best friend.'

He took her hand. 'If she's your best friend and you want her to be your bridesmaid, I'm very happy.'

'Why don't you like her? You could at least try.'

'I will,' he promised.

He was as good as his word. Isabella watched anxiously. Camilla was making a supreme effort, too. It turned out to be a wonderful party, after all. Isabella preened herself and showed off her gorgeous ring and fiancé, managing by the sheer force of her personality to give matrimony a bold and risqué air. Everything was going marvellously until she went to get herself another drink. She looked back across the room to cast a smile at her beloved and saw him in conversation with Luke. Bugger. She turned back to the drinks with her face scarlet. What was the smirking bastard saying? Why did you trust to his discretion, you fool? He wouldn't grasp the concept if you gave him a dictionary. She poured a glass of wine with a trembling hand.

When she turned back Luke had disappeared. A pair of legs were sticking out from behind the sofa. Barney was staring down at them bewildered.

'Leave him. He's drunk,' explained Isabella in relief. 'He's always passing out like that.'

Barney shrugged and allowed Isabella to lead him away.

They danced until Big Ben began to chime.

> Should auld acquaintance be forgot
> And never brought to mind?

Definitely, in Luke's case, thought Isabella. Barney had a service at eight the following morning, so they did not linger. He went to de-ice the car while Isabella tried to find Camilla and her mother to thank them. They were both in the kitchen standing over Luke. He was groaning in a chair with a packet of frozen peas clutched to his face.

'He passed out and hit his head,' she heard Camilla explaining. Luke removed the packet to reveal a glorious black eye. He mumbled something but Camilla clamped the peas firmly back in place.

'What did he say?' asked Camilla's mother.

'Didn't catch it,' replied Camilla.

But Isabella had: 'He hit me. He bloody hit me!' She turned and fled without saying goodbye.

They drove a couple of miles in silence.

'You hit him.'

'Yes.'

'I don't believe it! Why? What did he say?'

'I'm not telling you.'

'You're mad, Barney! You can't go around punching people. You're a clergyman, for God's sake! What happened to turning the other cheek?'

He made no reply. What have I done? she thought. He could be had up for assault. Isabella had always assumed it would be wonderful to have men fighting over her. Now she just felt sick and hollow. I can't make you faithful to me, he'd said, but I can make you very, very sorry if you're not. Would he turn out to be one of those terrible possessive monsters? She pictured him socking his parishioners at the church bazaar because she flirted with them. It was too awful to contemplate.

But the terrible thing was that, as the miles went by, she started to find it funny. Luke's legs sticking out behind the sofa. Barney staring down innocently. Camilla clamping the peas over Luke's face to shut him up. Before long she was giggling out loud.

'You're outrageous, Barney!'

'We'll make a lovely couple, then.'

CHAPTER 19

Saturday morning came. Annie felt sick with dread. Something had changed that previous Wednesday and she knew she would spend the afternoon alert for clues, trying to read something in Will's manner or tone, some difference that would tell her how soon the whole thing would be over. I mustn't let him see, she told herself. It'll drive him mad. He frequently cursed her for being too apologetic and placating. 'I'm asking what *you* want,' he'd snarl. 'Stop trying to guess what I want the whole fucking time.'

He was waiting for her at Newcastle station as usual, but his first words confirmed her fear: 'It's a beautiful day. Why don't we head out to the moors?'

'OK.'

As they drove out of Newcastle Annie puzzled anxiously. Why the moors? Did he want to talk? They usually went straight back to his house, barely making it out of their clothes or up the stairs before falling on one another. But maybe he was just planning a spot of *al fresco* sex.

'Everything all right, Annie?'

'Oh, yes. Thanks.'

They were out in the countryside now. The narrow twisty roads and hills were beginning to make her feel queasy. At last he pulled up and they got out.

'Beautiful,' she said, taking a deep breath. Not a moment too soon. Her knees were trembling.

The sky was full of larks glorying in the sunshine. New bracken was uncurling fresh and green against the old heather.

They began to walk. Edward always came armed with an Ordnance Survey map and compass when he set off for a stroll. Annie grinned at the thought and tucked her hand through Will's arm. He smiled down at her and led her off the path towards some rocks and gorse bushes. Her heart pattered. Sex, not serious conversation. It would be all right. His hand was already burrowing under her skirt. She was gasping by the time they reached the rocks. He pulled her down and started kissing her. She clung to him in relief.

'What are you doing next Wednesday?'

'This, I hope,' she replied.

'It's my birthday. Spend the night with me, for once.'

'Oh! I –'

'We'll find some hotel in the middle of nowhere, have dinner, get pissed and spend the whole night . . .' She gasped again – that *vibrato*! – '. . . doing this.'

'But I can't. Someone's bound to notice I'm not there and –'

'Tell them, then.'

'I can't possibly tell them!'

'Please.' He was smiling. Joking. He had to be joking.

'Don't push me!'

His fingers slid away. 'OK.'

She watched him anxiously to see if she had offended him. He leant down to kiss her again, then stopped. She saw one of those quick mood changes she dreaded.

'No. No, it's not bloody OK. If I mean anything to you, spend the night with me. Tell your friends about us.'

'I can't! You must know I can't.'

'Then it's over. This isn't a relationship, it's a bad habit. I'm sick of being your dirty little secret.'

The skylarks sang in the silence. Annie tried in vain to think of a way out, some way she might escape for a night without anyone knowing, some way to explain about Will.

'But I thought this was what you wanted,' she said.

'Not any more. I feel used. I've had enough.'

She closed her eyes. It's not fair! she wanted to cry. You can't do this – present me with an impossible choice so that I'm the one who appears to be finishing it.

'Oh, drop the fucking martyr act,' he said.

'But –'

'You can't go on like this. You don't know what you believe, you don't know what you want. You think if you do nothing, everything will –'

'I was all right till I met you!' she burst out.

'Yeah, yeah. Riddled with doubt and desperate for sex.' She sat up and pulled her skirt down with a sob. 'Just admit you don't want to be ordained. Say it.'

'Stop trying to make me choose between God and you.'

'Why? You can't have everything, honey child.' He lay down and closed his eyes.

She stared at him numbly. It was unworthy of him, this kind of dishonesty. If he wanted to end it, why didn't he just say? Surely they could part sweetly, reasonably? Why was he making it all her fault?

He opened his eyes suddenly. 'Well? No comeback? Nothing you'd like to add? It's over?' His eyes seemed to be hunting for something in her face.

She didn't know what she was supposed to say. 'I'm sorry.'

'You always are, Annie.'

'Shall we . . . Do you want to go now?'

'Well,' he said, 'unless you fancy a "last ride together", as Browning has it.'

'Don't!' She got to her feet. 'Don't joke about it.' They walked back to the car in silence.

'Look,' he said, as he dropped her at Newcastle station. 'I didn't mean to be this brutal. Come back if you want to. If you manage to sort yourself out.'

Annie made her way slowly back to college up the steep path along the riverbank which led to Palace Green. She was forced to rest half-way on a bench. It's as if I'm ill, she thought. Her energy had drained away and there was an ache in her chest. She half laughed. This is why people say your heart is breaking. I can feel it. Not breaking, though – tearing. An unbearable slow rending of fine silk. She had not known grief could be so physical.

Tears, shivering, sickness. I am ill. Sick at heart. Will, I want you so much.

Come back if you want to. He'd opened the door again a fraction at the last moment. Supposing he wanted a serious relationship, something more than a bad habit? Had he been implying that? It was a frail hope. She couldn't, for instance, go back to teaching on the strength of it and look for a job near Bishopside. He might turn round and say he wasn't interested. Come back if you manage to sort yourself out. I can't sort myself out! she sobbed to herself. She didn't know what she was supposed to be choosing between. It wasn't as though he'd asked her to live with him. Perhaps if she got a curacy near Bishopside . . . But at once her conscience shrieked. She wouldn't be able to live with that degree of hypocrisy.

She sat for a long time with these thoughts, but at last a dull misery settled over her. No, he'd had enough, and for some reason he was unable to take the responsibility for ending their affair. She tried to summon the energy to walk the rest of the way back to college. She could almost have stretched out on the bench and slept, but she forced herself to her feet.

Muriel was in the hallway examining the noticeboard. 'Heavens, you're looking pale, Annie. Are you feeling all right?' The nurse's watch jiggled on her broad bosom.

'Actually, I'm feeling a bit . . . It must be something I ate.'

'You poor old thing.' Muriel gave her a quick hug. 'Why not go and lie down?'

'I think I will.' They went up the stairs together.

'I hope you'll be well enough to hear Edward preach tomorrow,' said Muriel. 'You won't want to miss that.'

Annie forced a smile as she unlocked her door. 'I'm sure I'll be fine.'

She stood in her silent room. That's it. It's over. Now I must skulk back to God again. But she was too weary to repent. Too weary to weep, even. She lay down on her bed and slept.

The next morning she felt worse, if anything, but she set off with the rest of her Coverdale group to the church on the marketplace to hear Edward. The fine weather had vanished. Wind buffeted the City, tearing down tender green leaves and whirling them along the streets in a parody of autumn. Blossom swirled in the gutters. Annie could still hear the wind bouncing off the church windows while Edward preached.

It was a well-constructed sermon. Three points all beginning with R. Annie would have found it easy to listen to if she weren't having to fight back waves of nausea. Edward was boisterously commending God's forgiveness to the largely undergraduate congregation. Why is this church so warm? Annie fretted, struggling out of her coat. I must be ill. Whatever had she eaten?

Then she felt a white hot bolt of fear. What if I'm pregnant? For a second Edward's voice seemed to be booming down a long tunnel. No. I can't be. Of course not, she realized in relief. Will was a doctor and conscientious to the point of paranoia about condoms. The fear receded, leaving a nasty taste in her mouth. She focused guiltily on Edward again, who was saying, 'Let me end with a story.'

He told them about a pastor with a poor widow in his congregation who couldn't pay her rent. Knowing that the woman was living in dread, the pastor called round with a gift of money so that she could pay her landlord. He called several times but got no answer. The woman was in all the time, but so sure it was the landlord that she was too terrified to open the door.

'And aren't we like that sometimes?' concluded Edward. 'God comes knocking at the door of our lives to bring forgiveness, to pay our debts for us, but we're too scared to open up and let him in.'

The words thudded home like an arrow into a target. That's what I'm like. Cowering away from the eternal Landlord. Then she felt again what she had experienced the morning she had visited Bishopside: the loving eye of God on her. He had been there all the time, watching, waiting, totally absorbed in Annie Brown and what she would do with her life. And what could she do but offer herself back to him? He had called her and she would try to be faithful.

She managed to hold onto herself until the last hymn:

Pardon for sin and a peace that endureth.
Thine own dear presence to cheer and to guide.
Strength for today and bright hope for tomorrow,
Blessings all mine with ten thousand beside.

All around people were singing, 'Great is thy faithfulness, great is thy faithfulness'. She let it bear her along, feeling the tears streaming down her cheeks and Ted's comforting arm round her shoulder.

He walked back to college with her, leaving the others in the throng drinking coffee.

'It's just . . . I've felt so far from God recently,' Annie tried to explain. 'And that story about the widow and her rent . . . That's me. I find forgiveness so hard to believe in.'

'Ah, now that's your Nonconformist roots,' said Ted, who had been brought up a Baptist. 'You believe God loves you out of a grim sense of duty, but you know he doesn't really like you.'

Annie gave a reluctant giggle. 'Exactly. I feel so unworthy.'

'Well, we all are.'

I *really* am, though, she thought. They walked on a little in silence.

'But you feel things have been set right now?' he asked, after a while.

'Yes,' she whispered. It's over. Perhaps that was what Ted was really asking. She feared he'd known about Will all along, although she couldn't work out how. He gave her a hug.

'Well, your friends like you too, Annie.'

'I sometimes think they wouldn't if they knew what I was really like.'

'You underestimate us.'

'I know. I'm sorry.'

They were back at college. She was feeling sick again. Ted invited her for coffee but she excused herself and went to lie down. She started to feel guilty about Will. What if he were waiting for some kind of explanation? I ought to tell him I've decided to go on with my training, she thought. I'll write. But would he think that was cowardly? She knew she should explain face to face, but she was scared he would demolish her newly recovered faith. He was too clever for her. Her sense of vocation always withered under his scathing green eyes. I'll plan what to say, she decided as she curled up on the bed then tried to banish it all by retreating into her novel, but it was impossible. She couldn't bear her heroine's happiness. It's all right for you, Isabella Deane. You've got your man. Even though Annie knew what Isabella didn't – that Barney was impossible to live with and the marriage was destined for an early shipwreck – she couldn't help feeling jealous. Libby howled in her kennel for Will. That sweet, ruthless lovemaking, those languorous, oil-drenched massages. The grace of God was a Lenten fast in comparison.

Her friends were starting to worry about her again. Even Tubby noticed something was wrong.

'Gosh, Annie, you're looking frightfully peaky.'

She mumbled something about a tummy bug. If she was honest she was beginning to get anxious herself. At least she wasn't pregnant. Her period had arrived. Never before had she greeted it with such a cry of welcome. But why was she feeling so wretched? Not ill exactly, just sick and tired. She had to leave one of her exams to throw up. Only mint imperials seemed to keep nausea at bay. She munched her way through packets of them. It must be misery, she decided. Misery and stress. She still hadn't found the courage to contact Will. A week and a half had passed. What if he turned up suddenly and demanded an explanation?

I didn't even send him a birthday card, she thought one morning as she crept into morning prayer. Her lip trembled at the thought. She gave Edward a wavering smile and sat beside him. The chapel felt stifling. The pews faced each other across a central aisle and Annie felt as though everyone opposite was watching her. She slipped off her cardigan, but could still feel sweat forming on her forehead. The service dragged. They all stood for the Creed.

'"I believe in God, the Father Almighty",' boomed Edward beside her, refusing stubbornly to turn east like everyone else. She ended up murmuring the words into his sleeve. The phrases seemed to swirl and roar around her. The floor tilted and she reached out to clutch him.

She was outside, lying on the chapel lawn looking up at Edward and Muriel. They were fanning her clumsily with copies of the Alternative Service Book.

'What. . .?'

'You fainted,' said Muriel soothingly. 'Don't worry. Just lie there till you feel a bit better.'

Annie closed her eyes.

'I'm going to call a doctor,' said Edward threateningly.

'I'll go this morning,' promised Annie. 'I'll be OK in a minute.'

'Hah!' said Edward. 'I'll take you in the car.'

In the end she managed to fob him off. She walked to the doctor's, sucking yet another mint imperial. I'm getting addicted to them, she thought. Fancy fainting like that! clucked her mother's voice. Annie felt extremely foolish. She'd still been lying on the lawn as the service ended and everyone poured out and went to breakfast. Muriel had explained over and over again like a recorded message, She just fainted, that's all. She's all right now.

But am I, though? What if something serious is wrong? She tried to brush the worry aside. The doctor would be able to tell. Just stress, probably.

It was a woman doctor, fortunately. 'Come in. I'm Dr Buchanan. What can I do for you?'

Annie sat. 'Um, well . . . I've been feeling a bit poorly. Sick. And exhausted. Possibly something I ate. I can't seem to shake it off. And then I fainted this morning . . .'

The doctor was watching her assessingly. 'Are you always pale?'

'No, I'm . . .'

'Sick, you say? Have you actually *been* sick?'

'Once, but I feel sick . . .'

'And tired?'

Annie nodded.

'Are you getting enough sleep?'

'I can't seem to stay awake, funnily enough.'

'No chance you could be pregnant, I suppose?'

Annie flushed. 'I can't be.'

'Well,' said the other woman, with a friendly smile, 'if you've been having sex there's always a possibility.'

'But I've just had a period.'

'Doesn't prove anything, I'm afraid. Some women get break-through bleeding for the first few months.'

Annie stared aghast. 'But I can't be!' She heard her tone of voice saying the opposite. The other woman raised an eyebrow. 'But he's a doctor!' she burst out.

Dr Buchanan's lips twitched. 'Even doctors are fallible. What type of contraception were you using?'

'Condoms.'

'With spermicide?' Annie nodded. 'Hmm. That's usually pretty reliable. Why don't you hop up on the couch and I'll have a feel of your tummy?'

Tummy? thought Annie as she climbed up. What happened to abdomen? This can't be happening. The doctor's cool hands pressed and stroked.

'Hmm. Can't feel anything.'

'You mean . . .?'

'Might just mean it's too early.'

Annie sat up and swung her legs over the edge of the bed. 'Can you . . . do a test, or something?'

'I could. But you won't get the results for several days. Why not buy one of those home testing kits? Any chemist'll sell them. The sort with a stick thingy you wee on. They're the best. It'll tell you in a couple of minutes.'

A stick thingy to wee on, thought Annie numbly.

'Then at least you'll know,' said the doctor. She had crossed back to her desk and was scrawling on Annie's notes. 'If you are pregnant come back and we'll have a chat about what you want to do.'

'OK.'

'Listen, come back anyway. If you're not pregnant we'll need to find out what's making you sick, won't we? You're a student? Which college?'

'Coverdale Hall.'

The doctor's biro paused. 'Isn't that the . . .?'

'The theological college. Yes.' Annie blushed scarlet. Was this a foretaste of the mortification that lay ahead?'

'Well, do that test and come back for a chat.' She crossed to Annie and gave her arm a pat. 'Goodbye.'

Oh, God help me! Annie was out on the street not knowing which way to turn. A chemist. But I might meet someone I know. She walked up the road, then turned and began to walk back. What shall I do? She tried to calm herself. You probably aren't pregnant. Will wouldn't have made a mistake like that. She remembered his face when he said condoms weren't half as inconvenient as an unwanted pregnancy. Go to Newcastle and buy a kit. It'll be fine. You'll see.

She caught a train and made her way to the big anonymous Boots, blushing furiously as she bought the kit. She felt sure everyone in the ladies' would hear the rustling packet and know. I'm just doing this to set my mind at rest. There was the little stick thingy to wee on. Her fingers trembled till she almost dropped it. *Simply hold the indicator in your flow of urine*, urged the instructions brightly. *A blue line shows that you are pregnant*. She did as she was told, peeing haltingly, then waiting, not daring to look. The second hand crawled round her watch. One minute. One minute thirty seconds, forty, fifty. She could bear it no more.

There was the blue line. Annie doubled over and vomited wretchedly.

CHAPTER 20

Don't let it be true! Somehow she stumbled out of the shopping centre and hurried blindly along the street. It was raining and she had no coat. Before long she was soaked to the skin but she kept walking, walking, as though by doing so she might arrive at an answer. The rainy streets made no sense. Where was she? For a moment she lost herself and thought she was a student in Cambridge again with finals a day away.

> Why didst thou promise such a beauteous day
> And make me travel forth without my cloak?

Please help me, please help me! Her friends' faces crowded in on her. Shock, disbelief, disappointment. Ted. Isobel. Muriel. And Edward. Oh, God, Edward! A passer-by turned and looked at her and Annie realized she had cried out. She hurried on. I can't face them. I'll have to get rid of it. Her voice cried out again and she clapped a hand over her mouth. I can't. The poor thing. The little thing clinging to her against all the odds. I'm all it has.

What if Will tries to make me have an abortion? Wait – he was against abortion. Except in extreme circumstances. But this was extreme. She quailed at the thought of him. He'd be furious. He'd blame her. But it's not my fault! She was his worst nightmare – the demanding, accusing, pregnant ex-lover. I won't tell him. I'll manage. I'll find somewhere to live. I've got my savings. I can get a teaching job. I'll manage somehow.

But the shame! The streets might have been lined with all the people she'd ever known. People who would find out. People she would have to face and tell. The college staff. The students.

Her mother. Her bishop. She passed their staring faces. Oh, God, let it not be true! And the people she didn't know. They wouldn't just look at her and think she'd been careless or unlucky. She was an ordinand. She was insignificant, but she was still an ordinand. People expected more of the clergy and judged more harshly. An unmarried pregnant ordinand. It was the stuff of tabloid headlines.

The rain suddenly became torrential. Shoppers ran for cover. Annie continued to walk. If only she had someone to turn to. If only she could run to Will. She stopped her furious walking. What if he heard about it second hand from Edward? The rain slapped down, hissing onto the pavement, throwing up bubbles on the streaming road. Go to him, urged a voice. Go to him. It's Wednesday afternoon, she thought. He'll be in. She turned and hurried to the metro and waited for a train.

It was still raining as she walked the half-mile from the station to his house. Her lips mumbled and rehearsed what she would say. The streets were empty, everyone driven inside by the rain. She went past the dripping privet hedge and in through his gate. What if he's not there? But his shape moved behind the glass in the door. He opened before she could ring.

'Annie! God, you're soaked. Come in.' She saw his ravishing smile and staggered across the threshold. 'I was going to give you till Saturday, then –' He broke off. 'What's wrong?'

Her voice uttered another strange moan. 'I'm pregnant, Will!'

'*What?*'

'I did a test. I'm pregnant.'

They stared at one another wildly.

'Shit.'

She shivered, trying to wipe the rain from her face with her sodden sleeve.

He had his hands in his hair as though he was about to pull it out. 'Oh, *Shit.*'

'I . . . I just wanted you to know.' She groped for her prepared words. 'I'm not going to make any demands on you.'

'Why the hell not?'

'Because you didn't plan . . . I know it's not convenient –'

'It was convenient for me to have sex. Why should I escape the consequences?'

'But . . .'

He shook himself. 'What am I doing? You're soaked. I'll get a towel. Go and put the kettle on.'

He joined her in the kitchen a moment later and helped her peel off her wet clothes. She clutched his dressing gown round her, ashamed to let him see her naked body. He handed her a towel.

'Sit down.' He stood frowning and biting his lip. 'You're quite sure, Annie?'

She nodded. 'Unless the test –'

'No. They're accurate.' His hands went to his hair again. She looked away at the rain trickling down the steamed-up window. 'God, Annie, I'm so sorry. Your training – what will you do?'

'I'll resign.' She caught an expression on his face and couldn't help crying, 'I know you think I didn't want to be ordained, but I did! I was going to come and explain. I'd chosen . . .'

'And now this. Jesus. Have you considered having an abortion?'

'Oh, I couldn't! I'm sorry! Please don't try to persuade me.'

'Ssh. It's all right. I wouldn't dream . . .' He knelt in front of her and took her hands. 'Look, I'm here if you need me. If you need a place to stay. Or money. Or moral support. Anything.'

'I'll have to tell so many people!'

'Well, not yet. It's early days, Annie. There's a one in four chance of miscarrying in the first three months.' He was slipping into his professional manner. 'I wonder how far on you are. Can I see if I can feel anything?'

She lay down on the floor. He has to ask now if he can touch me. For the second time that day a set of hands worked their way down her stomach. His expression was remote and thoughtful. She banished the memory of his savage face the last time she'd lain on that hard cold floor.

He shook his head. 'They'll be able to fix your dates by scan. Go and see your doctor.' He leant back against the cooker wearily.

She sat up, wrapping the dressing gown close again. 'I'll have to tell my bishop,' she said.

'OK. Who is he?'

'Henry Melville.'

'Fuck.' He flushed scarlet.

'What?'

'He's my bloody godfather.'

Annie stifled a giggle. They sat on his kitchen floor laughing. A moment later they were both in tears.

'Jesus, what a mess,' he said. 'No such thing as a free fuck. I just thought I'd have all the fun and none of the responsibility for once. Selfish bastard.'

'Don't. It's not your fault.'

'It was a mistake, wasn't it? All that sex with no commitment. I was never sure you liked me, even.'

'But I did!' she protested. 'I do.' I love you. I love you.

'Yeah, well.' They were silent for a while. Then she saw it dawning on him: I'm going to be a father. She felt a jolt of something that might have been joy, saw it mirrored in his face. But it passed. She sat listening to the miserable drumming of the rain and started to feel sick again.

Annie spent the rest of the afternoon asleep on Will's sofa while her clothes dried. He drove her to the station. She caught a train and walked back to college. He had advised her to tell only one or two close friends and the Warden, and to wait till the end of term before trying to make any decisions. It was only two weeks away. Annie was relieved to have someone else telling her what to do. She felt stunned and directionless. They'll all come back after the summer vacation, she thought. They'll find out one by one what's happened to me. Or perhaps the Warden will make an announcement. At least she would be spared the staring and whispering and the sudden silences when she entered a room.

Annie, where the hell are you? What's going on? Edward. His big handwriting almost filled the message board on her door. She panicked. He'd bully the truth out of her and storm off to confront Will. She stood wringing her hands. Ted. She'd go to Ted.

She went to his room, praying he'd be in and that she wouldn't meet Edward on the way. She knocked and Ted called her in. 'Annie! Where have you been? We've been worried about you.' Her face crumpled. She knotted her hands together. 'What's wrong?' he asked gently.

'I'm pregnant.' Without a word he held out his arms to her. She rushed into them and cried brokenly on his chest while he rocked her like a little child. 'You're not surprised,' she got out at last.

'Well, I'd begun to wonder. Dr Sex, I presume?'

'You knew.'

'I'm afraid so. I saw you with him at Newcastle station once. And you seemed to vanish on Wednesday afternoons.'

'You never said anything.'

He sighed. 'I couldn't decide whether it was my business.' If I'd said something this might never have happened. She could sense he was accusing himself. 'Have you told William?' She nodded. 'What did he say?'

'Um . . .'

'Ah. My Sankey box runneth over.'

He doesn't like him. 'He was very good about it.' She saw Ted thinking. So I should hope. 'I mean, if there's anything I need, he said . . . Money, you know. A place to stay . . .' Her voice pleaded with him. 'Ted, it was all over between us. I can't expect him to . . . to . . . He'll do everything he can. I'm sure he will. I'm not asking . . .' She trailed off.

'What will you do, Annie?'

'I don't know.' She started to cry again and he hugged her close. 'Will says not to tell too many people. In case I lose the baby.' He nodded. She felt his beard tickle her forehead. 'Edward!' she yelped, suddenly remembering. 'He'll want to know what the doctor said!'

'Well, tell him you're all right, but you'd rather not go into the details with him.'

'But he'll have to know in the end. Everyone will.'

'Yes.'

Oh, Ted, I'm sorry, she wanted to say. 'I thought you'd be shocked. Disapproving.'

'There's not much point, is there? You know what I think –
sex is for marriage. Or for commitment, at any rate.'

'That's what Will said, more or less. He said it was all a big
mistake.'

'Did he now.'

'Please don't think badly of him,' begged Annie. 'He's . . .'
But what was he?

'Well, if there's anything I can do, Annie.'

'Thanks. You could . . . pray for me. I've got to go and see
Tubby now.'

'Yoicks!' said Ted, improvising a new episode of Tubby of
Tuckerman Hall. 'Bally old bun in the oven? What mouldy old
beastly rotten luck! Have a gobstopper.'

'Stop it!' pleaded Annie, giggling against her will. He gave her
another hug and she went. She pictured his shoulders sagging
after he shut the door. Oh, Annie, he would be thinking as he
shook his head sadly. Annie, Annie, Annie.

Tubby wasn't in his office, so Annie crossed the street to his
house to see if he was there. Megs opened the door and Annie
backed off, realizing it was Tuckerman tea-time. Megs could be
fierce in defence of quality family time, but on this occasion she
invited Annie in and gave her a cup of mango tea. Tubby must
have told her something, thought Annie, as she entered the land
of flying fishfingers.

'Do you want some honey in it? We don't have sugar,' said
Megs, pushing a sticky jar towards her. Annie shook her head.
Sweet Justice, said the label. *Honey from more than one country.*

The noise was immense. Annie couldn't decide if they'd run
out of sugar or if they never had any on principle. Megs was
spooning something wholesome into the smallest Tuckerperson.
The older three sat round the table playing with their food and
pretending to vomit mouthfuls back onto their plates. Annie
inhaled some of her perfumed tea. Megs seemed to inhabit a
non-stop Joyce Grenfell sketch.

'Let's see who can finish first, shall we? Look! Timmy's almost
finished already.' She turned to Annie. 'David won't be –
Bottom down, Lucy. BOTTOM DOWN! Or there'll be no yoghurt.
David's just on the phone to – No hitting, James, no, 'sorry' is

not enough – on the phone to Pauline about the – the – He won't be a moment.'

About the – Annie never discovered what Tubby and Pauline were discussing. Megs's speech was littered with missing nouns.

'So how's your – STOP BANGING – how's your course going?'

'Well, all right. I'm –'

'Good boy! Just one more mouthful . . .'

It was clear that Megs perceived a thread of continuity running through the conversation, but it eluded Annie. This will be me next year, she thought, swallowed alive by motherhood, unable to have three coherent exchanges of adult small-talk. Perhaps in the end you became hardened to the constant bombardment of your attention. She imagined Megs saying to Tubby later, Well, I had a nice chat with Annie. By now the little Tuckerpeople were chanting Annie pooh, Annie bum as Megs was trying to talk about fair trading, something Annie was in favour of, except when she was talking to Megs.

'. . . which helps the local people produce their own – Stop that now! ONE. TWO.'

They fell silent in the nick of time before the fearsome THREE was uttered.

Tubby arrived and rescued Annie. They retreated to his chaotic study. He shifted some books and files and waved her into a chair. Annie had forgotten a handkerchief and glanced around for a box of tissues. Perhaps Megs forbade the use of paper hankies.

'Have you recovered from this morning?' asked Tubby, sitting down.

'Um . . . yes.'

'You saw the doctor?' he prompted encouragingly.

She nodded and hunted pointlessly around her pocket for a tissue. 'I'm afraid I've been very foolish,' she burst out.

He handed her a roll of recycled pink loo paper and waited, although she knew he must have guessed.

'I'm afraid I'm pregnant.' She sniffed.

His hand clasped hers tight. 'Thank you for telling me.' He went on waiting while she wept into strip after strip of disintegrating pink paper.

'I'm sorry. I've let everyone down. I –'

His hand clasped hers again. 'Never mind all that. It's you I'm concerned about. How are you coping?'

She gestured helplessly.

'Do you mind awfully telling me who the father is?' he asked, after a while.

'Nobody in college.' She'd spared him that, at least. 'It's . . . it's a friend of Edward's. He's a doctor in Bishopside.' Tubby nodded. She saw she would have to say more. 'We, um, had an affair. Earlier this term. I know it was wrong. It was all over. And now . . .' She began to weep again.

'Have you told him?' Tubby asked.

She nodded. 'He . . . he's prepared to support me. Financially. Not . . .'

'Marriage isn't on the cards?'

She shook her head. 'Edward doesn't know!' she blurted.

'Don't worry,' said Tubby. He took his heavy glasses off and she noticed again how beautiful his eyes were. He rubbed them. She watched him sizing up the weight of the burden, steadying himself to shoulder it. He sighed and put his glasses back on.

'Well, a lecture would be completely out of order. You're not the first student who's slipped up – golly, no – and you won't be the last, I dare say. But there are obvious consequences we're going to have to think about.' There was a silence. '*Bath time!*' sang Megs in the distance. The consequences seemed to tower over Annie. 'I think I'm going to have to urge you to take a break in your training.'

'I'll resign,' she said hurriedly.

He raised a hand. 'Hold your horses. Let's think this through properly.' They waited while he thought. 'The other members of staff are going to have to know. And the Principal will want to have a chat with you, I expect.' Annie nodded miserably. 'Would you like me to have a word with your bishop?'

'Please.'

'I want to spare you the ordeal of the whole college talking about you. You'll have enough on your plate without that.' She nodded again. 'People are going to be jolly condemning, I'm afraid, Annie. I just want you to know we'll do everything we can to support you. Do you have a spiritual director?'

She shook her head.

'I'd like you to see someone.'

'All right.'

'I'll fix it up. In the meantime, why not go and have another chat with Pauline? I'll put her in the picture.' Annie nodded. She couldn't argue. He was being so good about it all.

'I'm sorry,' she said. 'I . . .'

'Take it to God,' said Tubby gently. 'Take it to God, Annie.'

'Where have you been?' asked Edward as she crept into her seat for College Eucharist. 'What did the doctor say?'

'I'm all right,' she mumbled.

'What's wrong with you? Eh? Eh?'

'Nothing serious. I just don't want to discuss it.'

'Why not?'

Isobel, who was sitting in front of them, turned round and hissed, 'Honestly, Edward! Are you going to barge about like a mad bull when you're a curate? You can't demand to know other people's intimate health problems.'

Edward flushed. 'OK, OK. I'm just worried about her.'

'I'm all right,' repeated Annie.

Edward opened his mouth but was quelled by a look from Isobel. Tubby entered in his robes and they all got to their feet.

' "Almighty God, to whom all hearts are open, all desires known, and from whom no secrets are hidden, cleanse the thoughts of our hearts . . ." ' Oh, God, undo it all for me! Annie wanted to cry. They came to the confession. ' "We are truly sorry and repent of all our sins." ' But 'sorry' was not enough. Even if God forgave her all that was past, the past could not be undone.

' ". . . pardon and deliver you from all your sins," ' Tubby was saying. From the sin but not the consequences. Let there be some way out, she pleaded. Don't make me go through this. But she knew what the answer would be: *This is the way. Walk thou in it.*

CHAPTER 21

Annie went through the next few days like a sleepwalker. The staff were marvellous. She could almost hear Tubby saying to them all, I must stress that this is primarily a *pastoral* matter. Nobody blamed her. Why didn't they, when she was so very much to blame? Would she feel absolved if somebody bawled her out? Perhaps they all thought her situation was punishment enough. Some mornings as she hung retching over her washbasin she felt they were right.

All she could do was survive. The staff were treating her like some kind of victim or refugee, steering her gently in this direction and that. She went obediently to see Pauline. Tubby arranged for her to visit a Franciscan brother later in the week. Then the Principal summoned her. Annie went up to her office full of dread. Dr Pollock was a tall formidable Scotswoman renowned throughout the university for cracking down on student misdemeanours; but instead of getting the universally feared Pollocking, Annie was treated to brisk sympathy and practical advice.

The following day she went back to her GP. 'Ho hum,' said Dr Buchanan. 'Bad luck.'

She talked to Annie for a while, then sent her on to the practice midwife who began the process of filling in forms. Mother's medical history. Annie racked her brains and tried to answer the questions. Although Mrs Brown muttered darkly about her health she seldom gave details. After a while the midwife paused. '*Mother's* medical details,' she said gently. 'That means you. You're the mother.'

I am the mother, Annie repeated to herself. *I am the mother.*
She tried to believe that there really was a child growing inside
her and that it wasn't all some ludicrous mistake. One night she
dreamt she had given birth, but nobody was sure whether it was
a baby or an egg and bacon flan. The Principal had to cut into it
with a knife to find out. 'It's all right, my dear,' she said. 'It's a
flan.'

All the time she ached for Will. He phoned one evening.

'Annie, I feel I've abandoned you. Come and see me. What
about Saturday afternoon?' She agreed, mostly out of fear that if
she said no he would come to find her in Coverdale. Their conversation was full of awkward pauses. When they finally hung up
she was crying yet again. She could no longer get straight in her
mind the reasons why they had split up. Surely this was the time
to talk about serious commitment, now that she was pregnant.
But he hadn't raised the subject. Money, a place to stay, moral
support – that was all he had offered. All? It was a lot. He hadn't
flung her out, for goodness sake. She couldn't complain. Ted
raised an eyebrow and said nothing when she reasoned like this.

Finals results came out. The hot news in Coverdale was that
Ingram had somehow missed getting a first. It had been very,
very close, Ingram explained. But then, it always was. Annie
smirked. At last, the ultimate place name for Ingram: 'Upper
Second.' She shared this thought with Ted, who read her the
latest poetic offering from his daughters: 'In Xanadu did Kubla
Khan a stately pleasure Dominican decree . . .' Annie laughed
till she wept at the words 'A dandelion with a dum-dum bullet
in a vitamin once I saw. It was an Abyssinian maisonette . . .' He
read on steadfastly to the bitter end: 'For he on hooch hath fed,
and drunk the millipedes of paraldehyde.'

Ted devised many little methods of cheering her up, and she
loved him for it, but the days seemed endless. Her novel was the
only place where she was still in control, where the sun shone
when she wanted it to, where months could pass in a flash and
acts of fornication could be crossed out and forgotten. She
needed Barney and Isabella as never before, yet as she sat down
to write they slid from her grasp.

★

The train trundled west across Northumberland. Annie was struggling to calm herself after her encounter with Edward, who had insisted on driving her to the station.

'Look, Annie,' he began as he parked the car, 'I dare say it's some boring old gynae problem you don't want to talk about, but at least reassure me it's nothing serious. I mean, it's not . . . you know . . .'

He thinks I've got cancer, she thought. 'No, oh, no.' It wasn't fair to let him worry like this. Besides, he would have to know at some point. Her fingers twisted round one another. 'It's just that I'm, um, pregnant.'

'You can't be!' There was almost relief in his tone, as though she were a naïve girl who thought you caught babies from dirty toilet seats, and he could soon put her straight about that.

'Well, I'm afraid I am.'

'But you haven't got a boyfriend!' She saw him relinquish his faint hope that she was joking. 'Annie! You can't be. Who – but – when – I bloody well hope he's doing the decent thing!' She hung her head. 'Annie! Don't tell me he's *married*?'

'No.'

'Then he should damn well do his duty. Listen, you don't just get girls into trouble and leave them to get on with it! Who is he? Come on.'

'I'm not telling you.'

'Hah! I know him, then. He's in college.'

'No. That is, I'm not telling you,' she corrected herself hastily. Damn damn damn. There was a long pause.

'I'll bloody kill him. It's William, isn't it?'

'I'm *not telling you*.'

'It is! The little shit.' Annie clamped her hands over her ears. 'Right. We're going over there NOW.' He started the engine.

'But I've got to see this monk. Stop, Edward!'

Annie winced at the memory of Edward roaring and swearing in such a confined space. She had only managed to calm him down by the shameful tactic of clutching her stomach and moaning. The fear that she might miscarry on the front seat of his car did the trick. She was ashamed of herself, but how else could she have extracted promises of good behaviour from him? He had gone very quiet. Perhaps dangerously so. Ought she to warn Will? She was seeing him the next day. That would be soon enough.

She watched the hedgerows out of the train window. They were creamy with may blossom. The wind feathered across the barley. She wished she were happy enough to enjoy the sight. But you always hated him! Edward had protested. She knew he was saying to himself in amazement, I thought it was me she was keen on. Was that the kind of unsavoury detail she would have to confess to this monk? Brother Gabriel, as he was improbably called.

The train pulled into the station and she got out. He was supposed to be meeting her. The phrase 'stately pleasure Dominican' flashed unhelpfully across her mind as she walked towards the footbridge. She looked up the steps and saw a slight robed figure standing in the sunlight. He was shielding his eyes and looking down, like an archangel scanning the four corners of the earth. His red-gold hair sprang from his head like a fiery halo. She decided his name was right. He came swiftly down the steps to meet her.

'Hello, Annie. I'm Brother Gabriel.'

They shook hands and he held her gaze with searching blue eyes. She tried to think of something to say as they walked to the car. Sunlight dappled down through the trees and went flickering across his brown habit. Her Nonconformist background had left her unable to cope with monasticism. She battled with hysterical mirth as he backed out the car and narrowly missed a passing Labrador. Wouldn't it be terribly bad form for a Franciscan to run over a dog? They managed a few exchanges about her journey and the weather. At last they were going down a long, wooded drive to the Friary.

'*St Francis and St Clare pray for us,*' requested a polite notice in the entrance. Annie averted her gaze in Protestant squeamishness.

'Let's get some coffee and find a place to talk,' said Gabriel. Another brother paused as he mopped the floor and smiled at her. He was built like a nightclub bouncer and had a pink apron tied over his habit. Annie grappled with mirth again. The sound of a microwave beeping in a distant kitchen caused her another spasm. It was the incongruity – habits, microwaves, crew-cut bouncer, pink pinny.

They went with their coffee into a small room. The box of tissues on the little table made Annie rebel inwardly. She hated Tubby for sending her here.

'Why don't you tell me all about it?' Gabriel asked after a while.

It seemed rude not to respond. She began to mumble. He listened intently. Suddenly it seemed like a relief to pour it all out to a stranger. She told him about her doubts and frustrations at Coverdale and about her affair with Will. She suppressed another wild surge of hilarity at the idea of talking about sex to a celibate monk. His eyes never wavered from her face. When she finished her jaws felt tight and her teeth almost chattered as though she'd just given a lengthy performance of some kind. Gabriel looked down at his hands and carefully and deliberately fitted the fingers together like two halves of a puzzle.

'It's a complete disaster,' Annie concluded.

'Tell me about your mother,' he said unexpectedly.

'My mother? Well,' she began. Then she stopped, finding herself confronting a closed door. The cupboard under the stairs full of useless broken things. Gabriel waited. How had he known to ask this? 'My mother,' she began again. Her voice trembled and out rushed all the misery of her horrible childhood. She groped for the tissue box and wept as she told him.

'Annie,' he said in the end, 'it seems to me that your whole life is governed by the fear of giving offence.'

'I know.'

'It shouldn't be like that.'

'I'm sorry,' she said, sensing anger vibrating in the air. For a second she seemed to see it sparking from his finger-tips and wild hair.

'What about *you*? You're offending yourself every minute of your life.'

He's right, she thought. Why can't I be more like Isabella?

'Who's Isabella?' he asked curiously.

She jumped and stared at him. I must have said it out loud. 'Um . . . nobody, really. Just a character in a book. Something I'm writing. It's nothing.'

'Tell me about her.' She obeyed, still watching him warily, not quite able to dismiss the idea that he had secret access to the Book of Life.

'I think I like her,' he said. They sat a while in silence, then Annie's stomach gave a horrible lurch.

'I'm going to be sick!'

He leapt up. 'This way!'

They sprinted through the house until Annie was overcome by the sound of slapping sandals and flapping habit. Her nausea deserted her.

'No, I'm not.' They skidded to a halt and she giggled helplessly in the silent corridor.

He smiled. 'Well, what about some fresh air?'

He led her out into the garden. A small statue of St Francis lurked in the rockery like a garden gnome. They wandered along wooded paths until they came upon a large painted crucifix in a clearing. Tacky, said Damn's voice.

'Not my cup of tea, either,' remarked Gabriel.

'There's no . . . well, passion,' she ventured.

'Come and see this.' He took her back to the house. She smelt fish cooking, then as they approached the chapel, the ravishing smell of incense.

They went in. Annie stood awkwardly while Gabriel genuflected. Behind the altar was a large window, which looked out over a gently sloping lawn to the sweep of wooded hills. A flock of pigeons rose into the blue.

'Look,' said Gabriel.

Above the altar was another crucifix, the figure on it twisted in agony.

Annie cried out in shock. 'I'm afraid I was brought up to disapprove of crucifixes,' she explained. 'The resurrection was supposed to be the thing.'

'Ah, but *this* is the victory,' said Gabriel, still looking up at it. 'The point of suffering and defeat. That's where he conquered. It's shot through with resurrection light.'

Annie looked again at the strong figure as it writhed up against the pain, head flung back in agony. Or was it triumph?

'Maybe your "complete disaster" will turn out to be the thing which sets you free, Annie.'

That's a bit pat, she thought.

'If your aim in life was not to offend, you've failed. Spectacularly.' She flinched. 'You can give up trying to please everyone now and please yourself instead.'

'But aren't we supposed to try to please God?'

'He might be pleased to see you happy.' A bell started to chime. 'Will you stay for the Eucharist?'

As the train carried her away the whole thing began to feel unreal. She thought about the Samaritan woman at the well. I know how she felt. *Come see a man who told me all that I ever did.* Did Gabriel have genuine telepathic powers, or was he just a very shrewd judge of character? Perhaps the two weren't so far apart. 'Your "complete disaster" will turn out to be the thing that sets you free.' If only it would. If only she could stop cowering the whole time and dare to stand up straight.

That evening she went with her friends to the cinema. Edward had somehow broken his hand rowing and didn't feel like coming. Annie feared she had mortally offended him and his injured hand was just an excuse. Still, the film was enjoyable, exactly the kind of escapist comedy she needed. And it had Sebastian Penn in it, who was 'such a good actor', as Isobel could be heard remarking to Muriel as they walked home. Good actor be buggered, Isabella might have said. Have him oiled and tied to my bed at once. There was something about him that reminded Annie of Will. The smile, perhaps.

When she rang Will's doorbell the following afternoon she reminded herself of her resolve to be less cowardly. Would she ever stop being terrified of him? He opened the door.

'Your face!' she cried out. Black eye, row of stitches under the eyebrow.

'You told Edward, then,' he said.

CHAPTER 22

'Oh, no! But he promised!' wailed Annie. 'Will, I'm sorry.'

'Yeah, yeah. Forget it. Coffee?'

She followed him to the kitchen wringing her hands. 'I made him promise! Are you all right?'

'Yeah. A few stitches, a night in hospital.'

'In hospital! Why?'

'Concussion. They keep you in for observation. I'm fine.'

'I'm sorry.'

'Stop bloody apologizing. You're not responsible for Edward's actions. He's been longing to punch me for about fifteen years. You gave him the perfect excuse. Did he break his hand?'

'How did you know?'

He grinned. 'Newton's third law of motion, honey child.'

She tried feebly to resurrect her failed O level physics. He made her some coffee and they went through to his oatmeal sitting room.

'So how are you doing, Annie?'

'Fine.' The smell of coffee reached her. 'Actually, I'm not,' she said boldly. 'I feel wretched and sick and tired. And I keep crying all the time. Why's pregnancy so lousy?'

'The unassumed is the unredeemed,' he replied. 'Our Lord didn't assume a woman's body, therefore female sexuality and childbirth are unredeemed. Or, medically speaking, it's your hormones, dear.'

Just for a second she was glad Edward had hit him.

'Have you told your parents?' he asked.

'No. I thought I might write to them.'

He nodded. 'Term ends on Wednesday, right? Where will you go?'

'I . . . I'm not sure. Ted and Penny have said I can go and stay with them, but . . .'

They fell silent. Annie tried to sip her coffee but gagged instead. She put the mug down.

Will was frowning. 'Look, wouldn't it be simpler all round if you moved in here, Annie? Until you know what you want to do. I've got two spare bedrooms.'

'Oh! But everyone . . . It would look . . .'

'It's a bit late to worry what it looks like. What have you got to lose?' She remembered Gabriel's words. Will reached out and took her hand. 'Sweetheart, I'm worried about you.' Her heart bumped at this unprecedented tenderness. 'I'm worried you're going to be lonely and miserable and short of cash but too scared to ask me for help. And I bet you'll feel you're imposing on Ted, won't you?'

She was forced to admit he was right. 'But I'd feel I was imposing on you.'

'I'm the bastard who landed you in it, for Christ's sake. Let me help.'

'Um . . .'

'Or am I impossible to live with?'

'Oh, no. It's not that. It's –'

'Give it a try, then. Please, Annie. I'd feel a lot happier.'

'Well, maybe I could.'

'Good. I'll collect you on Wednesday afternoon.'

'What if you meet Edward?'

'I'm not scared of Edward.' He caught her expression. 'I'm not! You bloody cheeky woman. How's Libby, by the way?'

'In the doghouse,' muttered Annie, with a blush.

He laughed. 'You're not by any chance expecting me to do the decent thing?'

'Of course not,' she said, flustered. 'Don't be silly.'

'Well, excuse me,' he drawled. 'Only asking.'

On the train home she went over this exchange. She couldn't decide if there had been a serious proposal lurking there and she had offended him. No – he'd told her he didn't believe in marriage. But why did he want her to live with him? On balance she decided it must be his sense of duty. She pondered the awkward ambiguity of living in her ex-lover's spare bedroom. Oh, why had she agreed? How on earth was she going to explain or justify it? Her thoughts turned to the college staff. Her friends. Edward. He would be outraged. She felt suddenly hot. After a moment she wondered if she was angry. Yes, she was. Bloody angry.

Buoyed by this novel sensation she went straight to his room to confront him. Unfortunately he was hosting an undergraduate Bible study and they ended up having a hissing argument in the corridor. Edward stuck to his guns: William had had it coming. Someone had to bloody well sort him out. Annie retorted that it was none of Edward's business, and they parted resentfully. She went instead to find Ted.

He sighed when she told him she was moving in with Will. 'If it doesn't work out, let me know. Our invitation still stands.' She nodded miserably in the face of his disapproval. 'You love him very much, don't you, Annie?'

'I don't know. Probably. Ted, I wish you'd give him another chance.'

'I hope I give everyone several chances.'

'Seventy times seven chances,' Annie reminded him.

'That's an awful lot of paternity suits,' mused Ted.

Tubby was not happy either. He felt he must press her to reconsider. It would make the issue of her continuing her training very vexed indeed. She would have to talk to her bishop about it.

A letter from her bishop arrived the following day. *I should be grateful if you would arrange a time to visit me. + Henry.* Annie wept into his expensive crested notepaper and made herself phone his secretary.

Only two days till the end of term. It would soon be over. But someone somewhere had been indiscreet, had shared Annie's situation with someone else as a matter for prayer, and suddenly the whole college knew. Groups fell silent at her approach. Eyes glanced furtively at her waistline. Tubby was forced to make a short announcement and insist on compassion and understanding, and to emphasize that none of us is above reproach. Annie burned with shame, but weren't Gabriel's words beginning to come true? She had failed spectacularly in her attempts not to give offence. Why try to salvage anything from the wreck? She packed her things and waited for Will to collect her.

It was a warm windy day when she arrived in Bishopside. She looked out of Will's spare bedroom window across an alley at the backs of terraced houses. Above a wall the wind tossed the syca-more branches till they danced. She watched the leaves turning their pale backs to the gusts. Homesickness crept over her. It was like the day she had arrived at her penfriend's house in Germany after a sleepless night on ferry and train with the other pupils. Now she was isolated in what felt like a stranger's house, as miserable as a frightened fifteen-year-old.

She was supposed to be asleep. Will was moving around down-stairs. At some point she was going to have to emerge and talk to him. The arrangement was beginning to feel far too civilized and grown-up for her. He expected her to make herself at home, but she felt like a difficult house guest there on sufferance.

Another problem was looming. She couldn't believe she'd failed to anticipate it. Libby, although banished to the doghouse, was nonetheless making her presence felt. Annie tried to block out her piteous whining. How on earth am I going to sleep at night with him in the next room? she asked herself. Any little thing might set off a new bout of baying in the back yard – the sight of the shiny bath taps, the smell of Johnson's baby shampoo. Why don't I just rush downstairs and tell him how I feel? But she knew that the resulting embarrassment would make it imposs-ible for her to carry on living with him. Why was she there, exactly? Was she hoping that he would gradually fall in love with her and want her to stay permanently? To share his bed? At this she was assaulted by such fierce lust that she almost howled out loud with Libby.

Time passed slowly for Annie in Bishopside. Her day had no structure. She could get up when she wanted and go where she liked. But this freedom was bondage. She had to make herself crawl out of bed. Each day she set herself little goals – join the library, visit the gallery, go for a swim. She knew that if she failed to go out one day she would never cross the threshold again. Agoraphobia stalked her. She fended it off bravely. Another swim, a walk in the park, anything to prove to Will that she was not depressed. Days passed without her having a single conversation with anyone but him. People in the street cast her friendly remarks in their baffling accent, but she had no one to talk to. Sometimes in the park she heard other southern accents and could barely prevent herself rushing over and startling the speakers with wild conversation. They were fellow ex-pats in an alien land. The Jewish family next door always greeted her when they passed. Annie watched in awe as the tiny pregnant mother – younger than Annie, surely – voyaged out, babe in the majestic pram, tot riding in a pram seat and two larger children swinging one on each side of the handle. The children were always neat and well behaved. How did she manage all this and never have a hair out of place? Part of the mystery was solved when it dawned on Annie that Hasidic women wore wigs, but she was still intimidated by such a demonstration of maternal competence. Part of her was wistful, too. She envied the women their close-knit community and companionship when she saw them chatting in the streets or outside the library.

Sunday came and went. Will asked her if she was intending to go to church and she shook her head. The ordeal of meeting a new group of people was too daunting, although she knew that this was precisely what she needed. He stared at her thoughtfully, but let it pass. The day felt hollow. How did agnostics fill the hours? Were all those heavy Sunday papers and bustling garden centres just there to fill the gap left in the national life by a redundant church?

'What would you like to do?' asked Will that afternoon. 'Shall we go to the coast?'

'If you like.'

'I'm asking what you'd like,' he said patiently.

'Well, yes, then. The coast would be nice . . .'

He drove in silence. She knew he was struggling to control his temper every moment they were together. Their conversations were always polite and restrained. He had not snarled at her once since she'd moved in, but she could hear the bomb ticking. She tried to be no trouble and saw this provoking him further. I can't help myself! she wanted to cry. What's happened? We used to have so much fun together. She could imagine his scathing reply, We used to have so much sex together, you mean. There was nothing left but the polite conversation of strangers.

They walked along the empty beach. It was a grey windy day, but someone was out surfing in the icy waves. They watched as he disappeared then emerged again riding the water.

'What if he got into difficulty?' said Annie

'Then I'd go in after him,' replied Will.

'But he's got a wet suit on,' she pointed out. 'You'd be worse off than he is. You'd both drown.'

'I'd still have to try.'

But what about me? You can't abandon me. She said nothing.

The surfer swam further out then rode back in perfect control. Annie and Will continued along the sandy shore. This is where he brought me that first Saturday, she thought. Libby let out a pitiful whine.

Another week loomed ahead. On Monday she decided to work on her novel. Instead she found herself fiddling around. At last I've got all the time in the world to write, she thought, but I can't bring myself to pick up a pen. She still hadn't got Barney and Isabella to the altar. It was partly because she was feeling sick. Mint imperials would for ever after be the taste of misery for her. She couldn't believe that pregnancy would ever feel like impending motherhood rather than a prolonged illness. I'm going to have a baby, she kept reminding herself. A thought lurked, too shameful to admit: I hope I miscarry. I don't want this child. It could have been a parasite growing inside her, sapping her energy and making her ill. I don't want to be a mother.

At the word 'mother' she gave a guilty start. She sat down at the kitchen table and began composing the long-deferred letter to her parents. Will had indicated that he didn't feel free to tell his parents until hers knew. What's the big problem? his expression seemed to say.

She'd got as far as 'Dear Mum and Dad, I'm afraid' when the

doorbell rang. She jumped. Not the window cleaners again! They had been once, demanding money with menaces. Frightening men with scarred faces and tattooed necks. She had a theory they went round the neighbourhood claiming to have cleaned the windows and people paid them five pounds to go away. She opened the door fearfully. It was Ingram with a crewcut and a bunch of roses.

'Ingram! How lovely to see you,' she exclaimed, astonished to find she meant it.

He came in and they engaged in a short bout of head-butting until he managed to plant a kiss on her cheek. 'Just the *briefest* of calls. We're all here doing our Bishopside placement.'

Ah, and he'd felt the need to contextualize his coiffure. 'I like your hair.'

'Thank you.' He ran his hand over it doubtingly.

They went through to the kitchen and she made coffee while he teased out the motif of power/powerlessness in post-industrial Tyneside. He was the same as ever, but Annie could no longer see why she had disliked him so much. He cared enough to visit her and bring news of her other friends. Tears welled up in her eyes.

'Isobel and Muriel would like to pop in, if that's at all convenient,' said Ingram. 'Ted's not here, of course. He and Dave will be spending a term here next year, instead.'

'Lovely. And Edward?'

'Ah, yes.' Ingram shifted in his seat. 'Edward finds the whole scenario a *leetle* complex, I fear. He hasn't quite owned his feelings yet.'

Edward, on the contrary, had owned them fully and frankly, telling Annie that he didn't wish to see her or Will until they'd got things on a proper footing. She'd been hoping he would relent – but when did Edward ever relent where principles were at stake?

Ingram finished his coffee and went, leaving behind him an intriguing nugget about realized eschatology in the inner urban arena for Annie to ponder. She returned to her letter instead.

I can't take much more of this. She was as lonely and miserable as Will had predicted she would be. Ingram's visit had forced her to admit how much she missed her friends. She longed to be reconciled to Edward, but it was hopeless. His rejection hurt her deeply. Her parents' reaction was going to be even worse. In the end she settled on a bald account with an apology for the unhappiness she had caused them. She went out and posted it before she lost her nerve.

It was Friday night and Will was out on call. The lack of sleep would make him bad-tempered tomorrow, but Annie was relieved he'd been out of the house for most of the evening. She went upstairs but could not sleep. Will came back at midnight and she listened to him going to bed. The police helicopter was hovering overhead. A voice boomed and the searchlight slid over Annie's window. It sent a worm of light slithering across her bed through the crack in the curtains. She went to the window and looked out. The beam was raking across rooftops as the helicopter circled the streets. Who was it hunting? She got back into bed. After about half an hour it throbbed away into the distance.

She still couldn't sleep. Perhaps she could spend the time with Barney and Isabella. Her notebook was downstairs in the kitchen where she had been trying to write earlier. She decided to risk the alarm – she could remember the code number, surely – and collect the book. She tiptoed down to the hallway and pressed the buttons. Her heart thumped as she reached gingerly for the door handle. Don't be silly, she told herself. It won't go off.

It did. The siren howled and Will came running. 'What the fuck are you doing?'

'I'm sorry. I must have –'

'Can't you remember a simple four-digit fucking number?'

'I'm sorry.'

'You've been using it for a week, for Christ's sake. What did you want?'

'A book.' She scuttled into the kitchen and grabbed it, hoping he wouldn't guess she'd been leaving the house each day without putting the alarm on. He made a visible effort to control himself.

'Look, I'm sorry, Annie. Ignore me. I'm knackered, that's all.' His hand touched her arm briefly. 'I'll change the number to something you can remember. Tomorrow. OK?'

Her voice trembled. 'Thanks.'

He set the alarm again and they went back upstairs. 'Sorry,' he said again. 'Are you all right?'

'It's not working,' she wept. 'I don't think I can go on living like this. I'd better go and stay with Ted.'

'OK,' he said, after a pause. 'If that's what you want.'

'It's just that . . .'

'Yeah. Look, Annie, there's nothing we can do now. We'll sort it out tomorrow, all right? But I've *got to sleep.*'

'Sorry.' But his door was already closed.

She curled up under the covers and cried bitterly. Nothing could be worse than this, she told herself. Even losing him altogether couldn't be as bad as the tension of living as they were. He'd never know what she really felt. Unless she told him before she left. I'll tell him tomorrow, she decided. But her tears would not subside. She tried to cry silently in case he could hear. I daren't disturb him again. But something desperate and Isabella-like took hold of her. What had she got to lose? A moment later she was hurrying to his room.

'Now what?' he snarled, turning the light on. 'This had better be good, Annie.'

'I – I – ' She got stuck on a hiccuping sob.

'*What?*' He stared with wild sleep-starved eyes.

'I love you. I want to stay.' I had nothing to lose, she told herself.

There was a pause. A slow smile dawned on his scowling face. 'Well, get in the fucking bed, then,' he said.

'What?'

'Get in.' He flung back the covers. 'And take off your rags, Cinderella. I'll bestow on you whatever you ask, up to half my kingdom. Though not my hand in marriage, admittedly.' He flung his arms wide like a mad Pentecostal preacher. 'Thank you, *Je*-sus!'

She stood bewildered. 'You mean – '

'I mean I love you. Passionately. Blasphemously, even – with my heart, soul, strength and mind. Not forgetting my body.' He was pulling her into bed and tugging at her grey T-shirt while she stuttered in shock at what she'd unleashed.

'But you never said.'

'You never asked. I didn't want to scare you off.' He was kissing her naked flesh. 'This last week has been hell, Annie. Having you in the house, but not being able to . . .' His tongue, his fingers! Mad glissandos of delight. She clung to him, weeping, and felt his tears on her face as he entered her.

'I thought you were tired,' she said afterwards.

He chuckled. 'Not that tired, honey child.'

They lay for a long time staring into one another's eyes.

'So you really want to make a go of this?' he asked. 'Live as man and wife and bring this baby up together?'

'Y – yes.'

'You don't sound sure.'

'It's just the . . . the baby. I can't quite believe in it, somehow. How big is it, do you think?'

'Depends how far on you are.' His hand was stroking her belly. 'Say ten weeks. Hmm. About two inches long. It'll have all its major organs by now. Eyes, fingers and toes.'

She thought about it. Two inches long. Maybe more. All its organs. 'What if I can't love it?'

He smiled. 'You will.'

Later she lay listening to his breathing as the sky lightened outside. One by one the birds began to sing. A new day dawning in Bishopside. Would it be the start of a new era? I'm living in sin, she thought. She wondered what God made of it all. For a moment he loomed wrathfully above her, his eye raking the streets in search of sinners. Then the image vanished. She reached out and touched Will's hand. His fingers closed round hers.

Outside the sky grew steadily paler. The sun rose over the quiet streets, shining like the grace of God on the righteous and the unrighteous.

CHAPTER 23

She woke the following morning to find him smiling at her.

'Good morrow, Mistress Comequickly,' he said and kissed her.

'And good morrow to you, my Lord Lackprong,' she replied unwisely. His lengthy retaliation made him late for work.

Annie stretched out in his bed and smiled. How would she fill the vast empty morning till he returned? You can stop trying to please everyone else now and please yourself, Gabriel had said. If she'd taken him seriously she might have spared herself weeks of misery. How much of her life had she wasted in her misguided attempts not to give offence? She thought about God again and wondered if he was pleased to see her happy, as Gabriel had suggested, even thought her situation was dubious. I really *am* happy, she thought. It was a daring idea, one that seemed to invite immediate divine retribution. But there was no thunderbolt, just a glorious day streaming in through the half-open curtains.

Annie stretched again and decided it was time to tie the knot for Isabella and Barney.

At last the day came. Isabella fed herself into her oyster satin. Hermione grumbled and plucked at her tight shot silk bridesmaid's dress. It was deep red to match Isabella's roses. The style had been Camilla's choice.

'Hey, you look stunning, Herm!' exclaimed Isabella in surprise.

'Hah,' replied Hermione bitterly, but she allowed herself to be kissed and fussed over for once.

226

Camilla twisted this way and that in front of the mirror, a cigarette drooping from her lips. 'My bloody tits are lopsided,' she complained. She was still hung over from the previous night and Isabella suspected she was regretting all those maudlin confidences. Interesting to know that Camilla had once made a very serious pass at Barney and had been, humiliatingly, turned down. No wonder they didn't like one another.

Isabella adjusted her vast rose-trimmed hat one last time, and they were off.

As she went down the aisle on her father's arm Isabella was amazed at the waves of goodwill that surged from all sides. All those smiling faces. She was a newly launched vessel and here were all her friends and family crowding the slipway to cheer her on. God bless this marriage and those who sail in her! And God did indeed seem to be beaming down on the proceedings. She reached Barney and he turned and gave her his wonderful slow smile.

They emerged in a swirl of confetti as the bells pealed joyfully. Isabella was made to be a bride. Self-effacement was not among her talents. Oh, heaven for one brief day! To revel unashamedly in the limelight, to queen and preen and float and gloat, to be, for all practical purposes, the only woman present.

It flew past too quickly. In no time they were sitting for the speeches. Isabella's father said the usual things about not so much losing a daughter as gaining a second row forward. Barney rose to reply, thanking everyone courteously and expressing his particular gratitude to his new parents-in-law for the lovely gift of their daughter. 'I look forward to unwrapping her later,' he concluded, amid cheers and scandalized expressions.

Not much later, as it turned out.

'Barney, we can't possibly!'

'Why not? We're married.'

She was still stupid with surprise as they got into the car and left for the honeymoon. The laughter and cheering faded behind them. Barney stopped in a quiet lane to remove some of the clanking cans and streamers. The silence of the countryside was vast. A bird sang in the hedge. Isabella felt herself telescoping dizzily downwards, shrinking from being the centre of the universe into nothing but a tiny dot in the landscape. Barney got back into the car and smiled at her. It's only him and me now, she thought.

They drove for a while in silence. That's it, thought Isabella. We've done it. We're actually man and wife. Her mind still boggled at Barney's precipitous consummation of their marriage. But she must remember he was a rookie. She would have to guide him. But how to drop a little hint without offending him?

'Bloody hell, Barney. That was a masterful performance back there.'

'Thank you.'

'Incredible. Straight in at the meat course. Maybe we could have something by way of a starter next time. You know, a bit of foreplay.'

'Foreplay,' he repeated thoughtfully, as though it was something he must remember to get along with the milk at the corner shop. She stole a glance to see if he was hurt and caught him wiping a grin off his face.

Annie paused and did a quick calculation. If they left the reception at four or five and it was a six or seven-hour drive . . . No, they'd have to break the journey to Northumberland. She promptly called up a beautiful old country hotel in the Peak District and ushered Barney and Isabella into the bridal suite.

'Right,' said Barney, picking Isabella up and flinging her onto the four-poster bed. 'More foreplay, was it?'

'Yes, please.'

He stripped her bare and set to work. It rapidly became clear that he needed no little hints from her. More hors d'oeuvres than she'd ever encountered in her life before. He hadn't learnt this at Latimer Hall. She whimpered and struggled, but he pinned her down, kindly but firmly, savouring, devouring, gorging until she pleaded with him to stop. At last he relented, rolled her over and pulled her to her knees.

'Wait!' she cried. 'I've never –'

'You have now,' he said.

'Oh, God!'

Like animals! And what with her squealing and him grunting it was more like a barnyard than a bridal suite. He ended with a mad taurine bellow and collapsed, exhausted. She stared down at him. He lay like a felled oak diagonally across the bed. There was no rousing him. She was forced to curl up bewildered and laughing in the space he had left. It was a long, long time before she fell asleep.

She woke the following morning and reflected that, in more ways than one, she'd been had. He'd deliberately fooled her into thinking he was inexperienced. She sat up indignantly. He was lying on his back still fast asleep. She gazed into his beloved face. He looked so innocent and cherubic that she forgave him. She pulled back the covers stealthily. He didn't stir. Sunlight gleamed in the golden hair on his chest. She lay down and rested her head on his warm belly. She was eye to eye with Hardstaff himself, who was all primed and ready to go although Barney was still dead to the world. She dropped an indulgent kiss on him. At once a hand was on the nape of her neck encouraging her down. She recoiled. I can't! The hand fell away.

Isabella cursed inwardly. Why had she always projected such a worldly image of herself? She thought in dismay of all the other things commensurate with her supposed experience that he might expect her to perform. A tear trickled down her cheek.

'Are you crying?' asked Barney. She snuffled into his belly. 'Isabella! What's wrong?' He sat up and cradled her in his arms. 'Don't cry.'

'It's just that I'm not very experienced,' she bawled.

'I know you're not.'

She stared aghast. 'You mean I was lousy!'

'*Lousy?*' He laughed and stroked her hair. 'I mean, I've always known you were basically a good girl just pretending to be bad.'

'And you,' she accused, 'are a bad boy pretending to be good.'

He gave her an angelic smile and lay back down. 'A very bad boy indeed, I'm afraid.'

She glared at him. 'How many girls have you slept with?'

'I didn't exactly cut notches in the bedpost, Isabella.'

'Come on,' she persisted. 'More than ten?' His eyes went

round with shock, but this time she wasn't fooled. 'More than twenty?'

'I don't know. Possibly.'

'I bet you know exactly. What number was I? Go on.'

'I can't remember.'

'Perhaps this will focus your mind,' she said sweetly, taking a firm grip between his legs. 'How many?'

'Honestly, I can't – Aargh! Sixty-three. Let go!'

'*Sixty-three?*' Isabella had only managed five.

'Over eight years,' he pleaded. 'That's less than ten a year. It was before I was a Christian.'

'Did they all go down on you?'

'Aargh! About half. For God's sake, Isabella!'

'Hah!' She dealt him a final squeeze and let go. Was she going to be outdone by so many predecessors? She frowned thoughtfully as he moaned and clutched himself.

'That's probably what gave me the idea of going into the church,' he remarked when he'd recovered. 'Seeing so many women on their knees.'

She spluttered in shock. 'I cannot *believe* you just said that, Barney!'

'I always returned the compliment,' he assured her.

'No!' she shrieked, as his blond head disappeared between her thighs. Isabella had never been able to take cunnilingus seriously. It always struck her as an absurd party game, like trying to eat avocado with your hands tied behind your back, or something. But – 'Oh, Barney!' – she gradually began to see the point.

'Everything all right?' asked the hotel owner, as they checked out.

'Wonderful, thank you,' said Barney politely.

'You're telling me,' said Isabella.

Annie giggled as she went downstairs. She tried to eat some breakfast, but could only manage half a piece of dry toast. The post came and there was still no reply from her parents. You can just stew in your own juice, Anne, her mother would be thinking. The long silence was all part of the punishment. 'Ring them, then,' Will had suggested. 'Take control.' She went out for a walk, sucking another mint imperial.

As the day passed her euphoria seeped away. By the evening she was battling, as usual, with tears.

'What's wrong, sweetheart?' asked Will, when he got back from work.

'Oh, I don't know. I just feel . . . I know I should be happy, but . . .'

'Why should you?'

'Well, because . . .'

'Look, you've lost one of the most important things in your life, haven't you?'

For a moment she couldn't think what that was. 'My vocation, you mean? But you never believed in it!'

'You did, though. What happened to it? Did it just vanish? How are you going to make your peace with God?'

'Stop it!' she cried. 'It's bad enough without you —'

'Come on, you've got to face it some day, Annie.'

'I *know*! I can't get my mind round it. It's all too much.'

'Why don't you go to church? Find some nice vicar to talk to.'

'Maybe I will.' Her voice lacked conviction.

'Please, Annie,' he wheedled, taking her hand. 'For my sake. I feel like such a shit when you're miserable. Like I've robbed you of your salvation.'

'All right,' she said crossly. 'You're shameless.'

'That's me,' he agreed.

The following day was Saturday. Annie set out to find a church of the right flavour. The streets near Will's house were full of Jewish families going to synagogue in their Sabbath best. The nearest church didn't look particularly evangelical. It was locked so she couldn't snoop around and peer at the hymnbooks and décor to gauge the churchmanship. She wandered towards the town centre. This was the place she had found so depressing the day Tubby had sent her to look round. Now she sensed a cheerful stoicism in the air as people went about their shopping.

Up above a little aeroplane was circling busily, towing a long ribbon across the blue sky. Annie squinted up. A rock concert. She ran the back of her hand across her forehead.

'Warm enough for you?' called an old woman at the bus stop.

'Yes, lovely, isn't it?' replied Annie, conscious of her southern accent. On impulse she drew closer. 'Is there a church round here at all? I wanted to go tomorrow.'

Immediately three or four other people in the queue joined the conversation. Annie listened to a lament for lost churches. All those lovely old buildings. All pulled down. Terrible, terrible. They'd pulled the old St James down. St Mary's near the bridge, well, that was an auctioneer's now. Ee, it's a shame. Lovely old church. Before it was burnt. Ee, terrible, terrible. Holy Trinity, just over there on the High Street, that was closed, too – No, it wasn't – It was, it was a community centre – Aye, but the old bit was still a church, our Kayleigh was christened there. Oh, aye, aye, she's right.

'Well, perhaps I could try there,' said Annie, who was struggling with nausea again.

'Just down there on the High Street. Opposite Woolworths.'

She thanked them for their help.

'It'll be locked, mind,' they called after her.

The church turned out to be Victorian. She crossed the road for a better look. Part of it was obscured by scaffolding, but seemed very old indeed, possibly Norman. The Victorian bit had been tacked onto the side. There were builders up on the scaffolding who might – or might not – bawl down at her. This unpredictability was their menace. She told herself not to be so feeble. While she hesitated one of them began to sing full-bloodedly from the roof top.

'"Amazing grace! How sweet the sound . . ."' He sang slowly with a great deal of semi-satirical ornamentation. '"Tha-at saved a-a-a wretch li-ike me"'. Annie listened. He seemed to be revelling in his voice, or the view, or the glorious day. She was depressed at the thought that he sounded as if he knew more of the grace of God than she did. The other men began to bay like wolves. There was laughter and shouts in the baffling local accent.

'I once was lost, but now am found.
Was blind bu-u-ut now I-I see.'

Annie scurried beneath them and tried the door. It was locked as the women had predicted.

A face looked over the edge of the scaffolding. 'Do you want in, pet?'

'It's not important.'

But the man was already roaring up to the roof. 'Vicar! Vicar!'

A dark man in his thirties came swinging down the scaffolding. He was wearing a hard hat and overalls. Clearly not the vicar, but he was in possession of a bunch of keys.

'"I've got the keys to the door . . ."' He was the one who'd been singing.

'Sorry to be a nuisance,' began Annie. 'I only wanted –'

'Nee bother.' He unlocked the door. 'Ha'away in.' He held it open with a strong brown arm. Her eyes skimmed the tattoos and glanced timidly up into his face to thank him. He grinned. Too close! Too good-looking!

'Thanks,' she gasped.

The door swung shut. She stood in the gloomy silence listening to the pounding of her heart. It was a small, plain building. Various Northumbrian saints stared down from the stained-glass windows. She stared back at them blankly, seeing instead the man's dark face and piratical smile. *Libby! Walkies*. But Libby remained curled in her basket. Annie was impressed. She had never regarded Libby as a loyal hound. Perhaps she was ailing.

A moment later Annie had to race from the building and throw up humiliatingly in a small shrub. There were shouts. Before long the man with the keys was at her side handing her a glass of water. She let him lead her to a low stone wall where she sat trembling and clutching the glass.

'Sorry,' she said.

He asked her something. She waited, but the alien sounds failed to resolve themselves into a meaning. He repeated the question.

'I'm fine,' she hazarded. 'It's morning sickness.'

'Congratulations. When's it due?'

'Goodness. Um, I don't actually know.' He sat beside her and took his hat off. She looked away. He was too much to contemplate entire. She'd have to take him in in a series of glimpses.

'New round here, are you?'

Glance: overall arms tied round waist, vest showing off impressive muscles. 'Um, yes. I've just moved in with my . . . boyfriend.'

'What do you do, then?'

Glance: fading lovebite at base of throat. 'I was a student. Until . . .' She flapped at her stomach.

'Oh, aye. Surprise, was it?'

'Yes.' Row of gold earrings, cigarette behind ear. Still no sound from Libby. *I'm going to get you to the vet, girl.*

'What does he do? The boyfriend.'

She wondered suddenly at his questions. Was this simply the legendary northern friendliness? She drew away slightly. 'He's a doctor.'

'Where do you live, flower?'

'Um, not far from here,' she hedged.

One of the other men called down to him from the scaffolding. He called back. It was banter, but she couldn't follow a word of it. He had been modifying his accent for her.

'What's your name?'

'Annie,' she said reluctantly.

'Are you lonely, Annie?'

Her eyes flew nervously to his face.

'What's wrong?' he asked. Then he fished in his overall pocket and improbably pulled out a Filofax. 'Tell me your address and I'll visit you.'

'Oh!' she said in relief. 'You really *are* the vicar.'

His laugh rang out. 'Why, aye. I thought you were looking at me a bit funny.' He handed her one of his cards. *The Rev. John Whitaker, Vicar of St Columba's, Bishopside.*

'Oh!' she exclaimed again. 'You're —' Johnny Whitaker. The boozer and bonker. 'You trained at Coverdale. They still talk about you.'

'Never. It was ten years ago! What do they say?'

'That you . . . um, drank . . .' she settled on eventually.

'Just putting the fun back into fundamentalism,' he said.

'Anyway, that's all in the past. I'm a respectable man of the cloth these days.'

She risked another glance at his face and saw a frank honk-if-you-had-it-last-night type of sexiness that no vestments were going to render respectable.

'So you were at Jesus College, were you?' he asked.

She gripped the glass tightly. 'Coverdale, actually.'

There was a pause as this sank in. 'Oops!' He chuckled and put an arm round her shoulders. 'Well, God is good, Annie.'

Her eyes filled with tears, then to her amazement she began to find it funny. They sat outside the church laughing in the sunshine.

'Ee. What are we like?' he said. The *enfants terribles* of Coverdale Hall.

'Why are you dressed like a builder?' she asked, unable to contain her curiosity any longer.

'Because I'm a builder,' he replied. 'Or was, until –' He drew his finger across his throat as though a dog-collar were a garotte. 'Chunks of masonry keep falling on the old ladies. Thought I'd better take a look. Forty-five grand, it's going to cost. You're well out of it, pet.'

'I know.'

'So where do you live, then?'

She told him. He wrote it down, then sat tapping his pen on his teeth. 'This boyfriend. It wouldn't be Dr Penn-Eddis, would it?'

'You know him?'

His laugh rang out again. 'What did he say when you told him you were pregnant?' Before she could answer he reeled off a string of obscenities in Will's voice. She stared in astonishment. Even his facial expressions were right. 'I play him at squash,' said Johnny, in his own voice again. 'The only person in Bishopside whose language is worse than mine. Listen, will he be in now? Why don't I run you home and I can offer my congratulations?'

'Um . . .' said Annie, mistrusting the look on his face. But, as always, she let herself be overruled by a stronger personality.

She opened the front door wondering how Will was going to

react. She led Johnny through to the kitchen where he was read-ing the paper.

'Um, I've brought the vicar.'

He looked up and saw Johnny. 'Did you have to?'

'Will!' Annie cast him a pleading look.

'I hear congratulations are in order,' said Johnny, grinning broadly. Will returned to his paper disdainfully. 'Well, that's the last time I send the wife to you for family planning,' remarked Johnny.

Will gave him a withering glance.

'Coffee?' said Annie desperately.

'White with two sugars,' said Johnny sitting down. 'Bad-tempered bastard, isn't he?'

'And what does that make you, I wonder?' asked Will, with-out looking up.

'Ah, no. I'm a bastard with a bad temper. There's a big difference.'

Annie fumbled with the mugs. What on earth am I going to do?

'So,' said Will putting down the newspaper. Annie recognized the glint in his eye and knew he was about to pick a fight. 'Still smoking, I see.'

Johnny's hand went to the cigarette behind his ear. 'Aw, don't start, man.'

'And what about your cholesterol levels and drinking habits?' went on Will. Johnny rolled his eyes at Annie who was hovering, helpless. 'Don't you care about your heart? When are you going to get yourself down to my surgery for a health check?'

'The day you get yourself down to my church for confession,' replied Johnny. 'Or don't you care about your heart?' He put the cigarette between his lips and waggled it insolently.

'Just get out of my face,' snarled Will.

'Fair enough. Stay out of mine.'

This is awful, thought Annie. Awful. There was a long taut silence.

'Mind if I smoke?' asked Johnny.

Will laughed and the tension broke.

Annie made the coffee. The two men began talking about the

cricket like old friends. She watched Will and decided she might as well give up any attempt to cover for his unspeakable rudeness. Her efforts to apologize or mitigate would only make things worse.

'What time is the service tomorrow?' she asked Johnny.

'Ten,' he replied. Then he looked at his watch, swore and leapt to his feet. 'I'm late. The wife'll play war with me. No sex for two hundred years. Oh, shit, shit, *shit*.' This was said in Will's laconic drawl. Annie stifled a giggle. They went with him to the door.

'See you tomorrow,' he said, lighting his cigarette at last. 'Ah, that's good. That's so good.' Annie had never seen smoking turned into a lewd act before. Will was laughing again. 'That's a good woman you've got there, William. Take care of her.'

'I do.'

'Good,' said Johnny. 'I hope I'll hear you say that again one day. In a more religious setting.'

'Piss off, Vicar.'

Johnny went away laughing.

'Did you put him up to that?' asked Will, closing the door.

'No, honestly.'

'All my worldly goods, yes. Wedding bells, no. Got that?'

'What about forsaking all others?' she asked. 'Till death us do part?'

'I'll think it over.'

She felt a shadow of fear. 'You mean you might find someone else, then?'

'Would a wedding ring stop me? Look around you, honey child. Marriages are breaking up all the time.'

'I know. It's just that I feel a bit insecure.'

'Yeah, I'm sorry.' He put his arms round her. 'What can I say? I love you. I'm besotted with the idea of being a father.'

'You are?' she asked in surprise.

'Of course I am. Look, I could make all these rash promises about it being for life but we've got to be realistic. Let's have lunch.'

They made love in the afternoon. Afterwards he lay stroking her belly. Besotted, she thought. If only I shared his enthusiasm for parenthood.

'Chosen any names yet?' she enquired.

He laughed. 'Well, it'll have to be something simple. Penn-Eddis is bad enough without –'

'Excuse *me*. Who said it was getting your surname?'

'Hah.' He rolled away, pouting.

'I know,' she couldn't resist saying, 'what about Edward if it's a boy?'

'No way!'

'He might be pleased.'

'I don't want him to be pleased. I want him to apologize.'

'He won't.'

'Well, he should. Narrow-minded hypocrite. He's only pissed off because I did what he was too fucking pious to do.'

'Don't be ridiculous!' Her cheeks flamed. 'Edward's not interested in me.'

'You should hear him on the subject of your stocking tops some time.'

'Oh! The ball. But that was . . . He . . .'

Will laughed at her confusion.

'Stop it! Anyway,' she persisted, 'couldn't you make the first move?'

'No, I fucking couldn't. I did my bit getting the police to drop the charges.'

'What? He was arrested?'

'The receptionists called the police before I came round. Now shut up about Edward bloody Hunter.'

They lay without speaking for a long time. So it had happened while Will was at work. She pictured Edward charging into the practice like a mad bull, as Isobel put it, pawing the ground in the waiting room . . .

'Did he –'

'I said shut up.'

She slid a glance at him. He was scowling in much the same sulky way Edward had done when she said goodbye to him. Big babies. Annie turned away to hide a smile, but she wasn't quick enough. Will pinned her down and began exacting his own specialized brand of revenge. She was gasping and pleading with him when the phone rang. 'Leave it,' she begged.

But he reached across her laughing and answered it. Suddenly his expression became serious. 'Yeah. She's right here.' He handed Annie the receiver. 'It's your mother.'

Annie sat up and clutched the sheet to her as if her mother could see. 'Hello, Mum.' Will put his head next to hers to overhear.

'That was *him*, was it?'

'Yes. His name's Will.'

'The one who makes dirty phone calls,' said Mrs Brown.

'Shit,' mouthed Will.

'I never forget a voice,' said Mrs Brown. There was a silence.

Annie knew her mother was not lost for words, merely loading up and taking aim.

'Your father took it very badly, Anne. He's not a young man, you know. You might have thought of that. It's not me I'm worried about. I've not got much in my life to boast of, I know. I never went to college or had a fancy *career*, but at least I could be proud of my home and of bringing up a happy, decent family. Well, it looks like I can't even say that any more, doesn't it?'

Annie had been expecting this, but she couldn't stop the tears trickling down her cheeks. Will slid an arm round her.

'Mum, it's nothing to do with the way you brought me up. It's –'

'Oh, it's always the mother's fault. I know that, Anne. I know better than to complain. You've got your own life to lead.' Annie sensed the tirade heading off on a new tack. 'I'm just worried about you, that's all. You *modern* thinkers, you've got it all worked out. Living together. Free love. Pah! Nothing's free in this life, Anne. It's all very well to start with, but you've got no security. He'll be up and off and you'll be left holding the baby. Free love's not going to pay the bills, is it? That's why the Bible's so clear about marriage.'

'Mum –'

'This *man* of yours, he can do what he likes, can't he? You should've thought of *that* before you leapt into bed with him. How do you know you can trust him?' Annie winced to hear her own fears so tactlessly articulated. 'He's got no legal obligation to –'

Will took the receiver. 'Hello, Mrs Brown, this is William. Today's Saturday. On Monday I've got an appointment with – no, you bloody well listen to me – I've got an appointment with my solicitor. I'm changing my will. If I die Annie gets everything. I've already arranged for her name to go on my bank account and credit cards. Satisfied?'

Annie stared open-mouthed.

'Let me talk to my daughter,' Mrs Brown was saying. Annie took the receiver back. 'You make sure you get that in writing, Anne.'

'Mum –'

'Promises are all very well. If he was a decent man he'd have married you by now.'

'What's so fucking wonderful about marriage?' muttered Will.

'Will, *please*.'

'Disgusting language!'

'Mum! If you'd only –'

'Well, it's your business, Anne. But I must say, I don't know how you put up with him. I suppose it's the *sex*.' Mrs Brown spat the word violently. 'Sex isn't everything, you know, Anne.'

Will took the receiver from Annie and laid it down softly on the bedside table. He began kissing her tears away. 'Forget her,' he whispered.

Annie could still hear her mother's voice ranting away tinnily five minutes later. Will was on top of her parting her thighs. *All very well, but what if. . .* Annie fumbled round and replaced the receiver.

CHAPTER 24

In contrast to Annie's parents, Mr and Mrs Penn-Eddis responded with joy to the news. They were much too civilized to express any dismay that their eldest son had impregnated an ordinand. Annie was cordially invited with Will to attend the Penn-Eddises fortieth wedding anniversary party. The prospect filled her with dread. She suspected that they would prove to be one of those highly competitive and fearsomely gifted families that flourished in North Oxford, and that she would be completely out of her depth. They would wonder what Will saw in her, although they wouldn't dream of asking.

Her morning sickness gradually subsided and Annie began to feel brighter, although a vitriolic letter from her mother cast a blight over her life for several days. 'Your father wants to make one thing clear,' wrote Mrs Brown. 'You're not welcome in this house until you get married. He's a deacon, you know. What will the Church think?' There were two whole sides devoted to Will. The language was so violent that Annie went as far as shredding the letter and dropping it in the bin. Her mother's vicious words continued to stab away in her mind.

But at least she had caring, accepting friends. Isobel and Muriel visited one afternoon, bringing with them tiny baby clothes. Annie fingered the little vests incredulously. They really believe I'm going to have a baby, she thought. Muriel asked various midwifey questions about blood pressure, and Isobel remarked that Annie was very brave.

'I don't feel brave,' confessed Annie.

'But you're going through with it,' said Isobel, turning slightly pink. 'A lot of women wouldn't.'

Afterwards Annie pondered this. She had assumed that for Isobel there would be no question of abortion. Bravery was neither here nor there; one just got on with it.

Ted phoned a couple of times to chat. Annie was glad he'd be living in Bishopside next term. He had received a letter from Edward, who was spending the summer in Uganda. Ted was angry with him for being so judgemental. 'I hope he doesn't take such a hard line when he's in a parish,' he remarked.

Ted's daughters sent her a version of Marvell's 'To His Coy Mistress' ('Had we but wormwood enough and tin,/ This crab apple, Lady, were no criminology'). They also sent a collage of Will assembled from a body-building magazine, a gardening catalogue and a detail from a postcard of the Cerne Abbas giant. It was called 'Dr Sex Docs The Garden'. Annie giggled and left it lying around for him to find.

She knew her mother's accusations had riled him. He reiterated his belief that marriage was an outmoded institution, but was doing everything he could to set Annie's mind at rest. She was overwhelmed by the speed with which he was making over his worldly goods to her. Every day there were new forms to sign, new cheque books arriving. Everything was in their joint names, even the house and the cottage. She tried to reciprocate by putting his name on her savings account, but he refused to sign the form.

'You can take me to the cleaners if I bugger off with someone else,' he said. 'Reassure Mother on that score.'

But Annie felt crushed by it all. She couldn't bring herself to spend any of his money, despite his insistence that it was now hers as well.

'I feel I've got no right to it,' she told him.

He was reading a novel and giving her about an eighth of his attention. 'Mmm.'

'It's all so one-sided if you won't take my money. What am I giving you?'

'Your lovely self,' he drawled.

'Seriously, Will. I feel bad about it.'

He put his book down. 'You're giving me my child.'

'That's nothing,' she said crossly. 'I can't exactly help it, can I?'

'You could spit in my face and have it aborted.'

'Don't!' she cried. 'That's hateful, Will.'

'Then don't say it's nothing.' He returned to his book.

After a moment she gave up and opened her notebook to remind herself where Barney and Isabella had got to. She had just lost herself in their honeymoon when her book was thrust aside and Will was on his knees burying his head in her lap.

'Will! What's wrong?'

His fingers gripped hers tightly as though she might slip away from him. He tried to speak but couldn't. She watched helplessly. Then a sick possibility occurred to her: some other woman had done that to him – spat in his face and got rid of his child.

'Bad memories?' she asked.

He nodded against her stomach, still clinging to her. After a while he sat up and sighed. 'Ancient history,' he said. 'Just . . . Oh, just some woman I lived with in London. Years ago. The most god-awful relationship, looking back, but somehow I couldn't seem to extricate myself. I did in the end, of course.' He fell silent.

'Was she pregnant?'

'I don't know. She claimed she was. Faxed me at work with the news she'd had my disgusting foetus aborted.'

'Will!'

'Yeah. That's about the level we'd reached.'

'I'm truly sorry.'

'Well.' He shrugged. 'As I said – ancient history.' She put her arms round him and hugged him tight.

'Um, I know you find it difficult, but do you have anyone you can talk to? Are you still seeing –'

'My father confessor? Yeah. Once in a while.'

'He's a therapist?'

'Of a kind. He's a Franciscan.'

'Not . . . not Gabriel? That's who the Warden sent me to see.'

'Shit!' He was furious. 'So the bastard's heard both sides of the story.'

'He's nice!' protested Annie.

243

'*Nice?* He's got the manners of a fucking rattlesnake. He spots a weakness, then *voom!*'

'Well, he was kind to me.'

'Hah.'

Annie remembered suddenly how Gabriel had laced his hands together like two halves of a puzzle. She found it reassuring that there was someone who knew them both, whose mind encompassed both their stories.

Will hugged her close again. 'I need you so much, Annie.'

This admission was worth more than all his worldly goods. Annie had never felt needed before in her life. At best she'd felt tolerated, provided she didn't make a fuss. Her spirits rose.

She was still lonely, however. Church had not provided the immediate circle of friends she had been expecting. The congregation was friendly but she found no real kindred spirit. There was some comfort in attending worship again, but it was also painful. She felt left out and judged during communion as the rest of the worshippers went up to the altar. Each week she was surprised by the pang of regret she felt that she would never be a minister herself.

Will showed no interest in going to church with her, and she hesitated to suggest it. He would hate it, Annie felt sure. She guessed his taste was for sung eucharists in exquisite cathedrals. Johnny's informal style was stamped across the liturgy and even Annie, who had a professional interest in these things, never felt quite safe. You can't do that! You can't say that! she kept wanting to cry. But he seemed to get away with it. The congregation accepted him and he was achieving the impossible: getting some of the 'unchurched' into church.

But each Sunday was harder than the last. 'Don't go if it makes you feel miserable,' snapped Will. Johnny was aware of her feelings, however. He invited her round to the vicarage. Annie wondered if this was just a pastoral chat or whether she would be introduced to his wife who never went to church. Perhaps she was about to meet the friend she needed so badly.

It was early evening. As she walked across Bishopside she tried to picture what Johnny's wife might be like. 'Curvaceous blonde' sprang somehow to mind. Someone with the same unabashed attractiveness as the vicar himself. An unmistakable modern boxlike parsonage came into view. It was the only detached house for miles around and Annie found it mildly shocking to come upon it like this after streets of terraced housing and council flats. She rang the doorbell. She had just begun to ask herself if she'd got the wrong day when she glimpsed movement in the hallway. The door opened and a tall thin woman waited with an unfriendly stare.

'Um, hello,' said Annie, her eyes veering away from the woman's nose ring. 'I'd arranged to see your . . . the vicar.'

'He's not in.'

Annie hesitated. 'Um . . . I'm afraid I'm a bit early.'

There was a silence.

'You can come in and wait, if you like,' said the woman grudgingly.

'No, no. I'll come back later.'

The woman appeared to have some swift debate with herself. She opened the door a fraction wider. 'No, come in.'

Annie crept over the threshold. 'Thanks. If you're sure . . .'

The woman turned and Annie followed her, envying the long thick black plait that hung down her back. She led Annie through to the sitting room and gestured for her to sit. Annie watched another fierce inner struggle take place. The woman had an oddly expressive face with intense pale grey eyes.

'If you're busy . . .' began Annie, guessing what the struggle was about. The woman was evidently tempted, but not quite rude enough to abandon Annie.

'Do you want a drink?'

'Um, just water, if that's not too . . .'

She had already left for the kitchen.

Annie looked round the room. It was crowded with vivid bursts of colour. She ran her eyes round greedily after the austerity of Will's décor. Rich brocade curtains and cushions, huge brass candlesticks, dark carved wood – had someone been pilfering from the church? The plants were so vast that a machete would come in handy for reaching the bookshelf. There was a sumptuous savagery not usually encountered in a vicarage. It was curiously at odds with the dour brooding abstracts on the walls.

The woman came back and handed Annie a glass of water. 'He said he'd be back at five,' she said abruptly. It was nearly six.

'I'm sorry if I've interrupted anything,' said Annie.

The woman gave a twitching shrug and began pacing the room and glancing out of the window. Annie sipped the water and watched her. She was wearing faded jeans and a paint-stained black T-shirt. Was that a tattoo on her upper arm? Her feet were bare. A strand of silver hair began at her forehead and Annie could follow it weaving in and out down the length of the plait. She began to feel sure she knew her from somewhere. Hair like ebony, skin like snow. Someone in a fairy tale. She was not exactly beautiful, but Annie couldn't take her eyes off her as she moved edgily round the room. The silence was starting to get awkward.

'I'm Annie, by the way,' she tried.

'I know.'

Silence again. I must introduce her to Will, thought Annie. They'd get on like a house on fire.

In the end a grumpy admission was forthcoming: 'I'm Mara Johns.'

'Oh! You were at Cambridge.'

So what? said Mara's expression.

'I think we were in the same college. In a different year, though.'

'I don't remember.'

This promising avenue of small-talk was cut off abruptly. Annie sipped her water again. Oh, well. So this wasn't the bosom friend she'd been hoping for. It was a warm close afternoon and she was feeling drowsy. She battled with a yawn.

'Sorry,' she said. 'I'm always sleepy at the moment. I'm pregnant.'

'I know,' said Mara again.

'Do you have any children?' asked Annie, beating the silence back valiantly.

'No.' This was clearly a blunder. Mara was biting her lip and tugging at a strand of her hair.

Annie coloured. 'Um, so what do you do? I mean —'

'Paint.' Mara jerked her head at the dour pictures.

'Um,' said Annie. She tried to summon an intelligent response. 'I'm afraid I'm pretty hopeless at abstracts.'

'I do other stuff, too.' She pointed to another bit of wall.

Annie turned. It was a pencil drawing of two young men. She crossed to take a better look.

'Oh!' exclaimed Annie. 'Wonderful. Are they brothers?'

'Yes.'

Annie studied them. They were undeniably beautiful. The older stared out in arrogant contempt, the younger in smug, cat-like self-satisfaction.

'Do they like it?' she asked.

'No,' said Mara. Annie glanced and caught a broad toothy smile. It was instantly suppressed.

'Does it have a title?' asked Annie.

The smile flashed again. ' "Big Shit and Little Shit." '

Annie giggled.

'They're William's cousins,' added Mara.

'Really?' Annie studied the picture in surprise. There was a likeness. The older brother, particularly.

'I knew them in Oxford,' said Mara.

'Do you know Will's family, then?'

'A bit.' Then she scowled as though she'd been betrayed into silly chattering.

'Have you done any others I could see?' asked Annie.

Mara muttered something. At that point they both heard the front door.

'Sorry sorry sorry!' said Johnny as he came in. He shot himself in the head with an imaginary pistol. 'The late Johnny Whitaker.' He grinned at Annie. 'Hello, flower. Has she been looking after you?'

Mara was wearing a no–sex–for–two–hundred–years expression.

'You'll not believe this,' said Johnny, slipping out his dog-collar and undoing a few buttons. 'I'd've been on time, only –'

'Don't even bother,' Mara said as she left the room.

'Fetch us a beer, pet,' called Johnny after her. A door banged. 'Lovely girl, my wife. So how's Annie?' He laughed at her anxious face. 'Don't worry. That's mild. She must like you.'

'How can you tell?'

But he only laughed again, and began asking her how she was settling in. She decided to take her cue from him and regard Mara's behaviour as ordinary. They talked for a few minutes, then to Annie's astonishment Mara came back in and handed him his beer. 'Aw, thanks, sweetie.' He caught her fingers and smiled up at her.

Annie looked away embarrassed. There was a short pause.

'Listen, I'll show you the pictures another day,' said Mara.

'Lovely,' replied Annie.

Mara muttered again and left.

'There you are, pet,' said Johnny. 'She likes you.' He opened his can and drank and asked how she was keeping. They chatted for a while about babies, and she thought she could detect a wistfulness in his tone. 'Now then,' he said, getting down to business. 'Why are you excommunicating yourself?'

'Oh! Goodness. Because I'm living in sin, I suppose. I thought you wouldn't want to give me communion.'

'I operate an open policy. If they're willing to come, I'm willing to accept them.'

'Whatever?'

'That seems to be the line God takes.'

'Mmm,' said Annie doubtfully.

'Well, he accepts me. He can't be that picky.' He lit a cigarette.

'Rubbish. I'm sure God –'

'Guess what I do on Saturday nights,' he interrupted.

'Um . . .' Annie banished her first thought. 'Write your sermon?'

'Exactly. Now, fifteen years ago my idea of a good Saturday night was to get drunk, get my leg over – unless I passed out first. Maybe smash a couple of faces in. Nick a car. And if I didn't get locked up, well, that was a *really* good Saturday night.'

'Which do you prefer?' asked Annie.

He leant his head back and blew a thoughtful smoke ring. 'Hmm. Tricky one. Sermons, I guess. No hangover.' The ring floated across the room. 'You know what I'm saying, though.'

'Yes. But maybe great sinners make great saints,' said Annie. 'I was only ever a rather feeble sinner.'

He grinned.

She remembered her circumstances and blushed. 'I meant . . .'

'I know.' He patted her arm. 'Don't be a stranger, flower. Come up for communion.'

'It's just . . . Will –' Annie broke off. Johnny took her hands. 'I think he loves me, but he won't hear of marriage. I keep trying to tell myself it doesn't matter, that it's the quality of the relationship that counts, but . . . It sounds so old-fashioned. I can't tell if he's really opposed to marriage, or if it's just because of bad experiences in the past. He's been involved with some really horrible women. Maybe he can't cope with commitment.'

'You'll be all right,' he said. 'He's a good man. You'll be fine.' Somehow his optimism began to infect her. 'God's good, Annie.' She looked up into his brown eyes. 'Trust me,' he said gravely. 'I'm a priest.'

She giggled.

'So what's going to happen to your vocation?' he asked.

'I've abandoned it.'

'How do you feel about that? Ee, I sound like a bloody therapist.'

'Most of the time I feel relieved,' she admitted. 'Perhaps I never had a vocation at all. But the sense of calling seemed so strong at the time. I don't know. I just can't seem to *hear* God any more.'

'Vocations don't just go away, pet. They lie low, maybe. He'll be in touch. What are you doing with your time at the moment?'

'Um, writing, I suppose.' She found herself telling him about her novel.

'Does Will know about it?' asked Johnny.

'No.' Annie was overcome by guilt that she hadn't told him. This was followed by a cold fear that she had been disloyal by confiding in Johnny. 'Um, what I said earlier . . .'

'All in confidence,' Johnny assured her. 'I know, why don't we form a self-help group? For people with bloody impossible demanding partners.'

Annie glanced fearfully at the door.

'Listen,' said Johnny, 'if you ever want a job in the church, just say the word. I could do with a pastoral assistant.'

'But the Bishop . . .'

'He belongs to the if-it-moves-bless-it school of thought.'

'But wouldn't your congregation object?'

'You'll give a whole new meaning to the term "lay worker".'
He grinned at her outraged expression. 'Bear it in mind, pet.'

She thought about him as she walked home, remembering his voice singing 'Amazing Grace' from the church top. She'd never met anyone so full of himself and yet so full of God at the same time. The two were supposed to be mutually exclusive in Annie's theology. Self must be banished and Christ must reign as Lord in every last nook and cranny of your life. *If he's not Lord of all then he's not Lord at all*, ran the slogan. And yet if Annie were God she'd have a soft spot for people like Johnny, be secretly proud of them in fact, and not want them to stop being themselves. Johnny was so brimful of belief. God is good. You'll be fine. It was impossible not to be swayed.

Libby, heel! Annie hurried home and channelled her energies swiftly into her novel before Libby could lollop off and mate with the vicar's trouser leg. After all, it was high time to rescue Isabella and Barney from the hotel car park. This was done easily enough. *At last they reached the cottage* . . . It was Will's cottage in Northumberland, but on a wicked impulse Annie filled it with flowery settees, festoon blinds and little china bowls of peach-scented pot-pourri. She gave the double bed a plush headboard and, as an afterthought, tossed a few heart-shaped satin cushions on the cover. There.

Isabella began to realize that she was on a steep learning curve. She wondered if Barney had got hold of the wrong end of the stick somewhere along the line and was under the impression that the national nookie average was two or three times a night, rather than a week. She could hardly sit down.

'Barney, I *can't*. You're a wonderful lover, but I'm really, really sore.'

'But I'll be really, really gentle . . .'

Bastard, she thought afterwards. What am I going to do? I've married a bloody sexoholic! She was not a girl to take it lying down, however. She caught him the next afternoon and tied him naked to the bedroom chair. He submitted to this whim tamely enough, confident he could escape at any point if he really wanted to. But Isabella had not been a Girl Guide for nothing.

She painted her lips slut red and knelt in front of him. Hardstaff nodded approvingly. After a long drooling moment Barney surreptitiously tested the knots. Isabella laughed. He made a more determined attempt. Finally the truth dawned.

She kept him teetering on the brink for nearly an hour. He raged and swore and struggled, but it was all in vain. She went to work with her lipstick, painting his face and chest like a Cherokee brave and putting rings round his totem pole. Sweat trickled down his body as he strained against those badge-earning knots.

'Darling, you're all hot and bothered! Are you thirsty? Let's open some bubbly.'

'I don't want any, damn it,' he said, through gritted teeth.

But she made him drink from the bottle till the champagne surged from his lips and ran in icy rivers from throat to groin.

'Oops!' cried Isabella. 'We don't want to waste any, do we?' She followed the path with her tongue down his sweating belly. By now his curses had turned to whimpering.

'Please, please, oh, please, Bella.'

In the end she was merciful.

He lapsed like a good cleric into the language of prayer: 'Oh, God. Oh, God-oh-god-oh-god, Isabella! *Aaah!*'

Hmm, thought Isabella dispassionately, taking a swig of champagne. So that's what all the fuss is about. She untied him. He collapsed on the bed a broken man.

The phone rang. Annie jumped with a guilty giggle to answer it. 'Hello?' she said.

There was a silence, then a man said, 'Have I got the wrong number, I wonder?'

'I don't know,' said Annie. The voice was very familiar, but she couldn't place it.

'I was wanting Dr Finlay. Is he no' there, Janet?'

'Oh! Um, he's out, I'm afraid. Can I take a message?'

'It's his brother Seb. But that's enough about *me*, he says implausibly. Who are you, darling?'

'I'm Annie.'

'Hello, Annie. And you're what? A colleague? The Avon lady? A live-in lover?'

'Um, well, the latter, I suppose.'

'Good God! The dead walk, rivers run up hill, Orlando has a love life! This is wonderful. When am I going to meet you? Are you coming to the family festivities?'

'Yes,' she said, assuming he meant his parents' fortieth wedding anniversary.

'Please don't worry. We're all painfully nice. You mustn't be offended, though, if I tell you you've picked the runt of the litter. We're all bigger and better-looking than he is. Even Babe. You're not cross, are you?'

'No. Do you have his sunny disposition, though?'

He laughed. I'm sure I know him from somewhere, thought Annie. 'I love you already. Listen, would you do me a huge favour and ask him to ring me when he's back?'

'Yes. Um, I'm afraid I've forgotten your name.'

There was a surprised pause. 'Sebastian. The luvvie one.'

'I'll tell him.'

'Angel.' He hung up.

Annie picked up her biro to scribble Will a note. She'd got as far as 'Your brother' when the penny dropped. I've been talking to Sebastian Penn! She let out a short scream. That wonderful voice! Of course. Familiar from countless films and coffee commercials. And Will had said nothing. His younger brother was one of the most outrageously successful actors around and Will had not seen fit to mention it to her.

CHAPTER 25

She waited for Will to come home, unable to remember where he'd gone and when he'd promised to be back. Ten o'clock came and went and she became anxious. She got ready for bed. The sound of distant ambulance sirens chilled her. What if he'd met with some kind of accident? By eleven o'clock she was unable to shake off her morbid fantasies. If he's not in by midnight I'll call the police. But what if the police were already on their way? Footsteps on the path, a ring on the bell, two officers on the doorstep. 'Miss Anne Brown? Can we come in?'

'Don't be ridiculous!' she scolded herself as her tears brimmed over. Then came the blessed sound of his key in the lock. She flew downstairs.

'What's wrong?' he asked. 'Have you been choosing my funeral hymns?'

'It's not funny! Where have you been?'

'Got held up at the drug abuse centre. I do a stint there on –' He broke off, seeing her tears. 'Annie! I'm sorry.' She sobbed in his arms. 'Listen, another time you can always get me on the mobile phone. I should've thought.'

They went up to bed.

'Your brother phoned,' she said, remembering. 'He wants you to ring back.'

'Which one?'

'Sebastian. You might have told me, Will.'

'Why? You've never been remotely interested in my family.'

'I have! I just thought you wouldn't welcome questions.'

'All right,' he conceded grumpily. 'I can see that.'

'So,' she said, only a few months behindhand, 'tell me about your family.'

'Well, my father's a vicar in North Oxford,' he began. 'My mother does endless committee work and so on. She's also training to be a therapist – typical North Oxford matriarch. They've been there about thirty years. I'm the oldest. Ben's next. He's a book dealer, married to a barrister. They have two vile daughters aged six. Twins. Then there's Seb, who you know about. Then Jake, who's a priest. Then Babe – Robin – who's in his last year at school. He was a happy accident.'

'And they're all bigger and better-looking than you are.'

He chuckled. 'But I can beat any of them in a straight fight.'

'What if all four jumped you at once?'

'It's been known. Still, my self-defence is pretty good.' He stroked her cheek and smiled. 'You needn't worry about me out there on the mean streets.'

'I do, though.'

'I know. Tell about your family, then.'

She did so, conscious that she was embarrassed by her background.

'I look forward to meeting them,' said Will.

'Um, I'm afraid we're not welcome. Until . . . unless . . .' She told him about her mother's hateful letter.

'I see.' He lay frowning at the ceiling.

'I'm really sorry, Will. It's not personal. They just disapprove.' Why do I have to have such a dreadful family? She blushed with shame.

'Are they disowning you?' he asked eventually.

'No, no. I expect they'll come round,' said Annie bravely.

'Yeah. A grandchild is a great bargaining tool.' He fell silent. 'How was the vicar?' he asked, after a while.

'Fine.' She told him about Johnny offering her a job.

'Good. Take it. Then I won't feel such a shit. Did you meet his wife?'

'Yes. She chattered unselfconsciously for about half a second.'

254

He laughed. 'I think I blundered,' she went on. 'I asked her if they had children. Do you know if . . .'

'Can't comment. She's a patient of mine.'

This confirmed her suspicions. 'She's got a picture of your cousins on the wall. "Big Shit and Little Shit", she calls them.'

He laughed again and turned the light out. She could tell he was lying awake, thinking. She couldn't sleep, either, and decided to redeem the shining hour by planning her next chapter.

For the first month or so Isabella enjoyed being a curate's wife. There wasn't much to do other than read novels and tackle the hideous house and make love to her gorgeous husband. The wonderful thing about parish ministry was that Barney was in and out of the house several times a day. Isabella suspected he carried a furniture inventory in his mind and was ticking items off one by one as he rogered her on them.

But before long tensions began to emerge. Barney worked too hard. There was never enough money. Isabella developed a passionate hatred of the swirly carpet. Barney was of the opinion that carpets were expensive and they could put up with it for two years. He came back to bare boards one afternoon.

'I'm going to have it sanded and varnished,' announced Isabella.

'How much will that cost?'

'Oh, I don't know. A hundred quid?'

'Isabella, we don't have a hundred quid.'

'Well, I'll do it myself then,' she replied.

She did. It was far harder than she'd supposed, but stubbornness kept her going. Nothing, however, would persuade Barney to spend a penny on getting that essential Persian rug. Isabella seethed each time she crossed the bare floor.

The summer ended.

'Well,' said Barney with a sigh. 'That's the slack period over.'

And he meant it. He grew busier with every passing week. Sermons, services, visiting, youth groups, school assemblies, meetings. Endless bloody meetings! Isabella vowed to smack the head of the next idiot who remarked to her that clergy only worked one day a week. Sometimes he was out five evenings in a row. She began to wish he had a nine-to-five job. Something he could leave behind and say, 'That's it for the day.' But there were always other things he should be doing. Worthy things. Old ladies wanting home communion, Bible commentaries to read, people dying of cancer. And above all – God. How was she supposed to compete with God for her husband's time and attention? I don't get a bloody look in, she stormed inwardly as she stood at the altar rails. But then she felt guilty for even thinking such things.

She tried to pray for patience. Barney was under pressure and her complaints would only add to his burden. Resentment found outlets in trivial things, however. Why did he leave his bloody dog-collars lying about the kitchen? Why couldn't he put the sodding answer machine on during meals?

'Why do you have to clutter up the dining-room table?' she snapped one day. 'You've got a study, haven't you?'

He looked up from his sermon preparation. 'But I want to be with you.'

'No, you don't, you wheedling prick,' she said. 'You just want your own way.'

He sighed like a martyr and carried on reading.

This was the last straw. 'Stop treating me like your mother!' she yelled.

'Stop behaving like my mother, then.'

'It's not me, you bastard! It's you. You just expect me to slot into your life. You haven't made a single concession to the fact that you're married, have you? The only difference is that you don't have to pay a cleaning lady any more and you get to have sex.'

'I also get to work my butt off and pay the bills.'

Isabella was so angry she almost felt her eyes bulge. 'Fuck you!'

She stormed out, got into the car and drove to the nearby town. I'm bloody well going to buy a new dress, she thought, slamming the car door. She strode to her favourite shop, which sold the kind of smart, sexy, expensive clothes she liked best. But by the time she reached it she was feeling like a silly spoilt bitch. Poor Barney! She stared mournfully at her reflection in the plate glass and vowed to become a better clergy wife. A notice caught her eye: *Full time Sales Assistant required. Apply within.* Twenty minutes later she walked out with a job.

If Barney was pleased by this development, he didn't say so, but for the next few months they rubbed along quite happily. Isabella got used to the mindless tedium and backbreaking hard work of her job. Christmas approached. She proved to be extremely good at persuading men to part with huge sums of money and reigned supreme in Lingerie.

Barney, of course, was insanely busy in the run-up to Christmas. Isabella watched him one evening as he stood in the kitchen bolting down a sandwich, tying his shoelaces and answering the phone simultaneously. 'Just a minute! Don't I know you from somewhere?' she asked.

He got back after midnight, too tired for sex.

'I'm worried about you,' said Isabella.

'Things will calm down in the New Year,' he promised.

He began double-booking himself. Isabella had to field phone calls from people waiting for him to arrive and take their meeting when she knew he was miles away with the youth group. He was so unhappy that she bit her lip and didn't complain when he couldn't come to her work's Christmas party, although weeks before he'd promised he would.

But at last it was over. They drove up to his parents' house after the Christmas morning service. Barney spent almost the entire holiday asleep on the sofa.

Mrs Hardstaff surveyed her poleaxed son sardonically. 'So how does married life suit you, Isabella?'

'It's wonderful,' said Isabella fiercely.

'If you're married to a sweet-tempered man,' agreed Mrs Hardstaff, with a smirk.

New Year came. Isabella made another resolution to be a better clergy wife. After all, she had known he was ordained when she married him. It was time to knuckle down and support and enhance his career in every way she could. This meant mundane things like not giving a derisive snort when the Crimplene ladies told her she was a lucky woman. It meant refraining from saying, 'I'm not his bloody secretary,' when people expected her to know Barney's movements or take complex phone messages for him. It meant not nagging when he was out every night and worked on his day off.

But these were all negative things. Isabella longed to do something positive. One evening inspiration struck. She rang the Bishop and invited him and his wife for dinner.

'You're kidding,' said Barney when she told him. 'Tell me you're kidding, Isabella.'

'I'm not. They're coming on the seventeenth. Make sure you don't arrange anything else.'

'You can't do this!' said Barney in horror. 'Isabella, I'm a very, very junior clergyman. Junior clergy do not just invite bishops round for dinner.'

'Why not?'

'Because it looks like courting favour.'

'Well, I am. I want to help you in your career.'

He let out a cry of anguish. 'Isabella, try to understand. The Church doesn't work like that. The surest way of not getting on is to look over-ambitious.' He sat down and sank his head despairingly into his hands.

'You want me to ring them and cry off?'

'We can't,' said Barney. 'They'll have to come. Just promise me you won't do anything like this again.'

'Only trying to help,' she said, offended. Bloody stupid organization, the Church.

The day drew near. Watercress soup, mused Isabella. And boeuf Wellington. Would Barney regard two desserts as sycophantic? He had grudgingly promised to be in early to lay the table and entertain His Right Reverence and wife while Isabella stirred the soup.

She got in from work on the seventeenth laden with shopping. Six fifteen. It was going to be tight. She made the pastry and began chopping the watercress. Where the hell was Barney? She opened the wine to let it breathe and started the lemon syllabub. Seven o'clock. She darted upstairs to change out of her work clothes. He's forgotten. The bastard's forgotten. She raced downstairs, scrubbed the potatoes and poured herself a glass of wine. By seven thirty the table was set, the soup was simmering, the oven was hot and Isabella was drunk. She wrapped the beef in pastry and put it on the baking tray. There was something suggestive about its pallid form. I mustn't, she thought. I mustn't, but I'm going to. She cut up the remaining bits of pastry carefully and stuck them on.

The doorbell rang.

'Bishop Michael! And Mrs Hibbert!' She clutched the door-frame. 'Come in!'

The Bishop's wife glanced sharply at Isabella as she handed her a bunch of carnations and a bottle of wine.

'Something smells delicious,' said the Bishop.

They went through to the sitting room.

'I'm afraid my husband has been inexplicably' – Isabella brought the word out carefully – 'delayed. Can I offer you a drink?'

'Sherry, please,' said the Bishop. 'How kind of you to invite us.'

'I'm told it isn't the done thing for curates to invite their bishop to dinner. I do apologize. I'm new to the Church,' said Isabella. She handed him a brimming glass.

'Not at all,' replied the Bishop gallantly. Sherry dripped onto his trousers. 'We're delighted.'

'Well, Barney thought you'd think he was currying favour.'

The Bishop made an urbane gesture.

Isabella gave him a sunny smile. 'Still, if I had to suck up to a bishop, you'd be the one I'd choose. As the actress has often remarked to you, no doubt. Sherry, Mrs Hibbert?'

'Fruit juice, please,' said Mrs Hibbert, forbiddingly.

And stuff you too, lady, thought Isabella. She slopped apple juice into a glass and handed it to her. A car pulled up.

'That will be Barney,' she said. Relief broke out on their faces. Isabella peered out of the window and had the satisfaction of seeing Barney stare at the Rover on the drive and mouth, '*Oh, shit!*' He flew in and shook hands with the Hibberts.

'Have you been here long? I got held up at a baptism rehearsal,' he explained, with his wonderful disarming smile.

'Don't worry, darling,' said Isabella. 'Everything's under control. I've been keeping them entertained.'

Barney stared at his wife with a wild surmise. She retreated to the kitchen but he shot out after her.

'You're drunk! I don't believe this.' He prised the glass from her hand. 'Don't you dare touch another drop!'

She squared up for a fight. 'Well, where were you, big boy?'

'Ssh!' He glanced at the door in agonies. 'Promise me, Bella.'

If he says sorry, she thought. If he says sorry, I'll behave. She waited. He mistook her silence for docility and went back to his guests, taking her glass with him.

Bottoms up, thought Isabella, swigging from the bottle.

The soup course swam past. Barney hissed threats at her as they cleared away the bowls and took in the vegetables. She gave him the finger.

'Don't do this to me, Isabella,' he begged.

She opened the oven door and viewed her creation. She was about to repent when she heard Barney murmur an apology for his wife's behaviour.

Right!

She bore the steaming boeuf Wellington triumphantly in and thumped it down on the table. Barney closed his eyes in despair. The Bishop and his wife found themselves staring at a vast pastry fertility symbol.

'Can I tempt you, Mrs Hibbert?' enquired Isabella.

Barney and the Bishop winced as she plunged in the knife and hacked off a bleeding chunk.

It was a short meal.

The Bishop was sure they would understand if he and his wife had to slip away. An early start the next day . . . Barney followed them out to the car and Isabella knew he was apologizing again. Mrs Hibbert had left her handbag, but Isabella couldn't have cared less. They drove off and she heard Barney coming back to the house.

'You owe me an apology!' she yelled, getting in first.

'I?' he spluttered. '*I* owe *you* an apology?'

'You promised you'd –'

'I'm not discussing it. You're drunk.' He began clearing the table.

'Talk to me!' she yelled, as he carried the plates to the sink. He made no reply. She grabbed what was left of the beef and hurled it at him. It bounced off his head in a shower of crumbs. He stood stock still with his back to her.

Oh Gawd! 'Barney . . .'

He turned and flung the jug of apple juice over her.

'You bastard!' she screamed, pelting him with potatoes.

'Right.' He picked up the cut-glass dessert bowl and advanced towards her.

She turned to run but slipped over on the wet floor. 'No!'

'Yes!' He sat astride her and daubed her with handfuls of lemon syllabub.

'I hate you, you pig!' She landed a sticky slap on his face while he peeled her clothes away.

'You asked for this,' he panted.

Before long she was mewing like one of the legendary kittens in his father's hayloft.

'Mmm,' she said afterwards. 'That'll teach me a sharp lesson.'

'You're impossible,' he mumbled into her neck.

The doorbell rang. Barney lurched up.

'That'll be Mrs Hibbert,' said Isabella dreamily. 'Coming back for her handbag.'

'*What?*'

'I'll go,' she said.

'You can't! Look at you.' He began mopping frantically at his clothes before hurrying to the door.

Isabella heard the Bishop's voice say, 'I'm so sorry. My wife – Ah, thank you.'

The door closed again.

'Dear God!' lamented Barney. 'What have I done to deserve this?'

'Did you interrupt a row?' asked the Bishop's wife as he got back into the car.

'I believe I interrupted *something*,' mused the Bishop. 'He had syllabub in his eyebrows.'

'What are you giggling about?' asked Will.
  'Nothing. Go to sleep.'

CHAPTER 26

Annie tried to spend some time each morning with her Bible. She wanted to pray and discern God's will for her, but she had never felt so spiritually lethargic. Restraining her wandering thoughts had always been difficult, but now it was worse than ever. She realized one morning that instead of praying she had been thinking for fifteen minutes about lemon meringue pie – whether she might bake one and eat it. I don't believe this! she wailed in despair. Here I am in the middle of the most difficult spiritual crisis of my life, and all I can think about is lemon meringue pie. Will laughed when she told him.

'What's the matter with me?' she lamented.

'You're pregnant,' was his reply.

A couple of days later she received a postcard that jolted her out of her lethargy. It was from Isobel. She was having a lovely time in Normandy. There was mention of churches and cathedrals, but not of cider and Calvados. Isobel would only ever visit Rome in order to disapprove of what the Romans did, thought Annie. Then came the thunderbolt: 'I've got my curacy lined up, by the way. I'm going to Asleby-on-Tees, where you did your placement last summer.'

Annie stared at the tidy writing. She placed the card carefully on the table. Without warning, a sense of all she had lost washed over her. Isobel had a curacy, and Annie did not. Asleby had felt so right. She had been a round peg in a round hole for once in her life. She remembered walking the streets with Harry the vicar, sensing how he loved and prayed for his parish, how he knew it and the people inside out. He was a born parish priest.

Lucky, lucky Isobel, sobbed Annie. To be part of that work, seeing lives change and wounds healed and the kingdom drawing nearer. That was what had fired her, the whiff of advent in the wind. *The night is far spent, the day is at hand; let us therefore cast off the works of darkness, and let us put on the armour of light.* But when she'd gone back to Coverdale her life had felt like a glory hole stuffed with useless broken things. Other people's views and creaky old frameworks had squashed her into a corner. She had seized on the nearest passing saviour – Will – only to find herself in a different corner mourning what she had lost.

Johnny was right. Her vocation had just been lying low. She could hear the call coming again, not in words; but there, slipping in between one heartbeat and the next, there – the soul's birthday, the advent wind.

That Sunday she went up for communion. She had a low view of the sacrament, being in some ways still a Nonconformist at heart, but as she queued in the aisle she knew this time would be different. Her pulse began to race. What if she had the kind of charismatic experience she had always half craved, half dreaded? Supposing she were 'slain in the Spirit' and lay unconscious on the carpet for twenty minutes with everyone tutting and stepping over her? The organ began playing as she reached the communion rails. Johnny made his way along the row. Her hands trembled as she held them out for the bread. *The body of Christ keep you in eternal life.*

At the time she thought nothing had happened, after all, but as she stood at the back singing the last hymn, she realized everything had changed. It was the same noisy church – she registered the toddler bashing a bunch of keys onto the pew. She was the same Annie Brown, pregnant failed ordinand living with her difficult lover. But there had been a shift of perspective. These ordinary things seemed caught up in something bigger.

She tried to explain this to Johnny after the service.

He grinned. 'So you want a job?'

'I think I do,' she said in surprise.

'Ha'away. I'll show you something.'

He led her out of the church.

'Where are you taking me?'

They were hurrying towards a nearby estate with him still grinning as though they were up to no good. Children's voices piped, 'Hiya, Johnny!' as they passed. He waved and called back. Annie gazed at the tower blocks and blocks of maisonettes. It was the place that had seemed so desolate to her the day Tubby had sent her to pray and wander. Nothing here to feast the eyes on, she had thought.

'Where are we going?' she asked.

He stopped. They were in the middle of a courtyard. Washing flapped on lines in the little yards.

'Is the Gospel relevant here?' asked Johnny. 'Can it work?'

She looked around, doubtingly, knowing what the right answer was supposed to be. 'Well . . .'

'Yes, it can,' he said passionately. 'It can. But I'm damn sure Anglicanism can't. I know these people. I baptize them, I bury them. Once in a while I marry them. But Sunday worship? Nah.'

'What's the answer?'

'You've got to start from scratch. Build something new. That's what I want to do.'

'You're frustrated with –'

'Too right, I am. I'm a builder, not a bloody maintenance man.'

'So . . . Church planting, then?'

'Aye. Are you in?'

'Um . . .' Something of his excitement reached her. 'Yes. Yes, I think I am.'

'Great.' His face lit up. 'It'll be pretty radical. I'm seeing the Bishop next week to talk it over.' She watched his eyes sweep round as though he could see it already. He's another born parish priest, she thought. What if this is the place I'm called to? Bishopside. It had been offered once before by Tubby and she had run, dodging and weaving, hoping to elude the hand of God. But here she was again, right in the heart of Bishopside.

Building something new, she thought, as she walked home. A church stripped of the clutter of tradition. Radical. Starting from scratch. He's mad. It'll be terrifying. But think what we'd be free from: the Bridge Illustration, the evangelistic supper party, Christian paperbacks – all those wonderful worthy things, which made her want to scream.

She paused. She was on the spot where she had felt the presence of God months before. A benevolent eye looking down intently at Annie Brown to see what she would do, what she would make of the life and gifts and opportunities she had been given. Gabriel's words whispered in her mind like a prophecy: Your disaster will be the thing that sets you free.

Annie was lying on a hospital examination couch. The waiting room had been full of other women in various states of bloom. The afternoon, like a good evangelical sermon, could be summarized under three headings: Weeing, Weighing and Waiting. She was now at the latter stage. Every so often a midwife would pop her head round the curtain and say, 'Mr Jones won't be long now.'

Annie knew about Mr Jones. She had been to a coffee morning earlier in the day and had met several young mothers and mothers-to-be. She had not known there were so many middle-class professional women lurking in Bishopside. They were going to be a useful mine of baby-related information. Mr Jones was a new consultant. He was young and forward-looking. The other consultants were old-fashioned. The women swapped birth stories. Perhaps one day Annie would be grateful for their companionship, but at the moment they just made her feel desperate. I'll turn into Megs, she thought. I'll breastfeed in public and discuss pooh and snot at the dinner table.

A midwife stuck her head round the curtain again. 'Mr Jones will be with you in a minute.'

Annie began to suspect Mr Jones was a convenient hospital myth invented to soothe and subdue worried women. But then the curtain swished and a large man came in.

It was Barney.

Annie gawped in shock.

'Hello, I'm Mr Jones,' he said. He was already riffling through her notes and she got a grip on her facial expression and mumbled hello. It was the man she'd glimpsed in the Cambridge

266

University Library catalogue room so many years before. She'd forgotten he was real. As his large hands began to feel her stomach she noticed with amusement that he had thinned out just as Camilla had predicted Barney would. *Mr Mark Jones*, said the badge on his jacket.

'So,' he said, starting to run through her notes and ask questions. He conveyed the impression that he was pushed for time but not in so much of a hurry that she was being a nuisance.

'Anything worrying you?' he asked. 'Any questions?'

'Not really,' she said. She could hardly ask, Weren't you at Cambridge twelve years ago?

'I'll see you again at thirty weeks,' he said. He gave one last glance at her notes and paused in surprise. 'William Penn-Eddis?' He looked at Annie as though she were suddenly far more interesting than just another patient. 'Good God. I was at Cambridge with him. Isn't he a GP in Bishopside?'

'Yes.'

'Send him my regards.' He chuckled. 'Not that he'll remember me. In fact, I doubt if he has more than the haziest memory of his Cambridge days.' He saw Annie's surprised expression and cleared his throat. 'That was the seventies, of course.' He handed her file back and left her wondering what he had meant.

Will laughed when she mentioned it to him.

'What did he mean?'

'That I spent half my Cambridge career stoned.'

'You didn't!'

Annie longed to tell him that she had unwittingly put her consultant into her novel, but she still hadn't found a way of mentioning her book. Will read such highbrow fiction that she feared hers would be beneath him.

While he was out at his evening surgery she wrote up the boeuf Wellington episode. At quarter to eight she set off reluctantly for the vicarage. They had been invited for dinner. Will was to come later. Annie supposed that she must construe the invitation as further evidence that Johnny was right and his wife liked her, but she was not looking forward to it.

The vicarage smelled of garlic and fresh basil. Johnny was out.

Annie's heart sank at the thought of prising conversation out of Mara until he returned. She was wearing a dark red dress and had her long hair loose. She looked so stunning that Annie decided to put her in her next book and give her peptic ulcers. 'Can I do anything?' she asked, as they went into the kitchen.

Mara shook her head. She poured Annie some wine.

'Could I see some more of your pictures?' ventured Annie. She expected Mara would be regretting the offer by now, but the other woman went off at once and came back with a large portfolio.

'Have a look through,' said Mara. 'I've got to do the salad.'

Annie knelt on the sitting-room floor and began to leaf through the drawings. There were sketches of Bishopside, lofty flyovers against the sky. Annie began to see that they were the basis of the abstracts on the wall. She looked at the paintings with new interest and thought she glimpsed sense in them – rushing of wind, a mad, dizzy drop, sky between blocks of concrete.

There were more drawings of people. Lightning sketches done in cafés and trains, then some portraits, possibly of Mara's parents. There were some of Will's cousin (Little Shit), still looking incredibly pleased with himself. Annie peered at the tiny writing underneath. *Andrew Jacks.* Annie smiled at the way Mara managed to weave her opinion of the sitter into her pencil strokes.

She turned to the next sheet and gasped. It was Johnny, lying naked. She looked away in confusion, feeling gauche and unsophisticated. Didn't he mind his wife doing this? She fumbled hurriedly to the next picture and started in shock. It's art, she reminded herself, blushing. But how could Mara let another woman see her husband's erection? Yet it was drawn so tenderly. Annie was moved by the devastating honesty, the naked love that showed in every line.

Mara rushed back into the room. 'I've just remembered –' She caught sight of the picture. 'Shit.' Her face was crimson.

'Oh! I'm sorry,' cried Annie. 'I thought you meant me to –'

'*Shit.* I'd forgotten they were in there.' Mara was yanking savagely at a strand of her hair. Annie turned swiftly to the next picture. The same.

'Oh! Um . . .' What if there were dozens? 'I won't if . . .' They were both blushing furiously.

'Well, you've seen now,' muttered Mara. 'Go on.'

Annie hurried on until she reached a picture of the cathedral. 'What lovely Norman arches,' she remarked. A second later they were overcome with giggles.

'Don't you dare tell him,' said Mara at last.

'You could donate one to the tombola at the Autumn Fayre,' suggested Annie. Off they went again.

'That'll give them something to think about.'

'I'm afraid it's crossed most of our minds already,' Annie admitted.

'William's very attractive, too,' said Mara. Then she blushed again and retreated to the kitchen muttering, as though she was unversed in this kind of girlish exchange and despised herself for trying.

Annie continued to work through the portfolio, envying Mara's skill. She got to the end, then went sneakily back to the pictures of Johnny. There was the sound of his key in the door. She shut the portfolio and tried to look negligent. He came in.

'Hiya, sweetheart.' He pulled out his dog-collar. 'She's been showing you her pictures, then?'

'Yes. They're very good,' said Annie brightly, at a loss to know quite where to look.

'Yeah,' he said affectionately. 'She's amazing, isn't she?' He stooped to leaf through, then stopped abruptly. Annie gazed out of the window twiddling her wine glass in her fingers. Johnny swept the pictures up in his arms and strode through to the kitchen. He shut the door after him, but Annie could still hear him swearing and expostulating.

Oh, no! This is awful. Awful, she giggled to herself, as she sat on the sofa. The doorbell rang. Johnny and Mara were still arguing. In the end Annie went. It was Will. She whispered what had happened and he laughed out loud.

'Ssh!'

They went through to the sitting room and waited. Silence had fallen in the kitchen. Eventually Johnny emerged. 'Dinner is served,' he said. When Annie finally dared to meet his eye she saw he was grinning. Mara was looking a little flushed when she appeared to serve the pasta. But perhaps the kitchen was hot.

'By, this is funny lettuce, pet,' remarked Johnny, prodding at a radicchio leaf with his fork.

'Pillock.'

It was a happy evening. Johnny kept them entertained with scurrilous stories and impersonations of prominent churchmen. Annie had never seen Will so relaxed and able to laugh at himself. This was fortunate, since Johnny included in his repertoire an impression of Dr Orlando Penn-Eddis performing an internal examination.

'Stop it!' protested both women. 'It's not funny.' The drooling expression, the pulling-on of surgical gloves – Will was helpless with laughter.

He was still chuckling as he and Annie walked home.

'Why does he call you Orlando?' she asked, after a moment.

'Because that's my name,' said Will.

'What?'

'Mothers,' he said darkly. 'William's my middle name.'

'You didn't tell me!'

His good humour evaporated. 'Well, there's plenty you don't tell me.'

'Like what?'

'Like what you're writing.'

'He told you!' she cried in shock.

'Who's he? Johnny, I suppose. Oh, great. You tell him, but you don't tell me. What else does he know?'

'He's a vicar,' she protested, hurrying to keep up with his furious strides.

'So what *are* you writing all the time? If you can bring yourself to tell me.'

'Nothing much. A novel.'

'Can I read it?'

'It's just a draft.'

'But you've got copies? Annie, you idiot! What if you lose it? Why haven't you got a word processor?'

'I can't afford one.'

'Yes, you can. How often do I have to say money's no problem?'

'It is! It's always a problem, whether you've got it, or whether —'

'Don't be so fucking stubborn! I'm going to buy you a computer.'

'You can take your money,' she cried, suddenly angry, 'and stick it up your *arse*.'

'Oh, well done!' he applauded sarcastically. 'Let's see if we can improve on that, shall we? "You can take your *fucking* money and stick it up your arse." Say it.'

'*Sodding* money,' corrected Miss Brown, getting the hang of it. 'You're mixing your metaphors.'

They strode on in angry silence for a while. Then he relented and took her hand. 'Oh, come on. Don't be mad at me, Annie. I want to buy you things. It makes me feel good. Please.'

'Why do I let you get away with this?' she asked in despair.

'Because you're basically a good sweet obedient girl.'

They reached the house. He led her upstairs.

'Where are we going?'

'To find you a study.'

They went up the last flight to an attic. Annie had never been up there, although she was aware it existed. It was a large room, bare, apart from a couple of leafy plants.

'They're pretty,' said Annie. 'What are they?'

'Oriental tomatoes,' he said, after a short pause. 'Don't worry. I'll shift them.' She crossed to the window. Bishopside lay spread out in the dusk. In the distance were the hills.

'Oh!' she exclaimed.

'Why don't you get it done out?' he suggested. 'Choose a carpet, curtains, a desk. Whatever.'

'Can I use colour?' she asked.

He nipped her arm and she squealed. 'Do what you like. Blow all my money.'

He slid his arms round her and they stood looking out across the town. The street lights wavered and winked in the haze. She could hear the wind stirring the sycamore leaves and the sound of traffic on the distant by-pass. His lips brushed the side of her neck.

'I don't suppose,' he murmured, 'there's anything else of mine you'd like to blow?'

CHAPTER 27

When Annie woke the following morning her stomach fluttered. She pressed her hands on the growing bump and moved restlessly. There was another tickling sensation. Wind, she thought. All that garlic last night. Pregnancy is so glamorous.

Will stirred. 'Are you OK?'

'Indigestion, I think. It's sort of fluttering . . .'

She saw a wide grin dawn. 'It'll be the baby moving.'

'Oh!' Her heart leapt. 'Do you think so?'

'Yes.' He slid his hand over her stomach. 'You're about seventeen weeks, aren't you?'

'They think so. I've got a scan this afternoon, so . . . Oh! It's doing it again. Tickling.'

'I love you, Annie.' There were tears in his eyes.

'You big softy.'

Annie phoned the vicarage later in the morning to say thank you. Mara answered the phone. They exchanged a few polite nothings and were about to hang up when Annie said on impulse, 'I don't suppose you're any good at spending money, are you?'

'Why?' asked Mara suspiciously.

Annie explained about the study and twenty minutes later Mara was there casting her artistic eye round the attic. 'Cannabis!' she said in surprise, pointing at the plants.

'Oh!' Annie flushed. Oriental tomatoes – I hate you, Penn-Eddis. 'He's getting rid of them,' she mumbled, hoping Mara wouldn't realize she hadn't known. The other woman was grinning.

'I'll help you decorate, if you like,' offered Mara.

'That would be wonderful. I've got a special dispensation to use colour.'

They caught the metro to Newcastle and, under Mara's direction, Annie spent a quite staggering amount of money.

'We can't carry all this,' she protested.

'Have it delivered,' said Mara, with a shrug. Her pale stare swept assessingly over Annie. 'You could have your hair cut while we're at it. And what about some clothes?'

Annie gave in meekly, chastened by the thought that Mara had been itching to get to work on her dowdy image.

'Let me buy you lunch,' said Annie, when the orgy of buying was over.

'Actually, I don't feel too good,' Mara replied. 'Stomach ache.'

'Oh! I'm sorry. You should've said. I –'

'It's nothing.' But she was looking pale. At Annie's insistence they got a taxi back.

Remorse set in that afternoon. She sat in the bedroom among piles of carrier bags and felt guilty. I'm as bad as Isabella, she thought. Why had she allowed Mara to talk her into spending so much money on clothes? Her hand wandered to the nape of her neck where the hair had been cropped short. She crossed to the mirror and examined herself. It was the first time she could remember looking chic and grown-up. Even Isabella would not have scorned the honey-coloured silk dress. Perhaps she could face the assembled Penn-Eddis clan that weekend with some degree of equanimity. Yes, you've done rather well out of all this, sneered a little voice inside her. Her reflection began to appear calculating to her. She went back to the bed and lay down.

She was woken by the phone. It was nearly seven o'clock.

'Annie. Henry Melville here.'

'Bishop! Um, goodness, hello.' She sat up on the bed and smoothed her hair. 'I'm coming to see you next week,' she stuttered.

'Yes. Now, it's come to my attention that you're cohabiting.'

'Um . . .'

'This is quite unacceptable,' he said testily. 'If I let you do it, everyone else will want to, and then where would I be?'

'Um . . . I'm sure . . .' What had come over him? There was a hiccup at the other end and it occurred to her that he was drunk.

'It's not easy being a bishop you know. Everyone carrying on with everyone else. Finances . . .' He trailed off with a sob. 'Forgive me. I shouldn't burden you like this.'

'No, no, it's fine.' Help! Then the sobbing gave way to laughter. 'Johnny?'

'You never fell for it!'

She seethed and wished she could swear with Will's insouciance.

'How is old Henry these days?' he asked. 'He was Principal of Jesus when I was at Coverdale. "We don't have to ordain you, John."' He laughed again, as if remembering some disgraceful episode. 'Listen, is your man there?'

'No.'

'Get him to give us a ring, pet.'

Annie remained silent.

'Ha'away, I'm sorry.' He blew her some kisses down the line.

'Vicars shouldn't behave like that,' said Miss Brown primly.

'Like what?'

'Playing tricks. And flirting,' she added.

'It puts bums on pews, flower.'

Annie squeaked with indignation. 'Some of us come because it's the nearest evangelical church!'

'Goodness! Heavens, Annie! I didn't mean *you*.'

She recognized her own voice and seethed again.

'Get him to ring us. Please. It's important.'

'All right.'

They hung up. Seven o'clock, she thought suddenly. Where was Will? A voice in her mind suggested he was dead or had gone off with another woman. To silence these fears she rang the surgery, only to be told that he had left an hour earlier. For the next half-hour she tried not to conjure up the tread of police footsteps on the path. At last she heard Will opening the front door. 'Sorry I'm late,' he called. 'Come and give me a hand.'

She went out to the car where he was balancing a large box.

'*J'accuse!*' he said, seeing her hair and her dress. 'You've been spending my money. Turn round.'

She obeyed. 'Is it all right? It was Mara's idea.'

'Mmm. Very nice. Here, take this end.'

They carried the box into the house and up to the spare room.

'What is it?' she asked.

'Your computer. Shall I show you how it works, or shall I just stick it up my arse?'

He set it up and demonstrated how to use it. Annie was surprised at how simple it was to operate. It was like a clever typewriter, really. How silly to have been nervous of them all these years.

'Now you can put your novel on disc and I can read it,' said Will.

'Later,' said Annie.

'What's it about?'

'A curate and his wife.'

'Any sex?'

She blushed. 'Some.'

'Great. I like a good cassock ripper. Can I just read the opening paragraph? Please,' he wheedled.

She handed him the first notebook with a smile. He opened it eagerly, then threw it aside in disgust when he saw it was in code.

'I'll let you read it when I'm happy with it,' she promised.

'Which will be never.'

He's probably right, she thought. She stared at the screen then typed *Chapter One*. Suddenly it looked official. Her heart fluttered. Will saw her excitement and laughed. He put his arms round her and began kissing the nape of her neck.

'I'm glad you came back,' she said.

'Were you worried?'

'No. It's just that Posthumous is such a silly name for a child. I gave those plants to the church bring-and-buy stall, by the way.'

'*What!*' he said in alarm, before he saw her laughing. 'God, you're so mean to me.' He pouted. 'It's just an ancient herbal remedy.'

'For what?'

He smiled. 'For reality.' He was about to kiss her again when the phone rang. Annie started guiltily, remembering Johnny. Will went to answer it, and she heard him say, 'Piss off. I've only just got in. Phone the surgery like everyone else.' There was a longish pause. 'OK. I'm on my way.'

He came back into the room. 'That was Johnny. Mara's ill, but she won't let him call the surgery. She's terrified of hospitals. I said I'd go round.'

'Is it serious?'

'Sounds like it.'

'Will you be long?'

He sighed. 'Depends. Don't wait up.'

A strong aggressive woman like Mara afraid of hospitals? And Will and Johnny were indulging that fear. Annie knew she was being uncharitable and offered up a guilty little prayer that Mara would be all right then started to put her novel onto the computer. The first notebook was missing, however. Will must have put it down somewhere. In the end Annie gave up the search and began with the second book.

At ten thirty she went to bed. Will rang to say he was at the hospital. 'It looks like an ectopic pregnancy, I'm afraid,' he said.

'Oh, no!'

'They're operating now. I'll stay here and keep Johnny company.'

'Of course. Will she be all right?'

'She'll probably lose an ovary.'

'The baby . . .?'

'No chance.'

Annie lay in bed feeling her own baby fluttering. Poor Mara and Johnny. Their desperately wanted child gone while my little accident is still thriving, she thought. *God is good*. Would Johnny still be saying that? Annie prayed that he would.

The following morning Annie was still too upset to write the next section of her novel and spent the time typing up the earlier chapters instead. The first notebook was still missing. What if she'd lost it altogether?

Will returned for lunch looking very pleased with himself. He handed her a typed sheet.

'Isabella Deane was downwardly mobile,' she read. 'Her older sister Hermione, who was not, deplored this tendency . . .' Annie stared in disbelief.

'But . . .' Her missing notebook was in his hand. He's deciphered it! Her face burned in indignation.

'You said I could read it,' he pointed out.

'I hate you!' Annie listened to her childish words in horror, but Will seemed unperturbed.

'Go and type the rest up,' he said. 'I love it. I want to know what happens next.'

She was too angry to be pleased by his praise.

'I hope it has a happy ending,' he said.

'No,' she replied.

'It has to. You've set it up as a comedy. You can't bugger your readers around like that.'

'I'm the writer. I can do what I like.'

'No, you can't. You're not God.'

Annie was still raging inwardly after he'd gone back to work. How dare he tell her how to write her own book? Eventually she calmed down enough to admit it was his violation of her secret shorthand that was angering her. It had been hers since childhood. It had repelled and thwarted everyone. He's too clever by half, said her mother's voice. But perhaps it had been a test she had unconsciously set him? He alone had bothered to decode her. And he loved what he'd found. She fingered the thought sceptically.

That afternoon Annie was sitting waiting to have her scan. It was a broiling day. *Please ensure that you have a full bladder*, the appointment card said. *And we will amuse ourselves at your expense by running late*, it might have added. Annie shifted in her plastic chair.

'Ee, I'm bloody bursting,' the woman next to her muttered.

At last she was called. A man in a white coat riffled disdainfully through her notes. 'Cold,' he warned her, dropping a dollop of gel on her exposed belly. He rolled the scanning device

278

this way and that over her bulge. Patterns filled the screen. Annie gazed eagerly, but it might have been a satellite weather map of the UK for all she could tell. The man seemed to be taking measurements and she didn't like to disturb him.

'First day of last menstrual period?' he asked.

'Um, I'm not sure. Sorry.'

He sighed. There was a pause for more measurements.

'Well, everything seems to be fine. One foetus. Sixteen weeks, four days. Due date . . .' he fiddled with a little cardboard disc, 'the eighth of December.'

He pointed out various bits of baby in a rather bored way. Stomach, spine, heart. . . Annie nodded, baffled by the jumble, but then suddenly she glimpsed a little hand and almost cried out.

It's real, she thought tremulously. My baby.

The man wiped her belly with a paper towel. 'Toilet through there.'

Annie bolted towards it.

Johnny was with Mara when Annie was shown into the room.

'Oh! I'll come back.'

'No, stay and talk to her,' said Johnny. 'I've got a couple of other visits to make.'

Mara flapped a feeble hand and Annie hoped this indicated agreement.

'If you're sure . . .'

'Aye. I'll run you home later.' He stooped to kiss Mara, then left the room.

'Um, I brought you some novels,' said Annie.

'Thanks,' whispered Mara. She was too ill to rouse herself, so Annie put the books on the bedside locker.

'I'm really sorry,' began Annie. Mara's hand flapped again. Annie perched on the edge of the bed.

'At least I know I can conceive,' whispered Mara.

Annie nodded, wondering if Mara realized she had lost an ovary.

'I've just been having my scan,' she heard herself say. She stopped short, wishing she could suck in her tactless bulge.

'Could you see much?' asked Mara.

'Not really. A hand.'

They fell silent. Annie thought again about the little hand. She felt strange, as though she'd been intruding, prying into a nest where the fledgeling slept.

'Are you scared?' asked Mara. 'Of labour.'

'I suppose I haven't really thought about it,' admitted Annie.

'I'm scared.'

'Oh, but it can't be as bad as what you've just been through.' Annie heard her tones coming out with an awkward jolliness.

'My sister had a baby. The brain never grew.'

'I'm sorry,' said Annie. 'Did she have other –'

'She died.'

Annie hesitated, unable to tell whether Mara meant her sister or the baby. Somehow she couldn't ask. Mara's eyes were closed. Annie watched as she drifted asleep, the blue-veined eyelids flickering. It was unbearably hot. Out of the window the lime-tree leaves hung motionless and the air shimmered over the hospital rooftops.

Johnny returned at last. Mara stirred. 'Say thank you to Will,' she whispered.

'Of course,' said Annie.

She walked with Johnny to his car, the melting tarmac tugging at her shoes.

'Thanks for coming, pet,' he said, unlocking the door.

'That's OK. I'm really sorry, Johnny.'

'Thanks, sweetheart.'

They got in. He started the car.

'Um, would you like to eat with us tonight?' she asked.

'I'd love to, but I've got my parents coming over.' He sighed. 'To look after me and generally tell me what a useless bastard I am.'

'But –'

'Know what my dad said when I rang? "Keep it in your trousers, son. You've caused enough bother."'

'That's horrible!' cried Annie.

'Aye, but he's right. I'm to blame,' he said. 'Putting her

280

through that. She was screaming, Annie. It was . . . I lost it. Completely. Thank God Will was there, that's all.'

Annie was appalled by the raw grief in his voice. She put a hand on his arm and said again, 'I'm sorry.'

'Maybe I'm just selfish, wanting a bairn.'

'But she wants one, too.'

'Only for my sake.'

Annie didn't know how to answer. They pulled up outside the house.

'Aye, well. That's life,' said Johnny at last. 'Tell him thanks, won't you?'

'Of course.'

She was getting out of the car when he said, 'Oh, I was forgetting. I saw the Bishop. He's given me the go-ahead with the church planting. And he says it's OK for you to help, only not in any official capacity. "We'll have to address the problem of her domestic circumstances at some stage," he says. Don't worry,' said Johnny, seeing Annie's mortified expression. 'He'll support you. He just can't commission you officially. "It's all a question of *order*, John."'

'I can't do it, then.'

'Don't be daft. They don't get to be bishops without a Ph.D. in being cautious. Think it over.'

'OK.'

She hurried into the house as he drove off. Her mother's voice was already crowing in her ears. Oh, you thought you could get away with it, did you? There's such a thing as common decency, you know, Anne. You should have thought of that before you stuck your neck out. Nobody's going to want you now. Well, you made your bed, didn't you? You can't blame the rest of us if you don't like lying in it.

Shut up. Annie tried to cling to the thought that God wasn't condemning her, that she could still be useful to him. Johnny accepted her. Why, even the Bishop accepted her. He was just being cautious. He would support her. It was just a question of order. But her mother's voice rambled on, jeering and accusing, refusing to be silenced. Annie was back where she had always been – in the wrong. I will never, never feel acceptable, she thought. Then her mother's voice changed tack. Oh, I know it's not your fault, Anne. You'd marry him like a shot, if you could. You'll just have to accept that you've landed yourself with a man who's too selfish to do the honours. He'd rather ruin your career than give up his precious so-called principles.

Annie stopped short. I don't think that, do I? To her horror she saw that part of her did. Any possibility of her working professionally in the Church was effectively being blocked by Will. She felt a wave of panic. She was trapped. If she tried to force his hand she would lose him. It was a choice between two losses. *Stop trying to make me choose between you and God!* she remembered herself saying to him once. And what had he replied? *You can't have everything, honey child.* Oh, was there no way of living honourably in all this?

That night she had her dream of hell again. She woke to feel Will shaking her.

'I was in hell,' she said.

'Well, that puts life with me into perspective,' he remarked.

She switched on the light and tried to shake off the desolate blackness. He was stroking her forehead. 'I'd lost God. I called but knew he couldn't answer.'

'Are you afraid of eternal damnation?'

'Don't worry. It's just the legacy of my upbringing,' she said.

'So long as it's not my fault.'

'No, no.' But her voice wavered. She saw him frowning as she turned the light back out.

CHAPTER 28

The next day she couldn't bring herself to read her Bible. She took refuge, as she had all her life, in her imaginary world. But Barney and Isabella were at a turning point, too. The plot was about to collapse into a deconstruction of the happily-ever-after myth. The prince sweeps the princess into his arms and gallops off with her to his castle, whereupon the marriage disintegrates. It would be open-ended, ambiguous at the last, like life. This was what she had planned all along. No easy happy ending. But now she realized how much she longed for a resolution, for some sense of closure both in her book and in her life. She skirted tentatively round the idea of marriage once more. Well, she would have to survive without a dénouement. She picked up her pen.

Before Barney and Isabella had fully recovered from the boeuf Wellington fiasco, disaster struck. The vicar announced that he was leaving. This would mean an interregnum of up to a year before a replacement was found, and during that time Barney would have to hold the fort alone. Of course there would be help from other clergy in the Deanery, but the greatest burden would fall on Barney.

Months went past. It struck Isabella one day that she couldn't remember when she last saw her husband smile. He was fading before her eyes. Concerned ladies popped round with meat pies and gave Isabella little hints about a man needing his food. He raced from one thing to another trying to keep the parish plates spinning. Isabella was torn between resentment and pity.

'Barney, this is terrible,' she said one day. He was sitting at the dining-room table, scribbling a funeral sermon. 'It shouldn't be like this. Can't you talk to the Bishop?'

'No.'

'Why not?'

'It would look as though I'm not coping.'

'But you're not coping!'

'I am.'

'You're not! The job's eating you alive.' He sighed and put on his resigned expression. She wanted to shake him. 'Look at you! You've lost weight, you've gone off sex, even. How can you say you're coping?'

'I'd cope a damn sight better without you whingeing,' he muttered.

'*Whingeing?*' she exploded. 'Listen, dickhead, these are real grievances. I'm beginning to wish I'd never married you. I saw more of you when we were engaged. At least I was a priority then. But now any lame duck in the whole sodding parish is higher up the list than me. All they have to do is phone and you go dashing round to minister to them! I'm your bloody *wife*! Doesn't that mean anything to you? What do I have to do to get a share of your attention?'

'Try growing up,' he suggested, returning to his sermon.

Isabella stared in speechless rage. This was how he'd looked all that time ago in the university library – working away, stubbornly refusing to look at her. He hadn't changed. He was never going to change. A kind of cold defiance settled on her.

'Well,' she said, 'if you're not going to make an effort, neither am I.'

He didn't even glance up.

For the next week they were locked in a silent battle. Isabella went out drinking each night with her workmates. She got back late, but he wouldn't ask where she'd been. She stopped cooking, but he didn't comment, just patiently made himself cheese sandwiches. His martyr act was beautifully understated. They lay side by side in bed each night until she ached with the effort of keeping her hands off him. She knew he was awake. All she had to do was stretch out a hand . . . How had he managed to occupy the moral high ground again? He was camped out there in his deck chair with a beer, waiting for her to crawl back. No, I'm damned if I will. Besides, she was having too much fun with the girls from work.

But on Friday they went to a nightclub and it stopped being fun. Isabella drank too much and found herself entangled with some slimy git who wouldn't take no for an answer. Maybe she'd given him the wrong impression during that slow dance. She extricated herself from a nasty bout of snogging and groping, and refused all offers of a lift home in his sports car. She was badly shaken. It could so easily have been a lot worse. However, a couple more Bacardis tamed it. Just a good anecdote to tell the girls. They left the club in the small hours whooping and screeching as they bundled into a taxi.

Isabella crept up the stairs. I'm still pissed. A pint of water. That's what they all said. Helps the old hangover. She found a glass in the bathroom and filled it. She was about to drink when she glanced in the mirror and saw a lovebite on her neck. Shit! The glass fell from her hand and splintered in the washbasin. She turned round and there was Barney at the door. Her hand clutched her throat and she giggled in fear.

'You're drunk,' he said.

'Nothing happened. I was just out with the girls.' Her stupid babbles echoed in the bathroom. 'I'm sorry, Barney. I'm sorry.'

He took a step towards her and wrenched her hand from her neck. She heard herself giggling again and tried to stop. He was shaking her. She could hear him shouting, calling her names.

'Why? Why, you stupid little slut? How could you do it?'

'I didn't,' she sobbed. 'I didn't do it!'

He pushed her into the bath and forced her head under the tap. Icy water beat on her face. 'You're like a sow. You're like a bitch on heat. You just can't say no, can you?'

She couldn't draw breath to explain. He's trying to drown me! She fought him in terror, snorting and choking until he dragged her from the bath and flung her across the room. She staggered and hit her head on the washbasin as she fell.

He'd gone. The water rushed on and on. She lay curled up, too scared to cry. In the end she got to her feet and turned off the tap. Oh, God, what am I going to do? She stood dripping, clutching the washbasin. In the end she peeled off her silly little dress and wrapped herself in a towel before creeping to the spare room. She lay shivering and hugging herself on the narrow bed. The room was dark and spinning.

Footsteps. She tensed. The light snapped on. He yanked the covers off her.

'You're my wife and you'll bloody well sleep in my bed.' He dragged her to the other room. 'You want sex? I'll give you sex.'

'No!' she screamed. 'Don't hurt me, Barney.'

He forced her down on to the bed.

'Don't! Don't!'

He slapped her across the mouth. 'Shut up! Just shut up and let me do it.'

At last it was over. Isabella lurched to the bathroom and threw up. She spent the rest of the night lying beside him rigid with terror. Sometimes she drifted asleep only to be jerked awake by the sound of him stirring. She wept inwardly. I want to go home. I want my mum and dad.

Morning came. Isabella lay trembling as Barney got up and went to the bathroom to shower. Would he say anything? He came back and began to get dressed. He wouldn't even look at her. She steeled herself. 'Barney, we've got to talk.'

'There's nothing to say, is there?'

'If you'd just let me explain!'

'No!' He caught her arm and pulled her to him. His face was inches from hers, taut with rage. 'Just do one thing for me, Isabella. Spare me the details.'

'I'm sorry,' she wept.

He let her go. She listened to his footsteps going down the stairs, then leaving the house for Morning Prayer.

Oh, God, help me! She lay sobbing. Did he really think she'd had it off? No, she'd told him last night she hadn't. She might be a lot of things, but she wasn't a liar. He knew that. Dear God, if this was what he dished out for a drunken smooch, what would he do if she actually slept with someone? His warning came back to her: *I can't make you faithful to me, but I can make you very, very sorry if you're not.* All she could do was show by her actions how truly repentant she was and wait for him to calm down and forgive her.

She went to the bathroom and looked in the mirror. Her right eye was black. Oh, God! Her reflection stared back, ashen. I hit my head on the washbasin when I fell. I'd had too much to drink and slipped and hit my head on the washbasin. It's the truth! Tears rolled down her cheeks. But how could she explain the swollen lip? This can't be me. This can't be happening. But somehow it was. She had slid overnight into the shameful ranks of women whose husbands beat them up. She was a useless liar, but she was going to have to learn fast. Her tears dripped into the shattered glass in the sink.

He preached the next day on forgiveness. No one observing his sweet gentle manner would have guessed how far he was from putting his words into practice.

Days passed. The house had never been cleaner and tidier. Meals had never been so carefully prepared. The ironing basket was empty. Isabella waited and waited to be forgiven. But still Barney wouldn't talk, wouldn't touch her, wouldn't look at her even. He was courteous, as though she were a new housekeeper. If he saw her weeping he left the house.

Their wedding anniversary came and went uncelebrated. Isabella was sick with misery. She sat alone in the empty house, sobbing in the middle of the varnished sitting-room floor. She had earned enough money to buy the Persian rug she had always wanted. But she knew she'd never buy it. She would need the money for something else now. She was leaving. She would go home to her parents. Now, at once, without even packing. She would take her credit card, catch a train and go.

She went to the hallway and dialled for a taxi to take her to the station. Someone at the other end had just picked up the receiver when Isabella heard the sound of Barney's key in the door. She hung up guiltily. There was no time to run.

'Who were you ringing?' he asked.

'No one. The clock. The speaking clock,' she gabbled. 'I wanted to know the exact time.'

He caught her by the wrist. 'That's easy enough to check.' He picked up the receiver and pressed the redial button. They waited, listening to the clicks then the ringing tone. Isabella was trembling. God help me! Let me think something up. Quickly.

'Dixon's Taxis,' said a tiny voice.

Barney hung up and turned to her, face rigid with fury.

'Oh, God, Barney –'

'So he's a cab driver?'

'No! I wasn't –'

He hit her. She crumpled to the floor.

'Don't! Oh, God, don't hurt me, Barney!'

He picked her up and flung her across the hall. She screamed in terror.

'Why? Why?' he was shouting. 'What have I got to do? What in God's name have I got to do to make you –'

'It's not what you think! I was getting a taxi to the station. I swear to God! I was just going home. Don't hurt me!'

She could see him clamping his arms tightly round himself, trying desperately to restrain his hands.

'Going home? Then why lie? Isabella, what am I supposed to think if you lie to me like that? I can't . . .' For a moment his face trembled, but he regained control. 'Look, I don't mind if you go to see your parents. It's all right. You don't have to sneak off. I won't try to stop you.' He was making his voice gentle, as though soothing a frightened dog. 'It's all right, Bella. Are they expecting you?'

She shook her head. It throbbed where he had hit her. No visible marks this time. He was learning.

'Why don't we both go?' he suggested.

She nodded.

'We could both use a break,' he said. 'I'll see if I can find a couple of days. OK?'

She managed a smile.

'Don't.' His voice cracked. 'I'm not a monster, Isabella. Don't make me into a monster!'

'Sorry,' she whispered.

He reached out to her. She saw he wanted sex. It was his way of putting things right. She sobbed as he undressed her. It was too late. There was no putting this right.

★

I can't write this, thought Annie, wiping away a tear. She laughed at herself for caring so much about made-up characters. I need a change, she decided. She picked up the first notebook. I'll start from the beginning and do it properly, she thought. It felt different, somehow, knowing she was writing it for Will to read. Would he like it? At one point she inadvertently leant on the wrong key and the computer obligingly swore for her in Will's voice. Annie shrieked and pressed it again. 'Oh, fuck it,' repeated Will. How on earth had he made it do that? She continued to type until he came in from work.

It was Friday. Annie had spent the whole of the previous day typing furiously and was feeling in need of a change. How am I going to end this book? she wondered. It might go either way. Will phoned in the middle of the morning to ask how much more she had done.

'I've been reading it between patients. I love it. If you give it a sad ending you're in serious trouble, honey child.'

'You'll just have to be very nice to me, then, won't you?'

He chuckled. 'All set for tomorrow?'

'Nearly,' she mumbled. She'd done a bit of half-hearted packing ready for their trip to Oxford.

'Listen, the car's playing up. I'll get it sorted out after work. That way we can leave straight after my surgery tomorrow lunchtime.'

'OK,' said Annie, experiencing another pang of dread about braving the Penn-Eddises.

'So don't worry if I'm late in.'

'I won't. Thanks for telling me.'

'My pleasure, honey. Get back to that computer.'

He rang off and she obeyed. She decided to see if she could save Barney and Isabella's marriage. Perhaps she should trust Will's instincts about the book and write a happy ending, after all.

CHAPTER 29

'I've got to talk to the Bishop,' said Isabella, as the door opened.
Mrs Hibbert had just got in from a hard day at the office. She
was usually a generous-spirited woman, but found herself giving
in to a little pettiness at the sight of her least favourite clergy
on the doorstep.

'I'm afraid you'll have to make an appointment like everyone
else.'

'Is he in?' demanded Isabella, stepping forward.

Mrs Hibbert, holding firmly on to the edge of the door, was
forced to admit that he was. 'But he's seeing someone. Perhaps I
can take a message?'

'Yes. Tell him from me he's a waste of fucking space. He's
supposed to be pastor to the pastors, but he leaves my husband
to –'

'Excuse me,' cut in Mrs Hibbert, two angry spots appearing
on her cheeks. 'I happen to know my husband phoned Barney
only last week to see how things were going. Barney assured him
everything was fine.'

All the fight went out of Isabella. Tears gathered in her eyes.

Damn, thought Mrs Hibbert. She foresaw a messy passing
session when all she wanted was to kick off her shoes and curl up
with the paper. She sighed. 'I take it that's not true?'

Isabella shook her head.

Mrs Hibbert's better nature impulsively took over. She held
out her arms and Isabella plunged into them sobbing. Well, at
least she'd spared her husband the ordeal of having an attractive
young woman weeping into his purple shirt. She led Isabella

e her some tea. 'I think you'd better tell me

...ella did – Barney's workload, the rows, his stubbornness, the awful nightclub incident. 'He won't forgive me,' she
sobbed. 'He won't talk to me even. It's over between us. I can't
take any more.'

Mrs Hibbert liked Barney and was inclined to see it from his
angle. 'How long have you been married?'

'A year.'

Mrs Hibbert patted Isabella's hand. 'Isn't it a wee bit soon to
be saying it's all over?' Isabella bawled. 'I know it's hell, my dear,
but nobody said marriage was easy. Have you tried counselling?'

'He won't.'

'You've suggested it?'

Isabella was silent.

Mrs Hibbert wanted to shake her. ' "For better, for worse, for
richer, for poorer" – they're pretty serious vows. God doesn't
expect us to be perfect, but he does ask us all to try.'

'But does he expect me to stay with a man who beats me up?'
burst out Isabella.

Oh, no, thought the Bishop's wife. Her heart sank. Not that.
Not Barney. She was a solicitor and had encountered many
women whose nice, intelligent husbands put them in hospital.
She took Isabella's hand. 'I'm so sorry,' she said. 'You poor child.
No, I don't think God expects that.'

'But I love him so much!' cried Isabella. 'If only I could get
him to talk or understand, then maybe he'd change. Maybe . . .'

The Bishop's wife leant back with a sigh. She knew she should
say, Get out now while you've still got a shred of confidence and
self-esteem. He won't change. They never do. Spare yourself
years of hell . . . She shook a mental fist at God. Why don't you
do something? she wanted to shout. Her eye fell on a crucifix
above the cooker and she heard her husband's voice reminding
her sternly that God already had. Then why doesn't it make a
difference? There should be a way, she thought. If your death
and our faith mean anything at all, there should be a way. And as
she stared, a plan began to form in her mind.

★

'Barney,' said Isabella, several evenings later ... talk.'

His jaw tightened. 'As far as I'm concerned, it's forg...

She steeled herself. 'It isn't, though. Don't you think marriage guidance –'

'No!'

Her courage wavered, but she forced herself on to the next tactic. 'Um, someone rang. A woman.'

He reached at once for his Filofax. 'Yes?'

'She wants to talk to you. She's thinking of leaving her violent husband.'

'What's her address?' he asked, unsuspecting, biro poised.

'She . . . she says she'll meet you in the church this evening. At seven thirty.'

He glanced at his watch. 'That's now! Why didn't you say earlier?'

'Sorry.'

'What's her name?' he asked, slipping in his dog-collar.

'I forgot to ask.'

He tutted in exasperation and hurried off.

She waited ten eternal minutes, then followed, heart pounding, solicitor's letter in hand.

The church door creaked as she let herself in. He was up near the chancel and turned expectantly at the noise. Her heels clipped as she walked up the aisle to where he stood waiting.

'She hasn't come,' he said.

'Yes, she has.' She handed him the letter.

'What's this?' He turned it over, puzzled, then saw his name and opened it. 'What . . .' His face drained of colour.

Tu es homo.

He ran his hand through his curls, tried to laugh in disbelief. '*. . . inform you of my client's intention to file for legal separation . . .*' She knew what he was reading and her tears spilled over.

'You can't do this!' He took a step towards her and she cringed back. He stared in shock at her terror. 'Bella! You can't! Why didn't you tell me you felt like this?'

'I tried!'

'Look, we can work things out. Don't do this to me! I know it's been tough, but things will change.'

Her sobs echoed in the empty church. 'It's over, Barney. Unless you talk things through, it's over.'

'I'll talk. Dear God, I'll do anything! This is terrible!'

'You'll come to counselling sessions with me?'

He struggled visibly. 'Yes. OK.' He stared down at the letter as though he might cry. He's nothing but a big baby, she thought wearily, as she dried her eyes. There was a long, long silence. He cleared his throat. 'Just tell me he's got the tiniest little willy you've ever seen.'

She could have laughed in relief. 'I'm sure he has.'

'You mean you were too drunk to notice?'

'I mean I've no idea. We didn't do it, remember?'

His eyes went round.

'Barney, I told you at the time we didn't!'

'Oh, God!' He wheeled round and took some hurried steps towards the altar.

'Is this what all this has been about?' she shouted at his trembling back. 'Is it?'

He turned to her, hands out, imploring as she strode up to him. 'Bella, please . . .'

'You useless stupid *bastard*!' She punched him on the nose with all her might. Blood dropped and flowered on his blue clerical shirt. He staggered. The altar rails caught him behind the knees and he crashed backwards into the chancel. Silence. Isabella registered dimly that his shoes needed resoling, then ran from the church.

She reached the house panting, rushed upstairs and grabbed a suitcase. She flung it on the bed and began tossing clothes into it. A moment later Barney burst into the room, wild and bloodstained.

'Bella, I'm sorry!'

'You're too late!' she screamed. 'I'm leaving.'

He swept the suitcase off the bed and pulled her into his arms. 'I'm sorry. Don't leave me. Please don't leave me!' He tumbled her onto the bed. 'I'm nothing without you.'

'Get off, you bastard!' She wrestled, but it was useless. 'You always do this!' she shouted. 'You think sex is a bloody aspirin!'

He was tugging her clothes off, weeping, begging with her not to leave him.

'Oh, all right. All *right*, you stupid, fat, useless . . . useless . . .' she raged as he entered her.

His tears dropped onto her face. He came with a shuddering cry. She pushed him away at once and got up.

'Where are you going?' he asked, clutching at her.

'For a pee, you twat.' She locked herself in the bathroom and sat on the edge of the bath wondering what to do. I hate him! He rapes me, he beats me up! Then it struck her. He said sorry. He *actually said sorry*. Bloody hell. For once he'd admitted he was wrong. What's more, he'd cried. He'd said he needed her. Surely this was a basis for a new start?

She unlocked the door. He was waiting on the landing as if to block off her escape. She sighed. 'You'd better soak that shirt in cold water.' He stripped it off. She went and lay down on the bed.

A moment later he joined her. 'Bella, will you forgive me?'

Her mind seethed. Why the hell should I? You wouldn't forgive me, you bastard. But God seemed to be waiting, hanging on her answer. 'Oh, all right,' she snapped.

'What was I supposed to think?' he pleaded. 'You came back drunk with no knickers on.'

'I went *out* with no knickers on,' she said. 'Haven't you heard of the visible pantie line? Get that wheedling look off your face.'

'So long as you haven't seen him again . . .'

Isabella blushed. The little git had taken to waiting in his sports car outside the shop, trying to give her a lift home. She'd been dreading Barney finding out.

'For God's sake, Isabella, tell me,' he begged. She saw all his fears leaping back.

'He hangs around wanting to drive me back from work,' she admitted.

'*Does* he. Right.'

'No!' she cried in alarm. 'Barney, if you lay a finger on him you won't see me for dust.'

He sat scowling. 'What sort of car has he got?'

She giggled. 'A red sports car. Like the one you sold.'

'Hah!'

The following evening Isabella glanced out of the shop window. The flash car was outside again. She had just turned to serve a customer when there was a loud bang and the sound of shattering glass. She whipped round again. The sports car was ten yards further up the road concertina-ed into a lamp post with another car in its rear. Isabella covered her face in despair.

'I can't seem to see the car anywhere,' remarked Isabella casually when she got in.

'Ah. Yes. I was coming to collect you from work,' explained Barney, 'only someone was parked outside the shop on double yellow lines and I went straight into the back of him. Unfortunately.'

She bit her lips.

'Silly me,' he added.

You dreadful, dreadful man, she thought, shaking her head at him.

The Bishop descended upon Barney like the Day of Judgement and ordered him to take two weeks' holiday. Barney unwisely demurred.

'Listen, matey,' said the Bishop. 'Me – big powerful diocesan bishop. You – insignificant little junior curate. Do as you're bloody told, or I'll suspend your licence and make sure you never work in the Church of England again.'

Mrs Hibbert stared when her husband related this. 'You can't do that, can you?'

'Oh, you'd be amazed what we bishops get up to,' he replied airily.

And so Barney and Isabella spent two weeks in bed in a cottage in the middle of nowhere.

'They've grown,' said Barney, cupping her breasts in his hands.

'Are you calling me fat?' she demanded.

'I'm calling you luscious,' he replied, running his tongue down her cleavage.

Damn, she thought. If she was honest, her clothes were a bit tight at the moment. She'd probably been comfort-eating during those horrible weeks. Up till now she'd always been able to eat like a pig and stay slim. I'll start dieting when we're back from holiday, she promised herself.

It was not as easy as she thought. She tried hard, but the weight wouldn't shift. If anything it seemed to be creeping up. But what the hell. She'd probably been too skinny before. I'm a woman, not a girl, for God's sake. Besides, life was good. Barney went with her to their counselling sessions like a good boy. Another little pep talk from the Bishop persuaded him not to work quite so hard. And the new vicar was arriving in another month.

Yes, life was good. Isabella's natural optimism had bounded back. She lay in bed one Saturday morning, languidly, running her hands across herself and thinking of Barney, who had just made love to her before sprinting off to church to say Morning Prayer. Suddenly her hand stopped. Dear God! What was that lump? Her heart pounded horribly. I've got cancer of the stomach! I'm going to die!

An hour later she was at the doctor's for an emergency appointment.

The doctor was young and a member of Barney's congregation. 'What can I do for you, Isabella?' she asked.

'I've found a lump in my stomach,' burst out Isabella.

'Well, hop onto the couch and I'll have a look.'

Isabella obeyed.

The doctor's hands began to feel around gently.

'Have you been putting on weight?' she asked.

Isabella nodded miserably.

'Noticed any changes in your breasts?'

'Barney says they've grown.'

'What about your periods?'

'Oh, all over the place. I'm hopeless at keeping track.'

The doctor got out a little ear trumpet and listened to Isabella's stomach.

'It's a growth of some kind, isn't it?' blurted Isabella.

The doctor straightened up and smiled. 'Yes. We normally refer to it as a baby, though.'

'*What?*' Isabella sat bolt upright. 'You're kidding!'

'No. I can hear the foetal heartbeat. I'd say you're about five months pregnant. Congratulations.'

'But I'm on the pill!' Her hand flew to her mouth and she giggled. 'Five months? Fu – Sorry. *Five months?*' She leapt down off the couch and ran to the door.

'Um, wait,' called the doctor. 'We've got some forms to fill in . . .'

'I'll make another appointment,' said Isabella. 'I've got to tell Barney.'

She ran all the way home. He wasn't in. Damn! He could be anywhere. She hurried to the church on the off-chance and found him in the vestry, photocopying the service sheet. He looked up in surprise.

'Good morning, Father,' she said with a smirk.

'I wish you wouldn't call me that,' he said irritably. 'It's a silly High Church affectation.'

She giggled. 'Better get used to it, big boy. Because that's what you're going to be.'

'*What?*' He dropped the sheets onto the floor.

'Yep. I've just seen the doctor. I'm five months pregnant.'

He stared, as if casting his mind back, then his wonderful slow grin dawned. He caught her in his arms and swung her round and round. They crashed dizzily against the photocopier, weak with laughter and tears.

'This calls for a celebration,' he said. He went to the church safe and unlocked it.

'Barney Hardstaff, you can't!' she said.

'Want to bet?' He pulled out the bottle of *vino sacro*. 'Now just remind me,' he said, edging her towards a convenient table, 'exactly how it was you got pregnant . . .'

There you are, Will. A soppy ending for you. I hope you like it. She felt oddly like crying. Well, that's it, she thought. It's over. They've gone. Goodbye, Barney and Isabella. Annie glanced at her watch – nine thirty – and went downstairs for a cup of chamomile tea. The car problem must be worse than Will had thought. Perhaps if it broke down altogether she'd get out of meeting his family. The doorbell rang and she went to answer it, wondering who could be calling at this time.

Their dark shapes loomed through the glass. She opened the door as if in slow motion and saw them waiting for her. Two police officers.

CHAPTER 30

Something was taking care of her, some kindly force shielding and guiding her, for although her body trembled and her teeth chattered, she was calm. Deep in her heart she was calm.

There's been an accident.

The two police officers, one male, one female, drove her to the hospital. Their radio played out a drama. Three youths breaking into a warehouse. A chase across rooftops in Bishopside.

There's been an accident. The car. He must have crashed. It would all be explained when they got to the hospital.

The policewoman held Annie's arm as they went into the building. Long corridors. A waiting room. Rows of chairs.

'You sit down and I'll find us a cup of tea.'

'Is he dead?'

'No.' The policewoman smiled. 'He was asking for you. He can't be that bad, can he? I'll find a doctor to explain what's going on. You just sit there, pet.'

'Why won't you tell me?'

Burns unit.

The car had caught fire.

He's not dead. He was asking for you. The doctor will explain. All this had happened years ago and she was dreaming it, watching the nurses and doctors passing backwards and forwards acting out their scene, backwards and forwards. Her hands were cold. Other people sat watching too. The end was already decided. It would be all right. It would not be all right. It didn't seem to matter which.

The tea was too hot and sweet. The thick-rimmed cup burnt

her lip. At last a doctor came. She was young, younger than Annie. She sat down.

'Annie Brown? William's been asking for you.'

'I want to see him.'

'I'm afraid they're still sorting him out. What do you already know?'

'Nothing,' her voice wailed. 'Nobody will tell me —'

'Ssh,' said the policewoman gently.

'Well, it seems there was a house fire and William stopped to help. There were some children trapped and he went in before the Fire Brigade got there.'

'No!'

'He was incredibly brave,' said the doctor.

The policewoman was holding Annie's hands. 'Ssh, it's all right, pet.'

'He got two of the children out before he was forced back,' the doctor went on. 'He had to jump from an upstairs window.'

'Is he all right?'

'Um, cuts to both hands. Third-degree burns on one arm. He'll need skin grafts.' She paused. Annie saw she was still new to all this having to break it to relatives. 'Annie . . . Look, I'm afraid he's fractured his spine as well.'

'Oh, God!'

'We're not sure yet how bad it is. If it's a stable fracture then he'll be all right in a month or two.'

'If it's not?'

'Then I'm afraid he could be paralysed.'

The doctor carried on talking. Annie could hear her voice explaining about the spinal column, the various possibilities, percentage chances — Annie nodded and nodded. The woman could have been saying anything, anything at all, the words were not going home. It was about someone else. It wasn't true.

The doctor left.

'Drink your tea, pet,' urged the policewoman.

Annie sipped and shuddered at its sweetness. The policewoman chatted about Annie's baby, when was it due, had she chosen any names yet.

Waiting, waiting. The nurses and doctors passed to and fro. It was midnight. The doctor came back. 'Annie, he's asleep. He's been sedated. I honestly think it would be better if you went home and got some sleep, too.'

'I want to see him!' Her voice rose. 'I want to see him!'

'Well . . .'

They led her at last to his bedside. His face was ashen, sunk to one side in sleep. His bandaged arms lay on the sheet. He looked dead.

'Will,' she whispered. 'Will.' She kissed his forehead but he didn't stir.

'Come along now, flower,' prompted the nurse. 'Let's get you home.'

'You'll phone me if . . .'

'Why, aye.'

The policewoman was waiting, smiling.

Annie pointed to the toilet door. 'I'll just . . .' She went inside and locked the cubicle.

Blood.

No!

Her hand clattered the bolt back. The policewoman turned.

'Please get someone. I'm bleeding.'

Faces floated over her. Nurses. Johnny. Barney. She must be dreaming. She swam up towards the light but couldn't break the surface. Down, down she sank again.

I must get up. She fought to a sitting position. But she was still on her back. Over and over she tried, pressing against the solid air, dragging herself upright only to find she was still lying down. I must get up. There was something, something important . . .

At last she woke properly. I'm in hospital. Why? It rushed upon her – Will! The baby! – and she cried out. A nurse hurried into the room.

'Will. I must –'

'No, stay lying down. Are you getting any pains?'

Annie shook her head and sobbed, 'I want to see him.'

'He's been asking for you,' said the nurse. She was shaking a thermometer. 'But you're not going anywhere till the consultant's seen you. He's doing his rounds now.' She slipped the thermometer in Annie's mouth. 'Cup of tea? Lunch is in an hour.'

Annie lay waiting. Tears slid down her cheeks. Will. He was lying in another bit of the hospital more helpless than she was. He might never walk again. Confined to a wheelchair. Will, who couldn't bear to be pitied or patronized. Had they told him about the baby? How could he bear it if she miscarried now? Suddenly she was weeping out loud, the thermometer bobbing in her mouth. Don't let me lose the baby! Please don't let me lose it!

The nurse came back and rescued the thermometer.

'That's right. You have a good cry.'

She sat on the bed and stroked Annie's hand. In the depths of her despair Annie felt a flicker of life. She stopped in mid-sob.

'I felt it move,' she choked.

'Why, that's wonderful,' said the nurse.

The door opened and Barney came in. Annie remembered he was only the consultant.

'How are you?' He checked her blood pressure and asked a series of questions.

'Well, Annie,' he said at last, 'I'm afraid there's not much we can say with a threatened miscarriage, except stay in bed.'

Her face quivered. 'What chance . . .'

'About fifty-fifty. But the bleeding seems to have slowed down, you're not getting any contractions, you felt the baby move—I'm cautiously optimistic.'

The door opened and someone wheeled in a machine.

'Ah, thanks,' he said. 'I'll just do a quick scan.' More cold gel. 'Yep. The baby's still there. Placenta in the right place. Good. Like a look?' Annie craned her neck, but could distinguish nothing. 'Heart beating there. Spine. That's a leg. Aha. Want to know the sex?'

'Oh! I . . . Yes, all right.'

'It's a boy. Hang on in there, son. Your father needs you.' He switched off the machine and smiled at Annie as he wiped away the gel. 'Any questions?'

'Can I see Will?'

302

'Mm. I'm not happy about that. I'd rather you stayed put for a couple of days,' he said.

Her lip trembled again.

'Things are looking good. I saw him this morning. He can move his legs. Look, why don't you phone him?' He smiled again as he rose to leave. 'We have the technology. . .'

Five minutes later the nurse wheeled in a telephone.

'Will?'

'Annie!' His voice was faint. 'Are you OK?'

'Yes. How –'

'The baby?'

'They think it's fine. The consultant did a scan.'

'Thank God. Christ, I'm so sorry, Annie.'

'Don't. How are you?'

'Still here. I can move my toes.'

'He told me.'

'Jesus, I'm sorry to do this to you.' He was weeping. 'Annie, I missed one.'

It took her a moment to grasp his meaning. Oh, no!

'I couldn't get to her, Annie. I tried.'

'You mustn't blame yourself, Will.'

'I could see her face. At the window. I was lying on the yard and I couldn't move. I was looking up. Jesus, Annie, I could see her face!'

She was crying too. 'It's not your fault, Will. You did what you could.' But she couldn't reach him, couldn't comfort him. All she could do was listen to that terrible broken sobbing. In her belly the baby stirred again.

'It's a boy,' she said. 'The baby. The consultant told me. You've got a son.'

But he couldn't speak. In the end he just hung up and left her weeping for him, wishing in vain she could make things right.

It was in the papers. *Local Hero – Bishopside Doctor in House Blaze Drama. Thirty-seven-year-old GP Dr William Penn-Eddis, risked his life in an attempt to rescue three children from a burning house yesterday night . . .* And in a different paper, the scoop: *Star's Brother in Heroic Rescue.* It had a picture of Will looking pale and plain beside one of Sebastian in his latest film. Ee, said the nurses. Ee, I never. Have you met him? What's he like?

Will was a hero. You must be proud of him, they said. *Greater love hath no man than this, that a man lay down his life for his friend.* And *he* had risked his life for complete strangers. Almost leaving his own child fatherless. Was that love? whispered a voice in Annie's head. Was it not a form of selfishness? What was a life worth? Will's life against the lives of two infants. Two infants against one little girl he had failed to reach. Who could pay the cost of a single life? What did atonement mean? She'd never grasped it. What was the point of the Crucifixion? She ground her knuckles into her forehead but she couldn't drive out the questions.

They gave her sleeping pills again.

That night an angel came and sat in her room. In the morning he was gone. He left behind him the scent of hope.

After a couple of days she was allowed to go home. Plenty of rest, they advised her.

Johnny drove her back. 'Will you be all right, pet? You can always stay with us.'

'Thanks. I'll be OK.'

Everyone wanted to look after her. Mrs Penn-Eddis was poised to swoop the moment Annie said the word. Nice old ladies from church had offered to pop in and do the dusting. 'If there's anything I can do —' these words were on everyone's lips. Except my mother's, thought Annie. Even if I told her what had happened, she'd only find some way of blaming me.

After Johnny had gone Annie gathered up the post and took it through to the kitchen. The house had been frozen in time, waiting for her return. There was the cup of chamomile tea standing cold beside the kettle. She went upstairs and found her notebook lying open. The happy ending, she thought. I was writing him a happy ending. She sat down weakly and began to cry again.

When she had last seen him Will was about to have his skin grafts. He was mending physically, but Annie was worried by his mental state. When he was awake he was stupefied by painkillers, and when he slept she knew he must be running endlessly through burning buildings hunting for the child he would never reach. Flowers and tributes had flooded in, but in his mind he had failed. Annie went and sat with him, but he turned away his face and said nothing. There was nothing she could do to stop him torturing himself. She prayed he would be released, absolved, but guilt still stared wildly from his eyes. He would see no one but her. His mother rang every day, but he wouldn't speak to her or allow his family to visit. Annie wept for them, hearing the terrible rending pain of motherhood in Mrs Penn-Eddis's voice. She hated to think of their blighted anniversary celebrations.

At last she went back downstairs to cook something. She leafed through the post. Most of it was cards for Will, but there was a small parcel for Annie. Her heart sank when she recognized her mother's handwriting gouged angrily with a biro into the brown paper. She opened it fearfully and found a little knitted white matinée jacket. 'It's not much, but it might come in handy,' said the note fastened to a sleeve with a safety pin. Annie smiled in relief. Soon she would have to write and thank her and explain what had happened, but she couldn't face it yet. That night as she fell asleep she could picture her mother knitting crossly, jerking the wool and muttering under her breath, 'Hah! She'll find out motherhood's not a bed of roses soon enough.' But perhaps there was a smile tugging at the corners of her lips? The thought going like a skipping song through her mind with every click of the needles: *I'm going to be a Grandma, a Grandma, a Grandma . . .*

When Annie saw Will the following day something had changed. He was snarling and swearing like his normal happy self. The skin grafts had been postponed, for some complex medical reason.

'They took all the dressing off,' Will was complaining. 'I must have felt every fucking nerve end. Then they said it's not ready yet! I'm going to have to go through it all over again. You're laughing.'

'Sorry. It's relief.'

'Wait till you're in labour, my girl. You realize I've got to lie here for six sodding weeks?'

'But at least you're not paralysed,' she pointed out.

'Oh, piss off, Pollyanna. Bring me something to read next time. Where's the rest of your novel? I'm bored out of my skull.'

'I'm so glad you're feeling better.'

'Hah.' He lay pouting.

'What happened?'

'Gabriel came.'

Ah, thought Annie.

'Everyone's been so *nice*,' he said bitterly. ' "Don't blame yourself, William." Trying to make me see reason. You know – without me they'd all have died, all that stuff. But, Jesus, this is beyond reason!'

'What did Gabriel say?'

' "It's not your job to save the world. Stop being such a fucking prima donna." '

'What?' gasped Annie.

'Yeah. Outrageous, isn't it?' He smiled for the first time since the accident. 'I hate that man so much. He sat all night by your bed last week, by the way.'

'Oh! I dreamt there was an angel in my room.'

'Give me a break,' he said in disgust.

A doctor came in. 'Right,' he said cheerfully. 'Let's have a look at that arm.'

'You'd better go, Annie,' said Will. His face was white. 'I want the rest of that book. Oh, and tell my mother she can come any time.'

Annie hurried away.

Over the next few weeks Annie divided her time between typing up her novel and sitting by Will's bedside. She met his family as they came up to visit him. One by one they slotted into place like bits of the jigsaw. Will himself grew clearer and clearer in her mind. No wonder, she kept thinking. That explains it. She also saw a danger of being eaten alive by the Penn–Eddis family. They would annexe her. She would become an honorary Penn–Eddis, despite her lowly background.

306

She found the courage at last to write to her parents. The phone rang the following morning *before cheap rate*.

'Anne, it's your mother. Why didn't you tell us, you silly girl? Your father's worried sick about you. I hope you're resting properly. You've got the baby to think about now, you know. You can't just fly about the place like you used to. And then there's William. He's got enough to cope with without having to worry about you and the baby. Make sure you're resting properly or you'll miscarry.'

'I –' tried Annie in vain.

'Your father wants to know if you've got anyone looking after you. He's all for sending me, but I told him, no, they've got their own lives to lead, I can't just go barging in without being invited.'

There followed a long uncharacteristic pause in her mother's monologue. Annie could hear her breathing.

'That's very kind of Dad,' said Annie cautiously. 'But I'm fine at the moment. The vicar's wife pops in.' Annie smiled at the picture of Mara that these words must conjure up. 'But if it all gets too much . . .'

'Oh, well. Don't stand if you can sit. Don't sit if you can lie down,' pronounced Mrs Brown.

'I won't.'

'Hmmph. Still making progress, is he?'

'Um, yes.'

'Silly,' said Mrs Brown. 'Should've waited for the Fire Brigade.'

'But the children wouldn't be –'

'Still. All's well that ends well, that's what I always say. And another thing – olive oil rubbed into the tummy. Stops you getting stretch marks.' With these gnomic words she was gone.

Will improved steadily, but his frustration turned him despotic. He finished her novel and ordered her to send it to an agent and write another. He demanded books, fruit, newspapers, whisky, oriental tomato leaves or, worse, oral sex. When she refused, he sulked. He summoned and dismissed her at whim, then phoned at three in the morning to apologize.

Annie confided in Mara one hot afternoon while the two of them were painting the attic walls dark red.

'Tell him to go fry his face,' suggested Mara.

'Go fry your face,' said Annie next time he phoned with a list of outrageous demands. She unplugged the phone and slept through the night for the first time since she could remember. The next day the florist's van brought a dozen bouquets all bearing the word *Sorry*. The house was full of their scent for a week. His reformed behaviour lasted almost as long.

Eventually Annie's new study was complete. Johnny had been round earlier to shift furniture under Mara's eagle eye. Now it was evening and Annie stood gloating over the colours. There was a framed sketch of Will on the wall, which Mara had done slyly the evening they had been round for dinner. Annie sat down at the desk and began to make a list of things to do.

> *Write thank you letters.*
> *Buy baby things.*

Megs had offered all manner of things, from fifteenth-hand vests to breast pumps. Annie felt overwhelmed by the need to grind some peasant faces by buying everything new.

> *Revise MS.*
> *Get hair cut again.*

It all looked a little trivial.

> *Make a new appointment to see bishop.*

She had missed the last one, of course, but he had been very understanding when he rang. Will was his godson, after all. She kept wanting to giggle while he spoke, unable to banish the memory of him spilling out drunken confidences to her, although she knew he never had.

She doodled on the paper. As usual the sight of this kind of list filled her with longing and wild resolve. *Be a better person,* she wanted to add. *Work out my salvation in fear and trembling.*

She got up and crossed to the window. The sun was going

down over Bishopside, laying dull gold on the rooftops. The police helicopter was busy in the distance over another bit of town. *What am I going to do with this life I've been given?* Annie asked herself. *What do you want of me, Lord?* The light was dying from the sky. She remembered another sunset: the disciples on the road to Emmaus. Weary feet, weary, weary feet. *We had hoped he was the one to redeem Israel.* But how had it all ended? Another failed messiah on a Roman cross. Then footsteps behind them, catching them up, a light-hearted tread. The risen Christ. Annie felt for those two disciples, their hearts burning with grief and rage as this stranger lectured them.

Foolish! Slow of heart! Wasn't it necessary for the Christ to suffer these things and enter into glory?

Who did he think he was?

They burned, but was it with a flicker of hope, wild, impossible hope, that leapt into a blaze of certainty as those hands broke the bread? Annie laughed out loud to think of them stumbling back to Jerusalem, panting as they crashed at last up the stairs into the upper room. Before they could draw breath their punchline was stolen: He is risen.

This is it, Annie realized. *This is what makes sense of the Crucifixion.* Without it what was left? Just one more deluded man dying a grisly death. She saw the sealed tomb that dark Friday night. It was over. Even the women had gone home weeping. Then slowly, slowly, that first Easter morning before the sun was up, the coming glory began seeping out round the edges of the stone door, until at last it burst forth. The guards gibbered that it was an earthquake, it was an angel.

This is my faith, thought Annie. Not just death, but resurrection and the hope of glory.

It was a Saturday in late September when Will came home. He was still in pain, but he could walk and sit for short periods.

'Annie, I've been a bastard. Thanks for putting up with me,' he said in bed that night. 'I'll make it up to you.'

'Idiot. You don't have to,' she said.

'Make love to me. You get to be on top.'

'Tricky. My bulge is too big.'

'Shit! After all these weeks.' They laughed till they cried.

The next day she got ready for church and he surprised her by announcing he was coming too.

'You don't have to,' she said.

'I want to.'

'You won't like it. It's terribly informal.'

But he was adamant.

They slipped into the back pew, but not before Johnny caught sight of them. He came up grinning broadly.

'About time, too,' he said to Will.

'Oh, fuck off.'

There was a long, scandalized *Eeee* from the pewful of women in front.

'Sorry,' said Will.

'Oh, it's Doctor William,' said one. And they were all off at once, telling him how brave he was and how they'd cried over the reports in the paper. He bore it well.

The service started. Annie winced inwardly.

'It's like bloody breakfast TV,' muttered Will.

'I warned you.'

'Yeah, yeah.' He braced himself to endure. She could see he was in pain from sitting for so long. In the end he was forced to get up and walk around at the back.

Eventually the service was over and Johnny was giving the notices. Will came and sat beside her again.

'OK. Listen up, everyone,' said Johnny. 'I publish the banns of marriage between Orlando William Johnson Penn-Eddis, of this parish . . .'

Annie turned to Will in shock. Some terrible mistake!

'And Anne Brown, also of this parish . . .'

'Yes or no?' asked Will. He was slipping a ring onto her finger.

'. . . any reason in law,' Johnny's voice was saying.

'But —' A moonstone, like Isabella's. 'You're mad. Yes.'

He bent his head and kissed her.

'This is for the first time of asking. Give them a round of applause.'

Annie was still laughing as they made their way out into the sunshine.

'You're completely mad, Will,' she repeated.

He smiled at her. 'I love you.'

She took his scarred hands in hers and gazed into his face as though checking he was still his irascible demanding self.

'Surprise!' called a voice. It was Ted. And Ingram and Muriel. And Isobel. And there was Mara talking to Gabriel. Annie gasped.

'Look,' said Will. 'Here comes our best man.'

She turned and saw Edward, tanned and grinning, bounding towards them in the September sunshine.

READ MORE IN PENGUIN

In every corner of the world, on every subject under the sun, Penguin represents quality and variety – the very best in publishing today.

For complete information about books available from Penguin – including Puffins, Penguin Classics and Arkana – and how to order them, write to us at the appropriate address below. Please note that for copyright reasons the selection of books varies from country to country.

In the United Kingdom: Please write to *Dept. EP, Penguin Books Ltd, Bath Road, Harmondsworth, West Drayton, Middlesex UB7 0DA*

In the United States: Please write to *Consumer Sales, Penguin Putnam Inc., P.O. Box 999, Dept. 17109, Bergenfield, New Jersey 07621-0120.* VISA and MasterCard holders call 1-800-253-6476 to order Penguin titles

In Canada: Please write to *Penguin Books Canada Ltd, 10 Alcorn Avenue, Suite 300, Toronto, Ontario M4V 3B2*

In Australia: Please write to *Penguin Books Australia Ltd, P.O. Box 257, Ringwood, Victoria 3134*

In New Zealand: Please write to *Penguin Books (NZ) Ltd, Private Bag 102902, North Shore Mail Centre, Auckland 10*

In India: Please write to *Penguin Books India Pvt Ltd, 210 Chiranjiv Tower, 43 Nehru Place, New Delhi 110 019*

In the Netherlands: Please write to *Penguin Books Netherlands bv, Postbus 3507, NL-1001 AH Amsterdam*

In Germany: Please write to *Penguin Books Deutschland GmbH, Metzlerstrasse 26, 60594 Frankfurt am Main*

In Spain: Please write to *Penguin Books S. A., Bravo Murillo 19, 1° B, 28015 Madrid*

In Italy: Please write to *Penguin Italia s.r.l., Via Benedetto Croce 2, 20094 Corsico, Milano*

In France: Please write to *Penguin France, Le Carré Wilson, 62 rue Benjamin Baillaud, 31500 Toulouse*

In Japan: Please write to *Penguin Books Japan Ltd, Kaneko Building, 2-3-25 Koraku, Bunkyo-Ku, Tokyo 112*

In South Africa: Please write to *Penguin Books South Africa (Pty) Ltd, Private Bag X14, Parkview, 2122 Johannesburg*

BY THE SAME AUTHOR

Catherine Fox's acclaimed first novel:

Angels and Men

Mara is still suffering from the wounds inflicted by the sinister sect she
and her twin sister Hester were involved in. To allow them to heal, she
has built an invisible fortress around herself.

Coolly rebutting the overtures of her fellow students in the halls of
their great northern university, Mara hadn't reckoned on the persist-
ent attentions of the heartwrenchingly handsome Johnny, the giddy
warmth of Maddy and May, the provocative charm of 'the polecat',
Andrew, or the noble desires of Rupert. Awkwardly succumbing to
the lure of college romance – and rivalry – Mara slowly begins to confront the raging dilemma that torments her . . .

'As original as its abrasive but engaging heroine' – Pat Barker in the
Sunday Times Pick of the Year

'Wow! I was enchanted by *Angels and Men*' – Barbara Trapido

'It is a real pleasure to find what many readers are always on the look-
out for: a new and original writer of a rattling good story told with
intelligence and depth' – Val Arnold-Forster in the *Tablet*

'Powerfully involving fiction' – Kate Chisholm in the *Sunday
Telegraph*